A DUAL WORLD ECONOMY
Forty years of development experience

A DUAL WORLD ECONOMY

ECONOMY

Forty years of development experience

Edited by
Willem L. M. Adriaansen
J. George Waardenburg

BOMBAY
OXFORD UNIVERSITY PRESS
DELHI CALCUTTA MADRAS
1992

Oxford University Press, Walton Street, Oxford OX2 6DP

NEW YORK TORONTO
DELHI BOMBAY CALCUTTA MADRAS KARACHI
PETALING JAYA SINGAPORE HONG KONG TOKYO
NAIROBI DAR ES SALAAM
MELBOURNE AUCKLAND
and associates in
BERLIN IBADAN

ISBN 0 19 562732 6

Typeset at Alliance Phototypesetters, Pondicherry 605 013
Printed at All India Press, Pondicherry 605 001
and published by S. K. Mookerjee, Oxford University Press,
Oxford House, Apollo Bunder, Bombay 400 039

Contents

PART 3: THE LEAST DEVELOPED COUNTRIES

Preface

JAN TINBERGEN

With pleasure I agreed to preface this collection of papers which stems from a joint effort of the Centre for Development Planning of the Erasmus University Rotterdam and of the Association of Post-Keynesian Studies. I am glad to have been closely associated with the Centre since its inception in 1968. At its twentieth anniversary a conference was held where these papers were brought together and discussed. The world is such that the subject of the Centre's activities, I submit, will be not less important in the next twenty years than it has been in the first twenty years of its existence. As a member of the Association I have also good reminiscences of the occasions when I took part in the exchange of ideas at its annual meetings, of which this conference constituted the ninth one.

The topic chosen for this book is one of the most important problems the world is facing. In the four decades after 1948 hardly any change in world income distribution occurred, as illustrated by calculations of Summers, Kravis and Heston for the period 1950–80 and published in the *Journal of Policy Modeling* of May 1984. These figures show that the incomes of the poor world citizens in comparison to those of the rich world citizens did not change. We know well that the incomes of the poorest are not adequate even for their food, let alone for their education. Understandably many of them attempt to find a job in the more prosperous parts of the world. In order to reduce this inflow of migrants the United States have erected a fence along their frontier with Mexico. In or around Europe there are no fences yet, but millions from the poorer side of the Mediterranean have already penetrated into the prosperous European countries.

Would it not be better for developed countries to assist the less developed countries in creating employment for their citizens in their own countries? This would help to avoid the difficulties caused by the rapid inflow of people with different cultures in the poorer quarters of the cities of the developed world.

To find an answer to this question could be an important contribution to the solution of this and many other problems. My own conviction is that the well-known official development assistance (ODA) of 0.7 per cent of GNP is clearly insufficient to accelerate adequately the development of the Third World.

It is my hope that reflection on these papers will contribute to an understanding of the long-term nature of the development problems and thus to the answers we need for them and to a better policy of development cooperation.

Contributors

Willem L. M. Adriaansen, Veir Windstreken, consultants, Gouda, The Netherlands

N. Amin, University of Harare, Harare, Zimbabwe

Lodewijk Berlage, University of Louvain, Louvain, Belgium

Colin I. Bradford Jr., Yale Centre for International and Area Studies, New Haven, and World Bank, Washington, DC, USA

Daniel van den Bulcke, University of Antwerp (RUCA), Antwerp, Belgium

Sukhamoy Chakravarty (1934–1990), Delhi School of Economics, Delhi, India

Ludo Cuyvers, University of Antwerp (RUCA), Antwerp, Belgium

Nelson P. Moyo, University of Harare, Harare, Zimbabwe

Hans W. Singer, Institute of Development Studies, Brighton, Sussex, UK

Servaas T. H. Storm, Centre for Development Planning/Tinbergen Institute, Erasmus University Rotterdam, Rotterdam, The Netherlands

Piet Terhal, Centre for Development Planning, Erasmus University Rotterdam, Rotterdam, The Netherlands

Jan Tinbergen, formerly Centre for Development Planning, Erasmus University Rotterdam, Rotterdam, The Netherlands

Harmen Verbruggen, Free University Amsterdam, Amsterdam, The Netherlands

J. George Waardenburg, Centre for Development Planning, Erasmus University Rotterdam, Rotterdam, The Netherlands

1   Forty Years of Experience in Development Theory and Practice: An Introduction

WILLEM L.M. ADRIAANSEN
SERVAAS T.H. STORM
J. GEORGE WAARDENBURG

1.1. Introduction[1]

This book is concerned with long-term development. It looks back at the post World War II development experience, first of all at the global level, and attempts to draw some lessons from it. The second part of the book analyses countries for which this experience is by many regarded as positive, the so-called 'newly industrializing countries' (NICs); in contrast to what is usually done, the analysis of the NICs' experience is not limited to the often mentioned four countries in East Asia. The last part of this book looks at countries for which the post-war development experience has turned out considerably less positive, the least developed countries or areas, sometimes called the 'Fourth World'; although other areas also qualify for this category, attention is concentrated on sub-Saharan Africa.

In the forty-odd years since World War II, the dichotomy between developed and developing countries has become somewhat blurred, because on the one hand the relative distance between them has decreased, and, more importantly, parts of the developing countries' economies have been integrated into the larger part of the world economy dominated by the developed countries. At the same time, disparities within the Third World have increased, both between countries and between social groups within them. We think that the experiences of both the NICs and the least developed

[1] The authors are very thankful for comments by Sukhamoy Chakravarty on an earlier version of this paper. This does not, however, disburden them from full responsibility for points of criticism in this text.

areas belong to the collective experience of mankind and as such deserve to be looked at in juxtaposition, in the continuing search for the depth and structure of development processes.

This introductory paper intends to provide some empirical material on aspects of global development as well as on several issues related to the domestic development processes in LDCs, viz. income distribution, employment, technical change and poverty, financing, and trade and state. These issues are considered central to the development process, indicating either yardsticks of progress or bottlenecks of policies. Alongside this empirical material, generally drawn from World Development Reports of the World Bank, we also provide references on these issues as well as an indication of some diverse views on them. We hope that in this way, the introductory chapter may serve as a framework against the background of which the more intensive discussion of certain issues in the papers of this book can get its full weight.

1.2. Global perspectives

Before discussing the post-war development experience at the global level, we will first briefly inquire into some major long-term trends in the world economy before the 1950s.

1.2.1. *Global development up to the 1950s*

Long-term development has been on the world's political[2] and economic agenda since the Second World War and this has increasingly found reflection in the economists' literature (cf. Chenery and Srinivasan [1988]). Before World War II, from the marginalists' revolution of the second half of the 19th century onwards, development and growth theories had been largely and remarkably absent from most of the economists' agenda which was dominated by the neoclassical (partial) equilibrium analysis and welfare economics, business cycle studies and of late, by Keynes. Yet Schumpeter

---

[2] For the political dimension it is not so much the end of WW II, as the related decolonization process, the beginning of the 'cold war' and the non-alignment movement which has played a role. President Truman's Point Four in 1948 was a significant but not unambiguous heralding activity for development cooperation and/or assistance. Yet WW II solidified some international cooperation, while its ending left room for applying it more creatively than fighting a war.

[1919, 1934] had taken up the subject, though he treated it within the framework of a limited formulation. It re-emerged in the economic discussion with the long-term studies of Clark [1941] and Tinbergen [1942]. These studies were followed by others including Tinbergen's [1945] more popular and policy-oriented book on international economic cooperation and the seminal studies of modern economic development theory of Rosenstein-Rodan [1943] and Nurkse [1953] (cf. Taylor and Arida [1988]).

In fact, development was prominent in economics in its formative stage, when the great 18th-century economists like Smith and Steuart had dealt with the problem in a way which has an eminently modern ring and their work would undoubted fall into the category of what we call 'development economics' today.[3] And indeed the figures in Table 1.1 give an indication that at least from the middle of the 18th-century onwards there was reason for economists, with an open view to their world, to wonder about development. The figures display clear growth in the presently 'developed' countries from 1750 onwards, which can be attributed largely to the industrial revolution.

Reynolds [1986:78] defines a sustained rise in per capita output as 'intensive growth', in contradistinction to 'extensive growth', which takes place when output is growing at the same pace as population, i.e. without changing per capita output. He notices that the countries belonging to the presently developed world did not start modern (intensive) growth all at the same time. Intensive growth started in the United Kingdom in the mid-18th century, in France, Belgium, Switzerland around 1800, in Austria, Western Germany and the United States around 1830, in Scandinavia and Australia around 1850, in Canada around 1870, in Hungary, Russia and Italy around 1880, in Poland and Czechoslovakia around 1920, but in Rumania, Bulgaria and Yugoslavia only after 1945, two centuries later than in the United Kingdom.

Despite the 'hazardous nature of historical estimates of GNP reaching back over long periods', Terhal's [1988] comparison of Bairoch's [1981] and Maddison's [1982] figures on long-term growth rates of per capita product of some present-day developed countries shows some basic similarities between them. In particular,

---

[3] See e.g. Lewis [1988].

TABLE 1.1:   *Estimate of historical evolution of GNP per capita in some presently developed regions and some presently Third World regions*
(in 1960 US dollars)

Year	Western Europe	Eastern Europe	North America	Japan	All developed countries
1750	190	165	230	180	182
1800	215	177	239	180	198
1860	379	231	536	175	324
1913	693	412	1333	310	662
1938	868	566	1527	660	856
1950	928	588	2364	405	1054

Year	Africa[a]	America[b]	Asia[c]	China	Third World total
1750	--	--	--	--	--
1800	130	245	180	210	188
1860	130	260	164	195	177
1913	142	357	182	188	192
1938	158	400	187	187	202
1950	183	467	178	166	203

Source: Bairoch [1981]
Notes: [a] Excludes South Africa
           [b] Excludes United States, Canada
           [c] Includes only market economies, except Japan

both sources indicate remarkably little difference in income level between the richest countries and the poorest countries[4] around 1800 before the beginning of the industrial revolution in most countries. Thereafter, growth rates began to diverge with little growth in the so-called Third World as a whole until 1950, i.e. during the colonial era. The latter statement should however be qualified by observing that there were considerable differences in growth even within the Third World itself. Starting from a higher level of GNP per capita than the average in the Third World, Latin American countries registered a relatively high rate of growth, while Japan displayed an even higher rate after 1860. For African

[4] Apart from primitive societies for which no estimates are available (cf. Terhal [1988], quoting Bairoch [1981]).

countries, available data appear far less reliable for such conclusions, and for most of Asia per capita income has stagnated.

Again Reynolds [1986:31 ff.] emphasizes in quite a precise way that the popular picture of growth occurring in the presently developed countries before 1945 in combination with simultaneous overall stagnation in the Third World is grossly distorted. He sees turning-points for (intensive) growth in Chile (1840), Malaysia 1850), Thailand (1850), Argentina (1860), Burma (1870), Mexico (1876), Algeria (1880), Brazil (1880), Japan (1880), Peru (1880), Sri Lanka (1880) etc. having occurred long before the 20th century and much earlier than Rostow's take-off period estimates which are all after 1930. It should however be noted that while Rostow's conceptualization does imply ensuing self-sustained growth, Reynolds' turning-point does not imply that explicitly.

The picture emerging from these long-term trends in per capita income growth before 1950 can be broadened by looking at long-term data on population growth and the world income distribution. Estimates[5] of long-term trends in world population size are given in Table 1.2. In spite of their roughness, these figures provide

TABLE 1.2:   *Very long period estimates of world population*[(a)]

Year		World population (in millions)	Average annual growth rates (%)
10000	BC	4	--
5000	BC	5	0.00
0	AD	193	0.07
1400	AD	350	0.04
1500	AD	425	0.10
1600	AD	545	0.25
1700	AD	610	0.11
1800	AD	900	0.39
1900	AD	1625	0.59
2000	AD[(b)]	5750	1.27[(c)]
2100	AD[(b)]	8250	0.36

Source: McEvedy and Jones [1978].
Notes: [(a)] For the reliability of these figures, see Durand [1974]
[(b)] Projections; for 2100 around the maximum expected, to be compared to the theoretical limit of 20000 million
[(c)] Todaro [1989:189] gives for 1900-50: 0.91; 1950-70: 2.09; 1970-80: 1.76

[5] For an evaluation of the reliability of these figures, see Durand [1974] who also gives references to other estimates.

some feeling for orders of magnitude of the former and future world population. Only after AD 1400, did world population begin to increase more rapidly than before. Strikingly, this already high rate of population growth even increased during the 20th century, but is expected to slow down thereafter.

Estimates of the distribution of personal income in the world are fraught with difficulties, as they should take account of exchange rate corrections[6] and national personal income distributions, which are hard to come by. Not surprisingly, the available estimates do not go back further than a little more than a century. Table 1.3 gives estimates of the long-term evolution of the personal distribution of income in the world. By any measure these figures display a remarkable increase in world inequality between 1860 and 1930. In the period after 1930, the share of the second quintile increased considerably at the cost of the three lowest quintiles. These last figures refer already to the period after 1950 to which now we direct our attention.

1.2.2. *Global development from the 1950s onwards*

Although, as we saw, the study of economic development dates back to classical economists such as Smith and Steuart, the systematic study of the problems and processes of economic development in Africa, Asia and Latin America has emerged only over

TABLE 1.3: *Historical evolution of the personal distribution of income in the world*
(estimated quintile shares)

Quintile	1860	1913	1930	1960	1970
Top quintile	50.0[r]	61.0	70.0	68.5	69.7
Second quintile	18.0	17.0	18.0	19.5	20.6
Third quintile	12.0	11.0	5.5	4.9	4.2
Fourth quintile	11.0	6.0	3.5	3.8	3.0
Bottom quintile	9.0	5.0	3.0	3.3	2.5

Source: Bertholet [1983]
Note: These estimates are rough calculations

[6] Instead of the nominal exchange rates purchasing power parities should be used for making the national incomes comparable. In the United Nations International Comparison Project by Kravis *et al.* [1982], it has been found that in international comparisons, without this correction, poor countries' incomes are systematically underestimated and increasingly so as the countries are poorer.

the past four decades, the period since World War II. Development economics has been concerned with structural changes taking place during the growth process both within the world economy and within the national economies of developing countries, and with the (economic) requirements for affecting these structural transformations in a desired way.[7]

The period since World War II has been exceptional both in terms of growth and structural change. On average, between 1950 and 1980 the GDP per capita in LDCs more than doubled notwithstanding high population growth (Table 1.4). Further, in most LDCs the manufacturing sector has grown particularly fast. The growth rate of LDCs' industrial production was 8.6 per cent during 1965–73, 6.4 per cent during 1973–80 and 3.7 per cent during 1980–86[8] which was higher than the growth rate of GDP in the same periods (cf. Table 1.5).

While the growth of the population of Third World countries from the 1950s onwards has been rapid, their economic growth has been just as exceptional. This becomes clear if we compare the growth rates of contemporary LDCs with the more limited rates of presently developed countries of Europe and the US at the beginning of their industrialization drive (i.e. the 19th century). During this period, the average annual growth rates of their GDP ranged from 2.0 per cent to 2.5 per cent and those of their GDP per capita from 1.2 per cent to 1.7 per cent (Bairoch [1975]). These are less than half the rates realized by the LDCs since World War II. Moreover, from 1950 to 1980, the GDP per capita of LDCs (excluding China) grew almost as fast as it did in the developed countries (3.0 per cent against 3.2 per cent). Consequently, the gap between these two groups has not decreased substantially.

Yet these overall results conceal important differences in growth performance between Third World countries, of which we will address the major demographic and economic ones. During 1950–85, the population of developing countries (excluding China) has more than doubled, increasing from 1.1 billion in 1950 to over 2.6 billion in 1985. Table 1.6 documents the variation in the demographic experience by region. We can make the following three generalizations

---

[7] With respect to the world economy, well-known examples are provided by Tinbergen's [1978] *RIO: Reshaping the International Economic Order* and Leontief *et al.* [1977].

[8] World Development Report, 1988, Table A.6 (p. 189).

TABLE 1.4: *Real per capita GDP and percentage distribution of world GDP of market economies by continent*

Region	Real per capita GDP:					Resulting distribution of real GDP and population.[c]			
	1950[a]	1950[b]	1960	1970	1977	1950	1960	1970	1977
(W) Europe	928	1944	2896	4181	4943	31	32	31	30
						(19)	(17)	(15)	(14)
North America	2364	4485	5225	6666	7795	35	31	28	26
						(9)	(9)	(9)	(8)
Africa	183	451	592	793	862	5	5	6	6
						(14)	(14)	(15)	(15)
Latin America	467	1257	1558	2069	2514	11	12	12	14
						(11)	(12)	(12)	(13)
Asia	178	441	627	992	1179	15	17	21	22
						(42)	(42)	(43)	(44)
Oceania	- -	646	784	966	1134	3	3	3	3
						(5)	(6)	(6)	(6)
Total	- -	1211	1555	2074	2348	100	100	100	100
						(100)	(100)	(100)	(100)

Source: I. Kravis *et al.* [1982]
Notes: [a] In 1960 US dollars as given in Table 1.1, here quoted for reasons of comparison
        [b] In 1975 US dollars
        [c] Population between brackets

TABLE 1.5: *GDP (in billion dollars) and GNP per capita (in dollars) in 1980, and growth rates, 1965–87*

Country group	1980 GDP	1980 GNP pc	Average annual growth of GNP per capita and GDP[c] (per cent)			
			1965–73	1973–80	1980–84	1987[a]
LDCs	2135	670	3.9	3.1	0.7	1.8
			(6.5)	(5.4)	(3.0)	(3.9)
Low-income LDCs	574	270	2.9	2.6	5.1	3.1
			(5.5)	(4.6)	(7.1)	(5.3)
China	284	290	4.9	4.5	5.7[b]	n.a.
			(5.7)	(5.2)	(6.2[b])	n.a.
India	162	240	1.7	1.9	2.5[b]	n.a.
			(7.4)	(5.8)	(7.1[b])	n.a.
Sub-Saharan Africa	203	600	3.7	0.7	−4.9	−4.6
			(6.6)	(3.3)	(−1.5)	(−1.4)
Middle-income countries	1561	1510	4.5	3.1	−1.4	1.1
			(7.0)	(5.7)	(1.4)	(3.2)
High-income oil exporters	216	14540	4.2	5.6	−7.7	5.7
			(8.8)	(8.0)	(−2.1)	(−2.9)
Industrial countries	7440	10760	3.6	2.1	1.3	2.2
			(4.5)	(2.8)	(2.0)	(2.6)

Source: WDRs [1985 and 1988]
Notes: [a] Preliminary
[b] Calculated from the projections in the WDR 1985
[c] GDP growth rates in brackets

TABLE 1.6: *Some measures of demographic change, 1950–90, by region*

Region	Population (in millions)		Annual population (in percentages)		Urban population (in percentages)	
	1950	1985	1950–55	1985–90	1950	1985
Africa	224	555	2.12	3.02	15.7	29.7
Latin America	165	405	2.73	2.16	41.0	68.9
Asia	1292	2697	1.96	1.67	13.9	24.9
except China	737	1637	2.04	2.00	16.1	27.7
LDCs	1684	3663	2.04	1.94	17.0	31.2
except China	1129	2603	2.13	2.25	20.4	35.5
DCs	832	1174	1.28	0.60	53.8	71.5
World	2516	4837	1.79	1.63	29.2	41.0

Source: A. C. Kelley [1988], 'Economic consequences of population change in the Third World', *The Journal of Economic Literature*, vol.XXVI (December), pp.1685-1728.

from this table. First, the post-war population growth rate of LDCs is exceptionally high (being 2.25 per cent per annum excluding China) as compared to the growth rate experienced by Europe during its period of rapid population growth. At this rate, the doubling time of the LDC population is only 28 years (Kelley [1988:1689]). This high rate of population growth is mainly the result of large reductions in mortality rates (Kelley [1988:1689]). Secondly, there is considerable variation in population growth by region, to a large extent due to differences in fertility rates. Currently, Africa is experiencing the highest rate of population growth (3.0 per cent per annum). Finally, the pace of urbanization in the Third World has been rather fast. Presently, almost 36 per cent of LDC population (excluding China) live in urban areas as compared to 20.4 per cent in 1950. The most distinguishing aspect of Third World urbanization is, however, not shown by Table 1.6, viz. the rise of exceptionally large cities such as Mexico City, Rio de Janeiro, and Bombay.

As could be expected on the basis of Pasinetti's [1981] structural theory of growth, a considerable change in the sector structure of developing countries has occurred. Pasinetti indicates population growth and technical change as the two main determining factors of the structural changes occurring in the growth process of an economy in the long run. Technical change gives rise to increasing welfare levels and a concomitant change in the demand structure, given the human hierarchy of needs and wants. We have already given some figures on population growth and will make a few observations in section 1.3.2 in connection with un(der)-employment.

Table 1.7 gives a rough impression of the global structural changes in the Third World's production since the mid-sixties. It shows that already in 1987 the percentage of GDP provided by industry had remarkably become the same in LDCs and developed countries. The share of agriculture in GDP was, however, radically different in both groups of countries. Moreover, in terms of employment provided, the picture would also be very different, the figures for agriculture all being considerably higher. A first statistical analysis of these structural changes or patterns of development was made by Chenery and Syrquin [1975], followed by much further work (see also Syrquin [1988]). These studies have led to the insight that three dimensions are important for distinguishing different development patterns: size of the country (in terms of population), openness towards the international market (in terms of relative level of exports), and trade orientation (in terms of the emphasis on exports of primary goods or manufactured goods). Pursuing the results of these analyses here would bring us to the consideration of national development processes which is the subject of section 1.3.

TABLE 1.7:   *Developing countries: structure of production, 1965–87[a]* (percentage of GDP)

Country group	Agriculture		Industry		Services	
	1965	1987	1965	1987	1965	1987
Developing countries	30	19	29	35	41	46
Low-income countries	41	32	27	33	32	35
Sub-Saharan Africa	44	34	19	27	37	39
Middle-income countries	22	13	30	36	48	51
High-income oil exporters	4	--	62	--	34	--
Industrial countries	5	3	40	35	55	62

Source: World Development Report [1988]
Note: [a] Preliminary

1.3 National perspectives

In the second part of this introductory chapter, we pay attention to some issues related to the national development processes in the developing economies, viz. income distribution, employment, technical change and poverty, financing, and trade and the role of the state.

1.3.1 *Development and income distribution*

Widespread poverty and considerable as well as often increasing income inequalities are at the core of all development problems. In fact, they define for many the principal objective of development policy. In order to get a feeling for the significance of the income distribution problems in LDCs, we begin this section by looking at recent data collected from 21 countries on the percentage shares in total national income going to different quintile groups. This is done in Table 1.8. Although methods of data collection, degree of

TABLE 1.8:   *Income distrubution figures for 21 selected countries*[a]

Country	Year	Lowest 20%	Second 20%	Third 20%	Fourth 20%	Highest 20%	Highest 10%
Bangladesh	1973–74	6.9	11.3	16.1	23.5	42.2	27.4
	1981–82	6.6	10.7	15.3	22.1	45.3	29.5
Nepal	1976–77	4.6	8.0	11.7	16.5	59.2	46.5
India	1975–76	7.0	9.2	13.9	20.5	49.4	23.6
Kenya	1976	2.6	6.3	11.5	19.2	60.4	45.8
Zambia	1976	3.4	7.4	11.2	16.9	61.1	46.4
Tanzania	1969	5.8	9.3	13.9	19.7	50.4	35.6
Sri Lanka	1969–70	7.5	11.7	15.7	21.7	43.4	28.2
	1981–82	5.8	10.1	14.1	20.3	49.8	34.7
Indonesia	1976	6.6	7.8	12.6	23.6	49.9	34.0
Philippines	1970–71	5.2	9.0	12.8	19.0	54.0	38.5
	1985	5.2	8.9	13.2	20.2	52.5	37.0
Ivory Coast	1985–86	2.4	6.2	10.9	19.1	61.4	43.7
Egypt	1974	5.8	10.7	14.7	20.8	48.0	33.2
Thailand	1975–76	5.6	9.6	13.9	21.1	49.8	34.1
El Salvador	1976–77	5.5	10.0	14.8	22.4	47.3	29.5
Peru	1972	1.9	5.1	11.0	21.0	61.0	42.9
Turkey	1973	3.5	8.0	12.5	19.5	56.5	40.7
Costa Rica	1971	3.3	8.7	13.3	19.8	54.8	39.5
Brazil	1972	2.0	5.0	9.4	17.0	66.6	50.6
Malaysia	1973	3.5	7.7	12.4	20.3	56.1	39.8
Mexico	1977	2.9	7.0	12.0	20.4	57.7	40.6
South Korea	1976	5.7	11.2	15.4	22.4	45.3	27.5
Venezuela	1970	3.0	7.3	12.9	22.8	54.0	35.7

Source: World Development Reports [1988]
Note: [a] The countries have been selected according to the availability of figures

coverage, and specific definitions of per capita income may vary from country to country, the figures in Table 1.8 provide a first approximation of the magnitude of income inequalities in these LDCs. We see from these figures that on average the poorest 20 per cent of the population receive only from around 2 per cent to 7 per cent of the total income while the highest 20 per cent group receive between 24 and 51 per cent.

An important question addressed by development economists concerns the many LDCs that had experienced relatively high rates of economic domestic distribution of the benefits from growth.[9] In many LDCs that had experienced relatively high rates of economic growth by historical standards, such growth has not led to a decline of economic inequality or a reduction of poverty. As is clear from Table 1.8, the income distribution in many LDCs is relatively unequal and in some cases such as Bangladesh and Sri Lanka, has become even more unequal over time.

Table 1.9 presents a summary of changes in income distribution in groups of non-communist developing countries in the form of changing Gini coefficients. We see that in general between 1960 and 1980, income inequality increased substantially for all non-communist LDCs—the weighted average of the Gini coefficients increased from 0.54 to 0.60 which implies an increase of an already relatively high income inequality. Socialist countries such as Czechoslovakia, Hungary and Poland which have the highest degree of

TABLE 1.9:   *Trends in income distribution, 1960–80*

Country group	Income distribution Gini coefficient	
	1960	1980
All non-communist developing countries:	0.544	0.602
– Low-income countries	0.407	0.450
– Middle-income, non-oil-exporting countries	0.603	0.569
– Oil-exporting countries	0.575	0.612

Source: Adelman [1986], 'A poverty-focused approach to development policy', in J. P. Lewis and V. Kalab (eds.), Development strategies reconsidered (Washington, DC: Overseas Development Council)

[9] During the last few decades, the long-run pattern of economic inequality within countries has been the subject of a considerable amount of theoretical and empirical work. For example, for industrialized economies such as England, the United States of America, Germany, France and the Netherlands, Bertholet [1983] has analysed the long-run pattern of income distribution in combination with the growth of personal income during the industrialization process. He comes up with a general pattern in which (i) the share of the upper 5 per cent of the income scale increases during the beginning of industrial development and decreases thereafter; (ii) the share of the 61st to 95th percentiles sharply declines at the start of the growth process, but thereafter increases; (iii) the share of the 21st to 61st to 95th percentiles steadily increases with per capita income growth; and finally (iv) the share of the quintile should be divided into a share of the lowest decile which gradually declines, and a share of the second decile which slightly increases.

equality in their income distribution, have Gini coefficients of around 0.2. Developed countries on the whole exhibit a relatively more equal distribution than most LDCs. The Gini coefficients of West Germany (1964), the Netherlands (1967), England (1968) and the USA (1970) are 0.45, 0.43, 0.32, and 0.31, respectively (Ahluwalia [1974]). In contrast to most LDCs, most industrialized economies have been able to develop effective mechanisms, such as social security systems, unemployment compensation, progressive income tax rates, to redistribute part of the primary income distribution which itself is already more equal in developed countries than in developing countries. From Table 1.9, we see that income inequality declined in middle-income, non-oil producing nations, while it increased in both low-income and oil-exporting countries. Further, the higher Gini coefficients of the last two groups reflect a worsening of income distribution both within individual LDCs and for the population of all developing countries as a whole.[10]

Within developing economies, the nature of the relationship between the level of economic development and income inequality has always attracted much attention. Already in 1955, Kuznets tested a hypothesis claiming that as economic development occurs, relative income inequality first increases and, after some 'turning point', starts declining. This came to be known as the inverted-U-hypothesis. As the analysis was based on historical data for industrialized countries, Kuznets was cautious in extending the pattern to include developing countries. Since the expected pattern of income distribution at various stages of development is an issue of major importance, the inverted U-curve hypotheses has been frequently tested for Third World countries. It is important to know that these tests were based on cross-country observations, because time-series data on income distribution for even moderate periods were not available for most LDCs. Studies by Paukert [1973], Adelman and Morris [1973], Ahluwalia [1976] and others tended to be favourable to the Kuznets hypothesis which almost gained the status of a 'stylized fact'. In recent years, however,

---

[10] Such an increase in inequality of the income distribution of the Third World's population is, of course, also connected with the low growth rates of the poorest countries as compared to the high growth rates of the relatively rich, oil-exporting countries. Middle-income countries registered in-between growth rates as has been discussed in the previous section of this chapter.

these studies have become subject to considerable criticism (cf. Saith [1983]). Besides the problem inherent in drawing inferences from cross-section data about expected dynamic income distribution patterns of individual countries, almost all previous studies suffered from two major data limitations (cf. Ram [1988]). First, due to differences in concepts of income, variations in income-receiving units, and disparities in geographical coverage, income distribution data were hardly comparable between countries. Secondly, the income variables generally used in the comparison were 'distorted' because the per capita dollar income measures were based on conventional exchange rates (see for this point Kravis, Heston and Summers [1982]). Analysis of internationally comparable income data of Third World countries gives only limited support to the inverted U-curve hypothesis as is shown by Ram [1988].

In contrast to the academic interest, in the 1950s and 1960s, economists and planners did not consider the distribution of income a major policy problem in developing countries. The prevailing view was that rapid economic growth would naturally (though with a time lag) lead to improved conditions for everyone. According to Adelman and Robinson,

Though many might have preferred to see more relative equality and faster improvement in the absolute incomes of the poor, even radical critics of the market economy and existing institutional arrangements were at the time much more preoccupied with failure to achieve adequate growth than with distributional issues. [1978:I]

By the mid-1960s, it became clear, however, that the expected trickle-down effects of growth did not materialize. Industrial growth has accelerated enormously in many Third World countries since the 1950s, yet a growing body of empirical evidence now indicates that relative inequality and sometimes even absolute poverty have not decreased, but rather increased as is illustrated by the figures in Tables 1.8 and 1.9 (cf. Chenery *et al.* [1974]; Fields [1980]; de Janvry and Sadoulet [1983]). Increasingly, the relationship between growth and income distribution became one of the major issues addressed by development economists. In the early 1970s, one of the major (policy) questions was whether there is a basic conflict between the goal of greater distributional equality and the goal of faster growth. In turn, this interest led to the question of identifying the societal causes of inequality, viz. how much actually can be done to improve the distribution of income in developing countries.[11] The answer to this question depends on the determination of income distribution. Opinions on the question of the determination of income distribution largely differ. In neoclassical theory, factor markets clear to determine factor prices and, consequently, the distribution of income. An alternative view presented by Marxist or structuralist theory assumes that factor prices are determined by class struggle or are given exogenously in the form of 'institutionally-determined' wage rates or mark-up rates. As a result, the distribution of income comes about in reaction to growth in neoclassical models, while in the demand-driven models of structuralists income distribution clearly affects the rate and pattern of growth (cf. Taylor [1983]).

Several attempts have been made to analyse the implications of each one of these approaches to the income distribution in developing countries within the framework of highly disaggregated macroeconomic models of the 'computable general equilibrium' type.[12] Results of simulation experiments which have been undertaken for a large number of countries have led to a proliferation of country-specific policy recommendations. Nevertheless, following de Janvry and Sadoulet [1983], we may classify all these recommendations into three main policy approaches to the problem of growth and income distribution:

(1) *Accelerate growth*
In order to reach the turning point of the inverted U-curve, growth should be accelerated. It is held that (i) in the early stages of economic development, growth is inevitably unequalizing; and (ii) growth itself creates the conditions for a more equal distribution of income at later stages through shifts in employment between agriculture and industry and through upward pressures on wages—as

---

[11] Notice that these questions are not unrelated to the issue of the inverted-U-curve hypothesis, but not the same either, as they address policy issues for which usually the horizon is shorter and the setting is smaller and more precise than for Kuznets' problem. In other words, whatever the answer to the latter problem, these policy issues are and will remain alive. But the other way round, the hypothesis might have suggested to some policy-makers that they didn't have to worry about the income distribution even though there might be a considerable problem in the medium and long-term.

[12] See, for instance, Adelman and Robinson [1978]; Taylor *et al.* [1988], Kravis *et al.* [1982]; Robinson [1988].

happens in the models of dualistic growth of Lewis [1954] and Fei and Ranis [1964]. Thus, the faster the rate of growth, the sooner trickle-down effects will lead to an improvement in the income distribution (see for this argument: Ahluwalia [1976]; Chenery and Syrquin [1975]).

(2) *Control the income-distributional effects of income*
Growth has to be accelerated as under (1) but the resulting increase in inequality has to be corrected by public intervention. This leads to the strategies of 'redistribution with growth' (Chenery *et al.* [1974]) and 'basic needs' (Streeten [1979]; Sinha *et al.* [1979]; Kouwenaar [1986]). Of particular importance in this context has been the formulation of the Approach to the Fifth Five-Year Plan of India which was based on a strategy of redistribution with growth and postulated a specific objective of poverty eradication along with the elimination of net foreign aid (cf. Chakravarty [1987]).

(3) *Change the conditions of growth*
At the outset of development, the structural conditions of growth have to be transformed in order to make the growth process itself more equitable. This approach is based on the assumption that the distribution of income is so deeply embedded in the structure of an economy (as it relates to the distribution of assets and property rights) that it can only be affected by a major change in this economic structure. Dasgupta and Ray [1987], for instance, show theoretically that an economy which is moderately endowed and capable of employing everyone and feeding everyone adequately, will fail to do so if the distribution of assets is highly unequal. This approach has given birth to the following three alternative strategies which can also be pursued in combination:

1. *The promotion of labour-intensive production patterns* that will create employment and upward pressures on wages (Stewart [1987]). Policy recommendations here include the generation of efficient labour-intensive intermediate technologies, the infrastructural support of small-scale (rural) industries,[13] and elimination of market distortions which have cheapened capital

---

[13] This recent interest in rural industrialization has already given rise to a large number of studies, see for instance: Haan [1988], Little, Mazumdar and Page [1987], Liedholm and Mead [1987], Islam [1987], and Suri [1988].

costs and increased labour costs; and, in general, the elimination of biases against appropriate technologies and small-scale industries.

2. *Integrated rural development programmes* to increase both labour and land productivity of peasant agriculture and increase peasants' delivery of marketed surplus (Mellor [1976]). An aspect which has to be taken into account when dealing with such programmes is their effect on the intra-rural income distribution. This effect crucially depends on the relative growth of labour productivity as compared to the increase in land productivity. A relatively larger increase in the productivity of land will imply larger benefits accruing to the (large) landowners as compared to the gains in income of the agricultural wage labourers.

3. *Redistribution of productive assets before growth.* An initially unequal distribution of assets is believed to set in motion an unequalizing spiral of growth, as in the Taylor-Bacha [1976] model in which the development process does not reach a turning point after which inequality declines as postulated by Kuznets. Therefore, equitable growth requires the prior equalization of assets in particular through massive land reform and education programmes such as those performed in Taiwan and South Korea (Adelman and Robinson [1978]; Fei, Ranis and Kuo [1979]; de Janvry and Sadoulet [1983]). However, the transferability of these South-East Asian development experiences is extremely limited for country-specific political and historical reasons. In both cases, for example, the land reforms were more or less exogenously brought about through foreign (i.e. United States) intervention. Furthermore, in South Korea a relatively well-functioning irrigation infrastructure in agriculture had been built up under the colonial rule of Japan, benefiting both large and small farmers.

1.3.2. *Employment, technical change and poverty*

Labour is by far the most abundant resource in low-income countries. One important characteristic of low-income countries is the large proportion of the labour force in agriculture as can be seen in Table 1.10. Between 1965 and 1980, on average, the share of agricultural employment in total employment declined from 70 to 62 per cent in developing economies. From Table 1.10 it is clear that there are considerable differences between individual LDCs

TABLE 1.10 *Changes in sectoral composition of the labour force,*
1965–80

| | Percentage share of labour force in: | | | | | |
| | Agriculture | | Industry | | Services | |
Country group	1965	1980	1965	1980	1965	1980
Low-income economies	**77**	**72**	**9**	**13**	**14**	**15**
– Ethiopia	86	80	2	3	4	5
– Bangladesh	84	75	5	6	11	19
– Mozambique	87	85	6	7	7	8
– Tanzania	92	86	3	5	6	10
– China	81	74	8	14	11	12
– India	73	70	12	13	15	17
– Sudan	82	71	5	8	14	21
– Pakistan	60	55	18	16	22	30
– Senegal	83	81	6	6	11	13
Middle-income economies	**56**	**43**	**17**	**23**	**27**	**34**
– Indonesia	71	57	9	13	21	30
– Philippines	58	52	16	16	26	33
– Zimbabwe	79	73	8	11	13	17
– Turkey	75	58	11	17	14	25
– Colombia	45	34	21	24	34	42
Upper middle-income	**45**	**29**	**23**	**31**	**32**	**40**
– Brazil	49	31	20	27	31	42
– Mexico	50	37	22	29	29	35
– South Korea	55	36	15	27	30	37
All developing economies	**70**	**62**	**12**	**16**	**18**	**22**
Industrial market economies	**14**	**7**	**38**	**35**	**48**	**58**

Source: World Development Report [1988] Table 31

with regard to the sectoral composition of the labour force as well
as to its development over time.

A second characteristic of low-income countries is the low proportion of workers who earn their income wholly or chiefly in the
wage labour market compared to the labour force in high-income
countries. In most LDCs, the majority of workers operate in family enterprises, both in agriculture and in industry. Consequently,
the behaviour of the family enterprise and its constituent members
has been extensively studied by development economists (cf. Singh
et al. [1986]).

It is now widely held in the literature that open unemployment must be regarded as only one aspect of the wider problem of underemployment and poverty in developing countries. In addition to the numbers of unemployed workers, many of whom receive minimal incomes through the help of family members, it is also necessary to consider the following three aspects of labour utilization:

1. Working time—many of those employed would like to work more hours per day, per week or per year.
2. Intensity of work—many can work only at a low intensity due to health and nutrition conditions (cf. Dasgupta and Ray [1986], [1987]).
3. Productivity—often labour productivity is also unduly low because of the technology used in production, the limited availability of complementary resources, lack of education, inefficient organization, etc. Taking these aspects into account, we are able to distinguish other forms of underutilization of labour such as underemployment which includes those persons working less than they would like to work, and disguised underemployment which includes persons employed on a full-time basis even though the services they render may actually require much less than full time.

Table 1.11 provides a summary picture of unemployment and underemployment trends from 1960 to 1990, both for developing countries as a whole and for Africa, Asia, and Latin America separately. Looking firstly at the unemployment figures, the projections to 1990 indicate that the rate of Third World unemployment will steadily increase to over 8 per cent. In fact, these projections which were made in 1975, were overly optimistic. Due to the debt problem and the slowdown in world economic growth during the 1980s, total LDC unemployment is at least twice as large in absolute terms as the estimate presented in Table 1.11 (cf. Todaro [1989:241]). Furthermore, in most LDCs open unemployment is a predominantly urban phenomenon and this has become a problem of increasing seriousness in the last two decades. Already in the early 1970s, Jolly *et al.* [1973] estimated that 15–25 per cent of the urban labour force are openly unemployed in many countries.

Underemployment is the predominant form of contemporary labour underutilization in LDCs as can also be seen from Table 1.11 where the combined unemployment and underemployment

TABLE 1.11: *Unemployment in developing countries, 1960–90*

	1960	1970	1980	1990
Unemployment rate (%)				
– All developing countries[a]	6.7	7.4	7.8	8.2
– Africa	7.7	9.6	9.8	9.9
– Asia	6.8	7.1	7.7	8.3
– Latin America	4.7	5.1	5.8	5.5
Combined unemployment and underemployment rate				
– All developing countries[a]	25	27		
– Africa	31	39		
– Asia	24	26		
– Latin America	18	20		

Source: Todaro [1989], Table 8.1; the figures are based on a projection made in 1975 which according to Todaro [1989: 238–41] is an underestimation of at most 50% of real unemployment levels.

Note: [a] Excluding China

rate amounts to 25 and 27 per cent in 1960 and 1970 respectively, which means levels two to three times higher than the calculated unemployment rates. This phenomenon of growth without adequate employment expansion has exposed the weakness of conventional development strategies based on the Lewis [1954] model of a labour-surplus economy with its emphasis on modern sector industrialization and GDP growth. As the rate of growth of manufacturing output exceeded the growth rate of industrial employment during the last two decades, the share of industrial employment in total employment increased less than the share of manufacturing output in total output.

The capacity of the modern sector to productively absorb the surplus labour in the economy has been seriously overestimated. Suppose, for example, that the labour force grows at about 3 per cent per annum and that the manufacturing sector employs, say, 20 per cent of the country's labour force. Then, in order to just absorb the increase of the labour force, manufacturing would need to raise employment by 15 per cent per year. Such industrial employment growth is virtually impossible to achieve in any economy. Moreover, the form of modern sector development, with its relatively high capital intensity, high productivity and high wages, has even worsened the situation by acting as a pull-factor triggering off large-scale rural-urban migration while not providing enough jobs.[14] For the first time in history, the pace of industrialization has been slower than that of urbanization. In almost all LDCs, the percentage of the population already living in cities greatly exceeds the proportion engaged in manufacturing. Given these demographic and structural economic circumstances, it would be unrealistic to rely solely on accelerated modern industrial growth to solve the problems of growing unemployment and underemployment.

Consequently, new types of development strategies have to be developed. Booth and Sundrum [1985], for instance, argue that LDCs must give greater emphasis to the role of labour absorption in agriculture in designing the development strategies appropriate to their present circumstances. According to them, all policy options open to LDC governments regarding technological progress, capital investment and interventions in the labour and product markets should be evaluated from the point of view of increasing productive labour absorption in agriculture. A second approach to the problem of unemployment and underemployment stresses the potential importance of combining labour-intensive production units outside agriculture. If the latter take place in rural areas, they also curb rural-urban migration. Stewart [1987] and others have drawn attention to the fact that price distortions sometimes have worked against such strategies. In the same way, multinationals and foreign connections in general have tended to use or induce relatively capital-intensive and large-scale production methods. Many studies and arguments have been made around this theme, e.g. in Suri [1988], Haan [1988], Islam [1987], James [1987] and Little et al. [1987]. This question of the 'choice of techniques' at any particular point in time leads on to a discussion of the question of technical change. This issue is not only important for an understanding of the sources of growth, as Tinbergen [1942] has indicated in a pioneering theoretical paper and as Denison [1967] has quantitatively shown for a number of presently developed countries, but also for an understanding of certain critical factors in regard to the processes shaping income distribution (cf. Stewart [1988:529 ff.], Schumpeter [1934], and Pasinetti [1981]). The question of technical change can be split into two strongly interrelated subissues: (a) tracing the growth of technology, the 'book of blueprints' from

---

[14] See the Harris-Todaro [1970] model of rural-urban migration. For a review of the literature on rural-urban migration, see Yap [1977].

which choices can be made both with respect to products and to methods of production, and indicating the underlying factors; and (b) understanding the factors which induce the actual historical behaviour of the relevant decision units with respect to the choice of technique from this book of blueprints. The present situation of developing countries has an added dimension to the two subissues insofar as they face in general a 'developed world' in which not only the per capita income and power in many senses is higher, but also the level of technology. The transfer of technology from this outside world is a permanent option, even though often not without disadvantages in terms of increasing dualism and dependency. This appears to occur especially if a minimally adequate indigenous science and technology system has not been established which can absorb these technologies and build further on them. It is important to see that in discussing these technologies much more is at stake than simply a choice between combinations of labour and capital in production lines, e.g. information and organizational patterns also play a considerable role.

For centuries, this technical change based on science and on corresponding institutional changes (see e.g. Dosi *et al.* [1988] and Kingston [1984]) has been a dominant source of growth in the presently developed countries, both in agriculture (Boserup [1965]) and in industry and services. Technological progress has enabled these economies to cope with population increases (Boserup [1981]). It can also be and it has already been an important source of growth in developing countries, but precisely the above mentioned interrelation between the creation of blueprints and the processes of choice from them, makes the adoption of foreign originated techniques a far from innocent affair (see e.g. Lall [1987]). Both the 'global' book of blueprints and the practice of transnational, and quite a few exporting national, enterprises in the Third World lean heavily on experiences and needs originating in the developed world, with prevailing relative factor scarcities radically different from those in the developing countries. Thus quite a few economic activities in the Third World are maladjusted to their environment. Although quantitative studies comparable to Denison's [1967] for developing countries are not directly available, it is clear that the high rates of un(der)-employment prevailing in LDCs today are not unrelated to such maladjustment.

There is a close relationship between high levels of unemployment and underemployment, widespread poverty, and unequal distribution of income. In most cases, those without regular or adequate employment are among the very poor. Those with regularly paid employment in the public and private sectors are typically among the middle- or upper-income groups. Of course, not all unemployed people are poor nor are all the employed well-off. Many self-employed workers in the so-called urban 'informal' sector, for example, are fully employed, but they are often still very poor due to their low labour productivity. Nevertheless, one of the mechanisms for reducing poverty and inequality in LDCs is the provision of adequately paying, productive employment opportunities for the poor. In this context, poverty and income inequality may be seen to be caused by the nature of technology, demographic forces and the prevailing payment system which is defined as the set of rules determining the primary distribution of incomes (cf. Stewart [1978]).[15] These rules include

1. rules governing how income from work is determined;
2. rules governing access to work; and
3. rules governing both the accumulation and distribution of assets, and determining property rights.

All economies in which impoverishment occurs are characterized by dualism with respect to the payment system and technology. In the modern, mainly industrial sector a mixed payment system prevails combined with advanced technology. In the urban informal and the rural sectors, elements of a traditional and a capitalist payment system exist simultaneously, combined with a mixture of modern and traditional technology (cf. Terhal [1988:136]). Due to its mixed payment system and capital-intensive technology, the modern sector can only absorb a small part of the incremental labour force. Nevertheless, public and private investment, public services and infrastructural outlays are concentrated in this sector due to strong political and economic pressure for preferential treatment by the government (cf. Lipton [1877]). In the rural sector, the scarcity of land and its uneven distribution prevent

---

[15] The secondary distribution of incomes which results from a transfer of primary claims—either informally through family, tribe and related social structures, or formally through state-imposed taxation and redistribution—is considered to play a minor role. As development proceeds, informal secondary shifts in income distribution tend to become less important whereas formal redistribution is still largely absent. For a review of these issues, see Terhal [1988: 134–8].

widespread adoption of new (green revolution) technologies (Griffin [1974]). In the rest of the economy, population growth combined with the lack of appropriate technological change leads to a worsening of capital-labour and land-labour ratios in the rest of the economy and, hence, to detrimental effects on income levels.

1.3.3. *The financing of development*

For developing countries, the provision of adequate resources to finance the requisite investment without engendering inflation is an important constraint on accelerating economic growth (cf. e.g. Chakravarty [1974]). This total supply of investable resources is equal to the sum of domestic savings and net capital receipts from abroad. Although foreign resources do contribute to the financing of economic development, most LDCs depend mainly upon domestic real resources (i.e. savings) for their development. Since, in a closed economy, savings equal national income less private and public consumption outlays, it follows that fiscal and monetary measures that succeed in restraining the growth of these two categories of consumption, without negatively affecting the growth of production, will also raise the ratio of savings to national income. Public intervention can play a two-fold role in raising savings for development. As the government is in a position to offset any contractionary impact of the curb on consumption by a corresponding rise in public investment, it may use resources released by cutting down consumption to promote investment, while maintaining the rate of growth of aggregate effective demand at the desired level. Early development models—such as the Harrod-Domar model and the Mahanalobis model—emphasize the role of domestic savings as the major source of capital formation and growth. In fact, an increase in the savings rate was seen as a necessary and sufficient condition for sustained growth as is illustrated by Lewis's statement that

the central problem of economic development is to understand the process by which a community which was previously saving and investing 4 or 5 per cent of its national income or less, converts itself into an economy where voluntary savings is running at about 12 or 15 per cent of national income or more.

From Table 1.12, it is clear that, already in 1965, the LDCs—taken as one group—had solved Lewis's central problem of development as their savings rate and investment rate amounted to 20 and 21 per cent respectively. There exist, however, large differences in savings and investment performance between Third World countries which may not be unrelated to their growth rates. Using data from the 1988 World Development Report, we have classified LDCs with populations of five million or more into three groups on the basis of their growth performance during the period 1960–86 (Table 1.12). We may now look at possible common characteristics of the individual countries in each of the groups.[16]

In Group III countries, GNP per capita grew at 1 per cent or less per year during 1965–86. A rather common characteristic of these countries is their relatively poor savings performance. In 1986, the share of domestic savings in GNP amounted to less than 10 per cent on (unweighted) average.[17] Even more striking is the dramatic decline in the savings rate and, correspondingly, of the investment rate of a number of Group III countries such as Ethiopia, Bangladesh, Zaire, Sudan, Zambia, Bolivia, El Salvador and Peru. In general, this low level or decline of the savings rate can be attributed to the fact that the countries concerned either do not have enough natural resources to yield enough savings for financing industrialization—as is the case for Bangladesh and Sudan—or else their economies have been disrupted by internal war or violence—as has happened in Ethiopia and El Salvador, and to a lesser extent in Bolivia and Peru. Possessing large mineral resources, Zaire is an exception to this rule. Nevertheless, it is clear that domestic peace is one of the conditions for growth and that the African continent is the most prone to economic disturbance due to internal wars.

Moreover, much of Africa also suffers from inadequate rainfall and/or inadequate irrigation infrastructure and this is one of the major causes of the recent severe droughts and famines plaguing the sub-Saharan African countries. It is also argued that the over-exploitation of the natural environment over a long period of time has at least aggravated this situation. Bangladesh, in contrast, increasingly suffers from annual floods. Adequate availability and control

[16] It should be clear, however, that in the framework of this introductory paper, we are not aiming at a thorough econometric analysis, but rather want to briefly elucidate and comment on some generally empirical data which the reader may pursue further.

[17] The two exceptions with savings rates in 1986 above 15 per cent, Peru and Chile, should be mentioned; they deserve a separate analysis which is outside the scope of this paper.

TABLE 1.12: *Share (%) of investment and savings in GDP, 1960–86; average annual growth rate (%) of GNP per capita, 1960–86*

Country group	Gross domestic Investment		Gross domestic Savings		GNP-pc growth
	1965	1986	1965	1986	1965-86
Group I: GNP growth of more than 3%					
– Indonesia	8	26	8	24	4.6
– Cameroon	13	25	13	28	3.9
– Rep. of Congo	22	29	5	30	3.6
– Egypt	18	19	14	9	3.1
– Thailand	20	21	19	25	4.0
– Ecuador	14	20	11	20	3.5
– China	25	39	25	36	5.1
– Tunisia	28	24	14	17	3.8
– Syria	10	24	10	14	3.7
– Malaysia	20	25	24	32	4.3
– South Korea	15	29	8	35	6.7
– Brazil	20	21	22	24	4.3
– Yugoslavia	30	38	30	40	3.9
Group II: GNP growth between 1-3%					
– Nepal	6	19	0	9	1.9
– Mali	--	21	--	4	1.1
– Burma	19	15	13	12	2.3
– Malawi	14	10	0	7	1.5
– India	18	23	16	21	1.8
– Rwanda	10	19	5	9	1.5
– Sri Lanka	12	24	13	13	2.9
– Pakistan	21	17	13	7	2.4
– Kenya	14	26	15	26	1.9
– Nigeria	19	12	17	10	1.9
– Dominican Republic	10	18	6	12	2.5
– Philippines	21	13	21	19	1.9
– Zimbabwe	15	18	23	20	1.2
– Morocco	10	20	12	13	1.9
– Guatemala	13	11	10	9	1.4
– Turkey	15	25	13	22	2.7
– Colombia	16	18	17	20	2.8
– Mexico	22	21	21	27	2.6
Group III: GNP growth 1% or less					
– Ethiopia	13	9	12	3	0.0
– Bangladesh	11	12	8	2	0.4
– Zaire	14	12	30	13	-2.2
– Uganda	11	14	12	11	-2.6
– Haiti	7	12	2	6	0.6
– Niger	8	11	3	7	-2.2

TABLE 1.12 (*Contd.*)

Country group	Gross domestic Investment 1965	Gross domestic Investment 1986	Gross domestic Savings 1965	Gross domestic Savings 1986	GNP-pc growth 1965–86
– Madagascar	10	14	4	10	−1.7
– Ghana	18	10	8	8	−1.7
– Sierra Leone	12	10	9	8	0.2
– Sudan	10	12	9	4	−0.2
– Zambia	25	15	40	13	−1.7
– Bolivia	22	8	17	5	−0.4
– El Salvador	15	13	12	7	−0.3
– Honduras	15	17	15	13	0.3
– Peru	34	20	31	18	0.1
– Chile	15	15	16	18	−0.2
All developing economies	**21**	**24**	**20**	**24**	**2.9**

Source: *World Development Report* [1988] Tables 1 and 5

of water, therefore, is also one of the fundamental requirements of growth. However, domestic peace, adequate water management, high domestic savings and investment will not generate growth in a simple, mechanical way.

Excluding Egypt, the Group I countries which are the fastest growing ones, all share high savings rates—25 per cent on average in 1986—and high investment rates—26 per cent on average in 1986. Indonesia, the Republic of Congo and South Korea experienced a rise in their savings rate of more than 300 per cent. It is noteworthy that a high growth rate of income associates with a relatively high per capita income—most of the Group I countries have per capita incomes in excess of $500. On average, as a percentage of GDP, they save and invest more than the Group II countries. A considerable number of LDCs belonging to Groups II and III have failed to promote domestic savings and investment to anything near the maximum possible. According to Eshag [1983:122], this is due to 'the unwillingness, or inability, to take the necessary measures to restrain growth of public and private consumption'. Instead of using their outlays for investment purposes (inclusive of health and education), governments—particularly those of Asian LDCs which account for almost two-thirds of the Third World population—spend them on defence.

With respect to private consumption, Eshag concludes that developing countries also failed to curb private consumption of luxuries by the upper-income groups through taxation or other measures. During 1970–75, the average share of total tax revenue in national income of 27 selected LDCs was 13.7 per cent, while the corresponding figure derived from 13 industrialized countries was 37.5 per cent (Eshag [1983:94–5]). Particularly, the revenues from direct taxation are relatively small in LDCs where vested interests—notably the large landlords—by and large escape the burden of direct taxation.

Looking at all these groups together, one is puzzled by the fact that for some LDCs an increase in savings (and investment) to above a level of 15 per cent of GDP has not automatically led to a substantial rise in the growth rate of their per capita GNP as was believed by Lewis. A good example is provided by India which through deliberate public intervention has succeeded in raising its savings rate to 21 per cent, but experienced a relatively disappointing per capita GNP growth rate of 1.8 per cent. As a discussion of the Indian development experience is beyond the scope of this introductory chapter (cf. Chakravarty [1987]), we will highlight only one important aspect of the Indian economy which is characteristic also of other LDCs and behind which one or more direct growth-constraining factors may be operative: its relatively high incremental capital-output ratios. Such constraints to growth for example, may arise from either insufficient agricultural production leading via real wage increases to cost-push inflation or insufficient availability of complementary inputs or inappropriate technology.

So far, our discussion has focused on the problem of financing economic development in a relatively closed economy and on the importance of promoting domestic savings. In an open economy, however, the argument changes. Suppose that the government of an LDC decides to step up the rate of growth for a period (say, of five years) by raising the ratio of investment in the national income. The additional investment required will now be financed by additional domestic savings and an inflow of foreign capital.   Foreign capital can perform two distinct functions:

1. By supplementing savings it can increase available investable resources.
2. By supplementing export earnings it can augment foreign exchange resources required for the purchase of imports—mainly capital goods, technology and intermediate inputs.

The relative significance of these two functions in promoting the development of individual LDCs will depend on whether their GDP growth rate is constrained by the availability of domestic savings or by foreign exchange resources. This is the familiar 'two-gap' analysis (cf. Chenery and Strout [1966]).[18]

The basic argument of the two-gap model is that most LDCs are faced either with a shortage of domestic savings to match domestic investment demand or a shortage of foreign exchange to finance needed imports of capital and intermediate goods. Suppose the first situation applies. If the country in question is unable to increase the domestic savings rate above the minimum level required to achieve the target growth rate of GDP, any attempt to raise the growth rate of investment beyond that rate, without the requisite inflow of foreign capital, would lead to inflation and a redistribution of income in favour of profits. For such a country, the growth process is constrained by savings. Foreign capital can make an acceleration of this growth process possible by filling the savings gap. According to Eshag [1983:127–8], the savings constraint is likely to be in operation in the poorest countries of Africa and Asia with a relatively small unexploited savings potential.

Most LDCs, however, are assumed to experience a binding foreign-exchange gap. These countries have excess productive resources—mostly labour—and all available foreign exchange is being used for imports. The existence of complementary domestic resources would permit them to undertake new investment projects if they had the foreign exchange to pay for the import of the required capital goods and associated technical assistance. Thus, foreign financial resources may help in filling gaps between the domestically available supplies of savings, foreign exchange and government revenue, and the desired level of these resources necessary for investment to achieve growth and development targets.

Foreign financial resources take two main forms:

1. Private foreign investment, mostly direct investment by large multinational corporations and financial capital by international

---

[18] Most two-gap models assume that the savings and foreign-exchange gap are unequal in magnitude and that they are mutually independent, i.e. there is no substitutability between savings and foreign exchange. This latter assumption of two separate types of constraints deserves further consideration. Note that to the extent that foreign resources are substitutes for domestic savings, only one gap exists.

banks whose lending activities accelerated greatly during the late 1970s.
2. Public and private development assistance (foreign aid), from national governments, multinational donor agencies as well as private NGOs.

The growth of private foreign investment in the Third World has been extremely rapid, increasing from $2.4 billion in 1962 to over $13 billion by 1985. Major recipients were concentrated among the higher-income LDCs such as Brazil, Mexico, Argentina, and Indonesia. In addition to export earnings and private foreign investment, the other major source of Third World foreign exchange is foreign aid. The money volume of 'official development assistance' (ODA) has grown from an annual rate of about $4.6 billion in 1960 to $37 billion in 1986. In terms of the percentage of developed country GNPs allocated to ODA, there has been a decline from 0.51 per cent in 1960 to 0.36 per cent in 1986. This external assistance is assumed to facilitate and accelerate the process of development by generating additional domestic savings as a result of the higher growth rates that it is presumed to induce. In practice, however, aid may have significant negative effects on growth on two accounts. First, by substituting for, rather than supplementing, domestic savings and investment, foreign aid tends to reduce the pressure on the public authorities to raise the share of savings in national income through fiscal and other measures (cf. Eshag [1983]). Secondly, as a result of the linking of aid to donor country exports, LDC balance of payments deficits are exacerbated. LDCs' balance of payments problems which have dramatically increased during the last decade will be the final issue addressed in this section.

The 1980s debt crisis originates in the period 1974–79 when there was a virtual explosion in international lending, precipitated by the first major OPEC oil price increase. In the face of high oil prices and a worldwide recession in which the growth rates of the industrialized countries fell from an average of 5.2 per cent in 1967–74 to an average of 2.7 per cent for the rest of the decade, many LDCs sought to sustain their high growth rates through increased borrowing. The second oil shock occurring in 1979 again added to oil import bills and affected industrial goods imports. There was also a large rise in the real interest rates caused by (i) the industrialized countries' economic stabilization policies, and

TABLE 1.13:   *Dimensions of the LDC debt crisis: 1970–89*

	1970	1975	1980	1985	1989[a]
Total external debt					
(in billions of $)	68.4	180.0	635.8	1,016.6	1,262.8
of which, sub-Saharan Africa	—	14.9	55.6	90.6	—
Debt/Export ratio (%)	99.4	76.4	81.9	148.8	139.0
of which, Africa	—	—	92.5	190.5	232.9
Debt Service ratio[b]					
(% of exports)	13.5	9.5	13.2	20.3	17.5
of which, Africa	5.7	—	14.4	28.8	24.9
Dept/GDP ratio (%)	13.3	15.4	24.4	36.6	34.5
of which, Africa	20.9	—	28.3	45.4	53.2

Source: Todaro [1989], Table 13.8
Notes: [a] Projections
           [b] Actual payments of interest on total debt plus actual amortization on
           long-term debt as a percentage of exports of goods and services

(ii) a decrease in Third World export earnings—resulting from a combination of slow growth in the more developed regions and a decline of over 20 per cent in primary commodity export prices. High real interest rates, in turn, led to a decline in buffer stocks of primary commodities and an increase in their supply on the world markets. This had a further negative effect on the international terms of trade of the countries exporting these primary commodities. As a result, the external debt of LDCs grew from $68.4 billion to $1283 billion between 1970 and 1989 (see Table 1.13). Although a major share of the debt is concentrated in four Latin American countries (Brazil, Mexico, Argentina, and Venezuela), recently interest has concentrated on the debt problems of sub-Saharan Africa which are made more troublesome by declining per capita incomes and stagnating economies. Both their debt:export and debt:service ratios are well above the overall LDC average. During the 1980s, a large number of LDCs sought debt relief from the IMF and, by the end of 1986, more than 25 countries were in the process of rescheduling or had already rescheduled part of their enormous bank debt.

1.3.4. *Trade and state*

In contrast to recent development research, early post-war concern with industrial growth was based on the view that development would largely take place in relative autarchy, a view that reflected the mood of export pessimism prevailing during this period (see Little [1982], chapter 4). Import substitution policies were pursued based on infant industry arguments as well as on the rapid growth in productivity that was expected during the stage when industrial skills were created and modern technology mastered. It was believed that domestic industries would utilize the period of protection to increase technical efficiency and move towards internationally competitive prices.

The high levels of protection remaining in force after two or three decades of intense industrialization suggest that many LDCs are not able to terminate protection when their domestic industries fail to meet international competition. There are, however, countries such as Korea and Taiwan which began their industrialization drives with high rates of protection, but gradually became more export-oriented. The willingness and particularly the ability of the political authorities of these countries to stop subsidizing enterprises that are not able to live up to the standards of international competition, is an important and only recently explored dimension of South-East Asian success (see Olson [1982]; Bradford [1987]; Chakravarty [1987a]).

The rapid growth of these South-East Asian NICs has led to a change in attitude with respect to trade policy towards more export orientation. Increasingly, exports are seen as generating greater productivity growth as a result of:

1. greater capacity utilization in industries in which the minimum efficient size of a plant is large relative to the size of the domestic market;
2. increasing familiarity with and absorption of new technologies;
3. greater learning-by-doing insofar as this is a function of cumulative output, and exports permit greater output in an industry; and
4. the stimulative effects of the need to achieve internationally competitive prices and quality (Pack [1988]).

Based on the success stories of the NICs in the 1970s, proponents of a liberal trade regime thus argue that the impact of an external orientation on growth will lie in its effect on allocative or technical inefficiency.[19] By enhancing competition with other producers in the world market, opening up the economy through a strategy of export promotion is believed to lead to greater enterprise efficiency and faster technical progress. Underlying this belief is the assumption that LDCs often suffer from 'distortions' between observed prices and some optimal set of prices, usually based on world market prices. These distortions are the main cause of existing inefficiency. 'Getting the prices right' then means equating internal price ratios to those ruling the international markets which, in practical terms, certainly is a non-trivial exercise (Taylor and Arida [1988]). Furthermore, we think that the impact of a policy of 'getting the prices right' may be much more limited than is believed by adherents of such a policy because the commodities which poor countries exchange internationally are in general of a non-competitive nature as is shown by McCarthy et al. [1987]. That is, export products are not consumed in large quantities at home and imports are not domestically produced or, in other words, the share of effectively non-traded goods in the production basket of most developing countries is high. The implication is that trade theory's 'law of one price' will play a minor role in determining resource allocation. Arbitrage will not enforce competition among domestic producers because large numbers of traders for the same commodity do not exist within the domestic economy (Taylor and Arida [1988: 179]). Furthermore, McCarthy et al. conclude that developing countries are strongly dependent on import of capital goods. With few exceptions (South Korea, India, Brazil) LDCs have had little success in penetrating export markets for capital goods. Finally, both the size of an economy and its history strongly affect its trading role. Larger economies are on average much more closed to trade than small ones (cf. Table 1.14). Many relatively small and poor economies thus suffer from their inherited dependence on primary commodity trade. Adherents of an export-oriented strategy do not adequately deal with these empirical regularities. Instead, their argument is based on the large losses of welfare due to price distortions which are commonly believed to be caused by public intervention. A major example of such intervention is the introduction of an import quota which provides

---

[19] According to Bradford [1987], there is a tendency in the literature to overdraw the contrasts between the kind of policy regimes which lead to success and failure: 'There is an effort to link strategies, policies, and politics to each other so that pure forms tend to emerge from the analysis while reality is indeed more mixed.' [1987:310].

opportunities for 'rent-seeking' behaviour of agents in LDCs. Suppose one owns rights to an import quota and can buy goods in the world market cheaply and sell them on the domestic market more dearly. The revenue of this transaction resulting from this price difference is called a 'rent'. Postulating arbitrarily large rents, proponents of trade liberalization argue that large welfare gains can be obtained by abolishing public restrictions. Numerous studies have tried to estimate these welfare losses.

TABLE 1.14: *Mean trade shares for the countries with population above and below 20 million in 1982*

	Large Countries	Small Countries
Merchandise imports	15.12	25.79
Service imports	5.10	9.48
Merchandise exports	11.95	20.94
Service exports	4.20	6.57

Source: McCarthy *et al.*[1987:29].

In a cross-section study of 31 LDCs in the 1970s which was summarized in the World Development Report 1983, Agarwala [1983] found a negative relationship between a 'distortion index' based on seven indicators and growth. Later work by Aghazadeh and Evans [1985], however, shows that only two out of the original seven indicators—real exchange rate appreciation and real wage growth in excess of labour productivity increases—bear a negative relationship with growth. The other indicators including tariff distortions for agricultural and industrial products proved unrelated. Aghazadeh and Evans further show that institutional variables such as military spending and planning capacity do influence growth. It thus appears that historical institutional circumstances (also influencing real wages and exchange rates) affect an economy's performance. The relationship between trade and growth has also been closely scrutinized, mostly in empirical terms. Assuming that the causality runs from trade to output, studies of this relationship in general show a positive regression coefficient of output growth on export growth (see Balassa [1988]). The causality may, however, run in the other direction: growth of output may lead to an increase in international trade. McCarthy, Taylor and Talati (1987) run the regression the other way around using a sample split by economic 'performance' to investigate trade patterns and asking if country growth differences have any impact on their observed patterns of trade. They find no strong relationships aside from a tendency of low-income countries to specialize more in primary exports than richer ones.

Everyone agrees that a country should specialize in the opportunities where it has a comparative advantage. In most LDCs, these opportunities have centred on natural resources (commercial crops and minerals), generally to the exclusion of producing food for export. However, one should analyse comparative advantages not only in a static context, but also dynamically. Through a strategy of planned industrialization based on import substitution, many Third World countries have tried to change their comparative advantage towards manufacturing. A more reasonable approach to the question of trade and growth is, therefore, to ask whether a strong outward-looking orientation fits naturally into a planning framework. For South Korea, Taiwan, Singapore and Hong Kong this appears to be the case as is shown by Bradford [1987] and Chakravarty [1987a]. For each one of these NICs, both authors conclude that economic decision-making is highly dirigible and that price signals do not play a central role in the process of taking investment decisions. Bradford's [1987:314] conclusions suggest that

. . . the conventional view of export-led growth deriving from an open economy with competitive market prices responding to world demand may not be the dominant pattern in explaining the surge of manufactured exports from the NICs. Rather the evidence here suggests that a supply-push development model with government playing a key role in stimulating capital formation through macro-policies and in accelerating structural change through sectoral strategies affecting the output and export mix may provide a more accurate framework for capturing the causal elements explaining rapid transitional growth.

Thus, by deliberate macro-policies the NICs have succeeded in obtaining their relatively high growth performance. We want to stress two important and often neglected components of these policies:

1. The legislation enabling a very intensive utilization of labour via a long working week—the average working week in South Korea's manufacturing industry was in excess of 59 hours, 16 per cent longer than Taiwan's 51-hour week (Scitovsky [1985]).

2. The use of a differential and generally low interest rate policy, especially for preferred groups of industries.

Within South Korea, these monetary policies, in combination with direct fiscal subsidies, have underpriced investment goods during the 1970s and were a powerful instrument for stimulating investment demand, facilitating capital formation, structural change and export growth of manufactures. Clearly, these results of careful study of the causes of the high growth rates experienced by the East Asian NICs contradict the main assumptions on which policies of the 'getting-the-prices-right' type are based.

Our final remark on the success of the NICs in changing from an inward-looking towards an export-oriented policy concerns the fact that it has been made possible by favourable conjunctural factors operating in the world market during the 1960s. During the 1970s, the situation changed due to the two rounds of price increases in the world oil market and the following worldwide recession in the first half of the 1980s. Consequently, the export opportunities for most Third World countries decreased. According to Lewis [1981], the rate of growth of world trade in manufactured goods which in large part drives the growth rate of LDCs' exports, is determined by two principal factors. The first factor is the demand of industrialized countries for primary commodities. Fast growth of manufacturing in the industrialized countries induced fast growth of the demand for primary commodities, mainly exported from LDCs. In turn, the demand of primary commodity producers for manufactures was stimulated. The other factor is related to protection. For instance, EEC countries opened up their markets to each other which had a restricting effect on trade in manufactures outside the EEC. To a lesser extent, the same is true for OECD countries. Therefore, Lewis argues that the ratio of net imports of manufactures—into industrialized countries from other industrialized countries—to consumption of manufactures is the other principal determinant of the share of manufactures in international trade. After the 1950s, this ratio has shown a tendency to increase. The export engine of growth in the Third World has thus slowed down and 'it is unlikely ever to repeat the experience of the 1950s and 1960s.' (Williamson [1988:28]).

What emerges most clearly from Lewis's analysis is the Third World's dependence on the economic performance of the industrialized economies. This will not come as a surprise to adherents of the dependency theory of economic development (Prebisch [1964]; Frank [1969, 1975]) in which the world economy is envisaged as consisting of a developed centre and a backward periphery. As trading partners, the LDCs, belonging to the periphery, are dependent upon the developed countries because the goods they usually produce (mainly primary commodities) are both price and income inelastic, whereas they themselves cannot produce the goods they want to buy. It is argued that this situation of dependency has led to 'unequal exchange' between the centre and the periphery (Emmanuel [1972]). Global economic growth is regarded as a zero-sum process in which the gains from trade accrue to the developed countries and the LDCs experience continuous (relative) impoverishment. Growth in developed countries in the centre is thus made possible by underdeveloping the already less-developed countries in the periphery. One way for developing countries to reduce their dependence is to increase their trade with other LDCs. In this respect, Lewis' argument may be seen as a strong plea to increase South-South trade.

1.4. A note on the other contributions to this book

The first group of papers is concerned with the experiences of four decades of Third World development at the global and international level. The central paper is that of Professor Singer on 'Lessons of post-war development experience, 1945–1988'. As distinct from our introductory paper, Singer presents a broad and critical overview of four decades of international development policy and the ideas at its basis primarily from an institutional point of view— looking at the development story as a process of 'learning-by-doing' in which the development economists if not inevitably then at least actually react with a clear time lag to the lessons of the past. From this point of view it is important to speed up and intensify this learning process, i.e. to absorb and integrate into policy suggestions new events more quickly and more adequately. In order to make a few steps in this direction, Singer draws some important lessons of post-war development experience—in particular referring to development policies proposed and imposed by the international financial institutions such as the IMF and World Bank. As his paper gives a very concise, decade-by-decade account of the evolution of encouraging and disappointing experiences during the 'golden years' and the crisis years, and of the insights gained, as well as a clear account of the lagged translation of these insights into development policies, we will highlight only two of Singer's major conclusions.

First, Singer argues that the policies aiming at restructuring, adjustment, stabilization, etc. which are nowadays imposed upon developing countries, disregard one of the basic insights of the early development period of the 1950s. In those days, development and growth were seen as a process of 'cumulative causation', i.e. a system of beneficial or vicious circles or spirals. The vicious circle of poverty, for example, says that poor people are poor because they are undernourished and/or illiterate, and they are undernourished and/or illiterate because they are poor. These same forces are also assumed to be in operation in the Taylor-Bacha [1976] model of unequalizing growth which we have discussed above. According to Singer, however, the present neo-liberal doctrine of adjustment is in danger of disregarding these cumulative effects. The argument in favour of these adjustment policies rests on the assumption that one can temporarily arrest growth, reduce government expenditure on physical and human investments, etc., while at the same time gathering strength for a period of new, sustained growth. This approach, Singer argues, disregards the possibility that each disruptive cutback may make it more difficult for an LDC to resume growth from a thus weakened basis. His argument seems particularly valid for the sub-Saharan African countries.

A second important conclusion drawn by Singer concerns the existing international economic order. On the basis of the experiences of the last two decades, Singer makes a renewed plea for an effective international development institution, close to the original idea of an International Trade Organization. From the inception of the post-war international finance and development institutions onwards, the ITO was intended to be a third element of the original Bretton-Woods system—together with the International Monetary Fund and the International Bank for Reconstruction and Development (World Bank). Its purpose was to stabilize primary commodity prices and promote world trade within a development perspective. The ITO was, however, not ratified. Some of its functions were shifted to GATT which was a weak version of the ITO as it did not include the vital function of commodity price stabilization. According to Singer, the lack of appropriate development agencies such as the ITO has led to an international flow of financial resources as a mirror image of part of the international trade flows, which is based on short-term criteria, instead of, for example, on a long-term evaluation of LDCs' needs and capacities. Instead of using the resources of OPEC members for development projects, these funds were deposited by commercial banks and, consequently, went almost exclusively to the middle-income countries (as we have seen in section 1.3.3), in disregard of the relatively even more affected poorest countries. In Singer's view, forty years of development experience have shown that the scope, priorities and effectiveness of the Bretton-Woods institutions have been too limited and urgently need to be enlarged.

Clearly, the issues addressed by Singer such as the IMF stabilization package, the debt crisis and the international economic order have given rise to an extensive literature. The best source of empirical information on the debt crisis can be found in the World Bank's annual edition of World Debt Tables. Cline and Weintraub [1981] provide a review of Third World stabilization programmes from a developed country's perspective. Streeten [1981], in contrast, gives a lengthy economic critique of the IMF stabilization policies and their effects on both the balance of payments and the overall economy. Other sources of interest are: Lever and Huhne [1985], Stewart [1985], Krueger [1987], and the entire *Journal of Development Planning*, issue no. 16 [1985] entitled 'The debt problem: acute and chronic aspects'.

Professor Chakravarty's commentary paper on Singer is complementary to it, discussing three major conceptual limitations of the development strategies that emerged during the 1950s and have been operative since then, and pointing out ways to overcome such limitations in future strategies. In order to do so, Chakravarty introduces the following three innovative concepts into development theory:

1. The transformation capacity of an economy.
2. The role of prices as a system of power relationships.
3. The distinction between 'tangible assets' and 'intangible assets'.

The notion of intangible assets in particular—which he attributes to Veblen—will have considerable consequences for development policy because it implies that technological innovation itself (à la Schumpeter) is not a sufficient condition to ensure long-run development. In order to be successful, technological progress should be accompanied by adequate institutional development, especially of institutions that operate innovatively in the domain of the generation of relevant knowledge and experience. Chakravarty's emphasis on organizational aspects of economic development and technological change (in terms of genesis, appropriateness and diffusion) is part of a recent interest amongst economists such as Nelson and Winter [1982], Stiglitz [1988], Bardhan [1989].

The second group of papers addresses features of the development experience of countries which have been relatively successful in achieving high rates of growth—i.e. the newly industrializing countries (NICs). These papers have been invited into this collection in order to highlight the differences in development experience between groups of countries within the Third World. On the one hand, one may be interested in the role these NICs play in the world economy. The extraordinary increase in manufactured exports from this small group of developing countries has stimulated many questions about future patterns of world trade and income distribution. On the other hand, one may wonder how precise the relationship is between the development experience of these much discussed and hailed countries and the development strategies they have followed.

In his contribution, Bradford mainly tackles the first set of questions, analysing the consequences of the rise of the NICs for world trade in the 1990s. Interestingly, he distinguishes between four groups of NICs of which the first, consisting of South Korea, Taiwan, Hong Kong and Singapore, is the one most familiar to us. The other three groups are

1. Latin American NICs—Brazil, Mexico and Argentina;
2. Mediterranean NICs belonging to the European Community—Spain, Portugal and Greece;
3. non-EC Mediterranean NICs—Yugoslavia, Turkey, Egypt and Israel.

In order to determine possible effects of NIC trade on the world economy, Bradford has developed an input-output based model describing world trade flows between 12 trading blocs of which 4 blocs are NICs. Given the current structure of world trade, the expected

GDP growth rates of the 12 trading blocs and the possible trade-strategies (import substitution versus export orientation) pursued by each one of them, Bradford determines the pattern of world trade for the 1990s. Extrapolating the trade strategies prevailing during the 1980s, simulation experiments with this model show that the group of low-income countries—consisting mainly of sub-Saharan African countries—has little to expect from world trade in the next decade. Their case stands in sharp contrast to the case of the 4 groups of NICs which have a far greater probability of reaping benefits from world trade. Bradford's results support our earlier conclusion that the potential of an export engine of growth in the Third World which has declined during the 1980s, is unlikely to gain importance in the near future. Moreover, because in the 1990s the differences in gains from trade accruing to the NICs on the one hand and the low-income countries on the other are likely to increase, the dualistic nature of world economic development will be strengthened even further.

Whereas Bradford investigates worldwide consequences of an increasing share of NICs' exports in total manufactured exports, Verbruggen focuses on the effects of this export-oriented industrial-ization strategy on domestic employment in particular. According to Verbruggen, all explanations of the growth of the East Asian NICs can be classified into the following four categories:

1. Studies arguing that this growth is caused by an export-oriented trade and industrialization strategy.
2. Studies designating the NICs' experience as atypical, i.e. not transferable to other LDCs.
3. Studies explaining the NICs' success as the result of highly centralized guidance.
4. Studies attributing the success of the NICs to social and cultural factors.

Verbruggen's contribution is concerned with the first category of explanations, discussing an important element of the export-oriented industrialization strategy, viz. the role of the production factor labour. For seven East and South-East Asian countries, Verbruggen empirically investigates the employment effects of an export-oriented industrialization strategy compared to those of a strategy of stimulating domestic market-oriented industrialization. His main conclusion is that, given the situation of these countries, the employment effects associated with one unit of foreign exchange gained in exporting (labour-intensive) products are clearly more extensive than corresponding employment effects associated with one unit of foreign exchange saved through (capital-intensive) domestic market-oriented production.

Cuyvers and Van den Bulcke discuss distinguishing characteristics of the outward-oriented development strategies followed by the Far Eastern NICs (or FENICs), South Korea, Taiwan, Hong Kong and Singapore. They conclude that direct foreign investment has played a significant role in the industrialization process of these Far Eastern NICs. This direct foreign investment has been encouraged by deliberate government intervention consisting of

1. industrial policy—stimulating joint ventures and attracting multi-national enterprises;
2. exchange rate policy—devaluation of overvalued exchange rates; and
3. investment and savings policy—in the form of raising the interest rates.

According to Cuyvers and Van den Bulcke, these policy measures cannot be taken as prescriptions for successful development by other LDCs because of the special circumstances under which the FENICs have been operating. The major factor limiting a successful transfer of the FENICs' model to other LDCs is the slowdown of the growth rate of the world economy, while at the same time the competition between LDCs has increased markedly. The three contributions to the second part of the conference are part of a growing body of literature on the NICs' experience. Of related interest are the papers by Bradford [1982], Bradford [1987], Chakravarty [1987a] and Cline [1982], and books by Balassa [1988] and Srinivasan [1985].

Whereas in the second part questions were raised on the causes and transferability of the 'success story' of the NICs, the third and final group of papers is devoted to the countries that experienced an almost exactly opposite path of development—that is, countries that experienced negative growth, deteriorating terms of trade and increasing marginalization within the world economy during the last ten or fifteen years. Together these countries are sometimes called the Fourth World of which the sub-Saharan African countries make up the largest part. The development experience of these African countries is evaluated in the paper by Moyo and Amin.

Sub-Saharan African development is characterized by declining export volumes; declining commodity prices and adverse terms of trade; and undiversified structure of industrialization; underutilization of production capacity; poor and sometimes even negative agricultural growth and rising food imports; mounting external debts and severe balance of payments deficits. The central question addressed by Moyo and Amin is whether the relative and absolute poor economic performance of sub-Saharan Africa during the 1970s and 1980s is caused mainly by internal factors or has to be attributed to external influences.

While the World Bank argues that domestic policies leading to over-valued exchange rates, price distortions, costly industrialization and the 'over-extension' of the government, were at the heart of this crisis, Moyo and Amin stress the negative influence of unfavourable external factors such as falling primary commodity prices on the world market, increasing interest rates causing a rise in the cost of borrowing, the instability of the exchange rates of the major international currencies, the increase in protectionist practices among the industrialized countries, and natural disasters. According to Moyo and Amin, the adjustment and stabilization policies imposed by the IMF and World Bank consequently do not deal with the real causes of the crisis but rather tend to deal with its symptoms. Nevertheless, they too are convinced of the necessity of domestic restructuring of the economies of sub-Saharan African countries. Important elements of their proposal for restructuring are

1. a reduction in the reliance on foreign capital by stimulating domestic savings and increasing the effectiveness of utilization of foreign aid and domestic savings;
2. an increase in intra-African or South-South trade which may improve possibilities to increase non-traditional exports;
3. strengthening of small-scale and/or informal production; and
4. stimulating the organization of collective and cooperative forms of production.

Further readings on Africa are provided by Bates [1981] who addresses the political origins of the shortfalls in agricultural production, Shankar [1981], Berg and Whitaker [1986], Mellor et al. [1987], and Helleiner [1986]. Lele [1988] provides a recent review of research and policy debates on Africa's development experience.

Berlage provides a brief comparison of the economic performance of the Asian low-income countries, Bangladesh and Nepal, and the sub-Saharan African economies. As the Asian countries show a relatively higher performance—especially during the 1980s—and do face an external environment comparable to the African LDCs, in Berlage's opinion, some of sub-Saharan Africa's problems may be attributed to inadequate economic policies and economic mismanagement. Berlage favours active policy intervention in line with some rules of economic behaviour which are of general applicability in any market economy, but have been neglected by a number of governments.

Finally, Terhal's contribution centres around the definition of the Fourth World. In Terhal's view, the Fourth World consists of those groups of people who are caught in vicious circles of vulnerability which are the inevitable consequence of development; under certain conditions, economic development tends to create relative impoverishment, i.e. making certain population groups ecologically, culturally and politically more vulnerable. Terhal discusses how, in reality, economic development has led to (a) rural impoverishment, (b) ecological degradation, and (c) international dependency in the Fourth World. Terhal pleads for a 'radical redefinition' of economic development incorporating elements of ecological, cultural and political sustainability and for growth policies which are revised accordingly.

References

Adelman, I. [1986], 'A poverty-focused approach to development policy', in J. P. Lewis and V. Kalab (eds.), *Development strategies reconsidered* (Washington, DC: Overseas Development Council).

Adelman, I. and C. T. Morris [1973], *Economic growth and social equity in developing countries* (Stanford: Stanford University Press).

Adelman, I. and S. Robinson [1978], *Income distribution policy in developing countries. A case study of Korea* (Oxford: Oxford University Press).

Agarwala, R. [1983], 'Price distortions and growth in developing countries', World Bank Staff working papers no. 575 (Washington DC).

Aghazadeh, I. and D. Evans [1985], *Price distortions, efficiency and growth* (University of Sussex: Institute of Development Studies).

Ahluwalia, M. S. [1974], 'Dimensions of the problem' in H. B. Chenery *et al.* (eds.) [1974], *Redistribution with growth*.

Ahluwalia, M. S. [1976], 'Income distribution and development: Some stylised facts', *American Economic Review*, vol. 66, pp. 128–35.

Bairoch, P. [1975], *The economic development of the Third World since 1900* (London: Methuen & Co).

Bairoch, P. [1981], 'The main trends in national economic disparities since the Industrial Revolution', in Bairoch, P. and Lévy-Leboyer (eds.), *Disparities in economic development since the Industrial Revolution* (London: Macmillan).

Balassa, B. [1988], *Change and challenge in the world economy* (London: Macmillan).

Bardhan, P. [1989], *The economic theory of agrarian institutions* (Oxford: Oxford University Press).

Bates, R. H. [1981], *Markets and states in tropical Africa. The political basis of agricultural policies* (Berkeley: University of California Press).

Berg, R. J. and J. S. Whitaker (eds.) [1986], *Strategies for African development* (Berkeley: University of California Press).

Bertholet, C. [1983], *Persoonlijke inkomensverdeling in ontwikkelingsperspectief, een internationaal vergelijkende studie* (Institute of Development Problems, Catholic University Tilburg).

Binswanger, H. P. and M. Rosenzweig [1984], *Contractual arrangements, employment and wages in rural labor markets in Asia* (New Haven, CT: Yale University Press).

Booth, A. and R. M. Sundrum [1985], *Labour absorption in agriculture* (Oxford: Oxford University Press).

Boserup, E. [1965], *The conditions of agricultural growth* (London: Allen and Unwin).

Boserup, E. [1981], *Population and technological change. A study of long term trends* (Oxford: Basil Blackwell).

Bradford, C. I. [1982], 'Newly industrialising countries', *The World Economy* (September), no. 2, pp. 171–86.

Bradford, C. I. [1987], 'Trade and structural change: NICs and next tier NICs as transitional economies', *World Development*, vol. 15, no. 3. pp. 299–316.

Chakravarty, S. [1974], 'Reflections on the growth process in the Indian economy', Foundation Day Lecture at the Administrative Staff College of India, Hyderabad.

Chakravarty, S. [1987], *Development planning: The Indian experience* (Oxford: Oxford University Press).

Chakravarty, S. [1987a], 'Marxist economics and contemporary developing economics', *Cambridge Journal of Economics*, vol. 11, pp. 3–22.

Chakravarty, S. [1987b], 'The state of development economics', *Manchester School of Economic Studies*.

Chenery, H. B. and A. M. Strout [1966], 'Foreign assistance and economic development', *American Economic Review*, (September).

Chenery, H. B. *et al.* [1974], *Redistribution with growth: An approach to policy* (London).

Chenery H. B. and M. Syrquin [1975], *Patterns of development 1950–1970* (London: Oxford University Press).

Chenery, H. B. and T. N. Srinivasan (eds.) [1988], *Handbook of development economics* (Amsterdam: North Holland).

Cheung, S. N. S. [1968], 'Private property rights and sharecropping', *Journal of Political Economy*, vol. 76, pp. 1107–22.

Clark, [1941], *Conditions of economic progress* (London: Macmillan).

Cline, W. R. [1982], 'Can the East Asian model of development be generalised?', *World Development*, June, pp. 305–10.

Cline, W. R. and S. Weintraub [1981], *Economic stabilisation in developing countries* (Washington, DC: Brookings Institution).

Dasgupta, P. and D. Ray [1986], 'Inequality as a determinant of malnutrition and unemployment: theory', *The Economic Journal*, vol. 96 (December).

Dasgupta, P. and D. Ray [1987], 'Inequality as a determinant of malnutrition and unemployment: policy', *The Economic Journal*, vol. 97 (March), pp. 177–88.

de Janvry, A. and E. Sadoulet [1983], 'Social articulation as a condition for equitable growth', *Journal of Development Economics*, 13, pp. 275–303.

Denison, E. F. [1967], *Why growth rates differ: Post-war experience in nine western countries* (Washington, DC: Brookings Institution).

Dosi, G., C. Freeman, R. Nelson, G. Silverberg and L. Soete (eds.) [1988], *Technical change and economic theory* (London: Pinter Publishers).

Durand, J. D. [1974], 'Historical estimates of world population: an evaluation', University of Pennsylvania, Population Studies Centre.

Emmanuel, A. [1972], *Unequal exchange* (London: New Left Books).

Eshag, E. [1983], *Fiscal and monetary policies and problems in developing countries* (Cambridge: Cambridge University Press).

Fei, J. C. H. and G. Ranis [1964], *Development of the labour surplus economy* (Homewood, IL: Irwin).

Fei, J. C. H., and G. Ranis and S. Kuo [1979], *Growth with equity: The Taiwan Case* (New York).

Fields, G. S. [1980], *Poverty, inequality and development.* (Cambridge, Mass.: Harvard University Press).

Frank, A. G. [1969], *Capitalism and underdevelopment in Latin America* (New York and London: Monthly Review Press).

Frank, A. G. [1975], *On capitalist underdevelopment* (Bombay: Oxford University Press).

Griffin, K. [1974], *The political economy of agrarian change* (London: Macmillan).

Haan, H. H. de [1988], *Alternatives in industrial development; sugarcane processing in India.* (New Delhi/Newbury Park/London: Sage Publications).

Harris, R. and M. P. Todaro [1970], 'Migration, unemployment and development: A two-sector analysis', *American Economic Review*, vol. 60, pp. 126–42.

Helleiner, G. K. [1986], 'Outward orientation, import instability and African economic growth: an empirical investigation', in S. Lall and F. Stewart (eds.) [1986], *Theory and reality in development* (London: Macmillan).

Islam, R. [1987], *Rural industrialisation and employment in Asia.* (New Delhi: ILO/Artep).

James, J. [1987], 'The choice of technology in public enterprise: A comparative study of manufacturing industry in Kenya and Tanzania', in F. Stewart (ed.) [1987].

Jolly, R. *et al.* [1973], *Third World employment* (Harmondsworth: Penguin).

Kelley, A. C. [1988], 'Economic consequences of population change in the Third World', *The Journal of Economic Literature*, vol. XXVI (December), pp. 1685–1728.

Kingston, W. [1984], *The political economy of innovation* (The Hague: Martinus Nijhoff Publishers).

Kouwenaar, A. [1986], 'A basic needs policy model. A general equilibrium analysis with special reference to Ecuador' (PhD thesis, Erasmus University Rotterdam).

Kravis, I. B., A. Heston, and R. Summers [1982], *World product and income*. (Baltimore: Johns Hopkins University Press).

Krueger, A. O. [1987], 'Debt, capital flows and LDC growth', *American Economic Review*, vol. 77, no. 2.

Kuznets, S. [1955], 'Economic growth and income inequality', *American Economic Review*, vol. 45, pp. 1–28.

Lall, S. [1987], *Learning to industrialize* (London: Macmillan).

Lele, U. [1988], 'Comparative advantage and structural transformation: A review of Africa's economic development experience', in G. Ranis and T. P. Schultz (eds.) [1988].

Leontief, W., *et al.* [1977], *The Future of the World Economy: A United Nations Study* (New York: Oxford University Press).

Lever, H. and C. Huhne [1985], *Debt and danger: The world financial crisis* (New York: Atlantic Monthly Press).

Lewis, W. A. [1954], 'Economic development with unlimited supplies of labour', *Manchester School of Economic and Social Studies*, no. 22, pp. 139–91.

Lewis, W. A. [1981], 'The rate of growth of world trade', in S. Grassman and E. Lundberg. (eds.), *The world economic order, past and prospects* (London: Macmillan).

Lewis, W. A. [1988], 'The Roots of Development Theory', in Chenery and Srinivasan (eds.) [1988: pp. 27–37].

Liedholm, C. and D. Mead [1987], *Small-scale industries in developing countries: empirical evidence and policy implications*, MSU International Development Paper, Department of Agricultural Economics, Michigan State University.

Lipton, M. [1977], *Why poor people stay poor: A study of the urban bias in world development* (London: Temple Smith).

Little, I. M. D. [1982], *Economic development: Theory, policy and international relations* (New York: Basic Books).

Little, I. M. D., D. Mazumdar and J. M. Page [1987], *Small manufacturing enterprises, A comparative analysis of India and other economies*. A World Bank Research Publication (New York: Oxford University Press).

Maddison, A. [1982], *Ontwikkelings fasen van het kapitalisme* (Stages of capitalist development) (Utrecht: Het Spectrum).

McCarthy, F. D., L. Taylor and C. Talati [1987], 'Trade patterns in developing countries, 1964–82', *Journal of development economies*, 27, pp. 5–39.

McEvedy, C. and R. Jones [1978], *Atlas of world population history* (Harmondsworth: Penguin Books Ltd.).

Mellor, J. [1976], *The new economics of growth*. (Ithaca, NY).

Mellor, J. W., C. L. Delgado and M. J. Blackie (eds.) [1987], *Accelerating food production in Sub-Saharan Africa* (Baltimore and London: The Johns Hopkins University Press).

Nelson, R. R. and S. G. Winter [1982], *An evolutionary theory of economic change* (Harvard: The Belknap Press).

Nurkse, R. [1953], *Problems of capital formation in underdeveloped countries*, (London: Basil Blackwell).

Olson, M. [1982], *The rise and decline of nations*, (New Haven, CT: Yale University Press).

Pack, H. [1988], 'Industrialisation and trade', in H. Chenery and T. N. Srinivasan (eds.), *Handbook of development economics*, vol. 1., pp. 334–380.

Pasinetti, L. L. [1981], *Structural change and economic growth. A theoretical essay on the dynamics of the wealth of nations* (Cambridge: Cambridge University Press).

Paukert, F. [1973], 'Income distribution at different levels of development. A survey of evidence', *International Labour Review*, vol. 108, pp. 97–125.

Prebisch, R. [1964], *Towards a new trade policy for development* (New York: United Nations).

Ram, R. [1988], 'Economic development and income inequality: Further evidence on the U-curve hypothesis', *World Development*, vol. 16, no. 11, pp. 1371–76.

Ranis, G. and T. P. Schultz (eds.) [1988], *The state of development economics* (New York: Basil Blackwell).

Reynolds, L. G. [1986], *Economic growth in the Third World. An introduction* (New Haven and London: Yale University Press).

Robinson, S. [1988], 'Multisector models' in H. B. Chenery and T. N. Srinivasan (eds.), *Handbook of development economics*.

Rosenstein-Rodan, P. [1943], 'Problems of industrialisation of eastern and south-eastern Europe', *Economic Journal*, vol. 25, pp. 202–11.

Rosenzweig, M. R. [1988], 'Labor markets in low-income countries', in H. B. Chenery and T. N. Srinivasan (eds.).

Saith, A. (1983), 'Development and distribution: a critique of the cross-country U-hypothesis', *Journal of Development Economics*, vol. 13, pp. 367–82.

Scitovsky, T. [1985], 'Economic development in Taiwan and South Korea, 1965–81', Stanford Food Research Institute Studies, vol. XIX, no. 3.

Schumpeter, J. [1919], *Theorie der Wirtschaftlichen Entwicklung*.

Schumpeter, J. [1934], *The theory of economic development* (Cambridge, Mass.: Harvard University Press).

Sen, A. K. [1966], 'Peasants and dualism with or without surplus labour', *Journal of Political Economy*, vol. 74, pp. 425–50.

Shankar, A. [1981], 'Perspectives and problems of development in sub-Saharan Africa', *World Development* 9, pp. 109–48.

Singh, I. *et al.* [1986], *Agricultural household models: Extensions and applications* (Baltimore: Johns Hopkins University Press).

Sinha, R., P. Pearson, G. Kadekodi and M. Gregory [1979], *Income distribution, growth and basic needs in India* (New Delhi: Vikas Publishing House Ltd.).

Srinivasan, T. N. [1985], *Dependence and interdependence* (Oxford: Oxford University Press).

Stewart, F. [1978], 'Inequality, technology and payments systems', *World Development*, vol. 6, no. 3.

Stewart, F. [1985], 'The international debt situation and North-South relations', *World Development*, vol. 13, no. 2, pp. 141–204.

Stewart, F. (ed.) [1987], *Macro-policies for appropriate technology* (Boulder, Colorado: Westview Press).

Stewart, F. [1988], 'Comments on Technology, Productivity Growth and Economic Development', in G. Ranis and T. P. Schultz (eds.).

Stiglitz, J. E. [1988], 'Economic organisation, information and development', in H. B. Chenery and T. N. Srinivasan (eds.).

Streeten, P. [1979], 'Basic needs: premises and promises', *Journal of Policy Modeling*, vol. 1, pp. 136–46.

Streeten, P. [1981], 'Stabilisation and adjustment', *Labour and Society* 13, no. 1, pp. 1–18.

Suri, K. B. (ed.) [1988], *Small-scale enterprises in industrial development. The Indian experience.* (New Delhi/Newbury Park/London: Sage Publications).

Syrquin, M. [1988], 'Patterns of structural change', in H. B. Chenery and T. N. Srinivasan (eds.), *Handbook of Development Economics*.

Taylor, L. [1983], *Structuralist macroeconomics* (New York: Basic Books).

Taylor, L. and E. Bacha [1976], 'The unequalising spiral: A first growth model for Belindia', *Quarterly Journal of Economics*, vol. XC, pp. 197–218.

Taylor, L. and P. Arida [1988], 'Long-run income distribution and growth', in H. Chenery and T. N. Srinivasan (eds.), *Handbook of development economics*, vol. 1., pp. 161–94.

Tinbergen, J. [1942], 'Zur Theorie der langfristigen Wirtschafts-entwicklung', *Weltwirtschaftliches Archiv*, Hamburg, 55 (1942, I), pp. 511–49.

Tinbergen, J. [1945], *International economic co-operation* (translated into

English by P. H. Breitenstein and E. Inglis Arkell) (Amsterdam: Elseviers economische bibliotheek).

Tinbergen, J. (coordinator) [1978], *RIO: Reshaping the International Economic Order: A Report to the Club of Rome* (New York: Dutton).

Terhal, P. H. J. J. [1988], *World inequality and evolutionary convergence* (Delft: Eburon).

Todaro, M. P. [1989], *Economic development in the Third World*. Fourth edition (New York and London: Longman).

Waardenburg, J. G. [1988], 'Small-scale leather shoe-manufacturing in Agra: A case study in small-scale industry in India's development', in K. B. Suri (ed.).

Williamson, J. G. [1988], 'Comments on Reflections on Development', in G. Ranis and P. Schultz (eds.), *The state of development economics*, pp. 24–30.

World Bank, *World Development Reports 1982, 1983, 1988* (Oxford: Oxford University Press).

Yap, L. [1977], 'The attraction of cities: A review of the migration literature', *Journal of development economics*, vol. 4, pp. 105–27.

PART 1

Global Perspectives

2   Lessons of Post-War Development Experience, 1945–1988

Hans W. Singer[1]

2.1. The story of development: differing scenarios

The story of development, the lessons of development experience, the evolution of our thinking about development, all these things (which are not exactly the same) can be written from any different angle. One could start the story with the high hopes for a Brave New World at the end of the Second War at Bretton Woods; comparing these hopes with the 'lost decade' of the 1980s, with its debt crisis, African crisis and development going into reverse—at least in Africa and Latin America—the story could then be written as one of steady deterioration, of the Brave New World of forty years ago ending in a developmental wasteland today. But that story would certainly not be 'wholly true'. It would not do justice to the many success stories in development nor to the 'golden years' spanning over two decades after Bretton Woods, nor to the fact that measured by such simple but compelling indicators as expectation of life, infant mortality, technological capacity, or progress with industrialization, the Third World as a whole is markedly better off than 40 years ago.

Another possible scenario when surveying the last 40 years could be as a story of ups and downs, of problems emerging and being solved, or left unresolved, only to be replaced by other problems requiring different solutions. This scenario would be somewhat nearer the truth than the first one. The development story is clearly a mixture of good and bad, of progress and regress, of success and failure. Indeed, it is this very mixture which leads to much confusion. Some people, institutions, or schools of thought tend to pick out the failures and draw from them lessons of what should be done to

[1] The author gratefully acknowledges assistance from Jonathan Perraton.

redeem them or avoid them in the future. Others will be more inclined to point out successes, and base their conclusions on what should be done to extend and support them. Obviously both approaches are justified: we should learn both from success and failure. But in practice, this polarized approach often leads to current debates with arguments based on selective anecdotal evidence. This often results in inconclusive controversies, for example whether food aid is beneficial or harmful to developing countries; whether the cause of the troubles of developing countries is internal or external; whether developing countries should practise inward or outward orientation; whether developing countries should use modern capital-intensive technology or traditional labour-intensive technology; etc. Generally, it is unhelpful to pose such questions and try to answer them in this polarized or categorical form of either/or. The truth broadly is that the right kind of aid or food aid is good and the wrong kind bad; that inward orientation is right for certain countries, certain sectors and in certain conditions and outward orientation for other countries, sectors and conditions, while usually a selective and phased mixture of inward-oriented and outward-oriented measures is best; a mixture of modern and traditional technology is best; in the present debt crisis the internal factors play a role and interact with external factors; etc. The problem is that in such polarized controversies the advocacy of either of the two alternatives often assumes the nature of a religious conviction, argued with fundamentalist passion. When one of these fundamentalist factions acquires ascendancy in and control over important institutions and governments it can do much harm. One illustration of this is the fervent belief in planning, the possibilities of the 'big push' and 'balanced growth' and import-substituting industrialization some 40 years ago; and the perhaps even more fanatical belief in outward orientation, market power and 'getting prices right' which has succeeded today in capturing the stage in powerful international institutions and governments. One can observe that the success stories tend to be based on a cool disregard of such fundamentalism—not so much a 'search for a middle ground' as a selective use of the limited truths contained in either of the contending doctrines.

This last point could well suggest a third scenario: one in which our approach to development problems and the lessons which we learn is simply the result of changing fashions and ideologies. If it was the Keynesian consensus 40 years ago, it is now the neoliberal tide of today, and goodness knows what tomorrow. This scenario, familiar to historians, is the counterpart of the proposition that history is not a meaningful evolution in which events in epoch B are meaningfully linked with events in epoch A and will in turn be equally meaningfully linked with future events in epoch C; but rather that history is 'just one damn thing after another'. Yet however tempted one may be today to think that development is 'just one damn thing after another', this again does not quite seem the whole truth. There was a sense in which the belief in planning and self-reliance in the 1940s and 50s was based on the experiences of the war and the preceding Great Depression; in which the later move towards outward orientation was based on the expansion of the world economy and world trade in the 50s and 60s; in which the temporarily successful OPEC action of 1973 and 1979 was linked with the experience of deteriorating and unstable terms of trade; in which the debt crisis of today is linked to the OPEC action and the response of the industrial countries to this action; in which the present African crisis is linked to the historical experience of new independence and the difficulties of giving political independence a proper economic meaning and foundation. So perhaps a better scenario would be to say the story of development is more than just 'one damn thing after another'; it is a story of unfolding, of one thing leading to another in a process which can be given some meaning. But the trouble seems to be one of time lags. Just as generals tend to fight the last-but-one war, so the development actors as well as the development thinkers seem to base their action and thought on experiences of the last-but-one decade or a last-but-one phase, only to be overwhelmed by the inappropriateness of such action and thought in the face of a tide of new events in new problems. It is perhaps a case of a problem for every solution, rather than a solution for every problem.

This last scenario seems to come close to the truth. It can be presented pessimistically as always reacting too late and to an obsolete situation; or more optimistically as a learning process. We react—although inevitably with a time lag—to the lessons of the past. Perhaps we can also learn to speed up this learning process, to react more quickly and more relevantly to new events. Even more optimistically, we can describe the last 40 years as a journey of discovery. For example, from the earlier emphasis on physical capital accumulation we have all—planners, Keynesians, neoliberals, structuralists or whatever we call ourselves—learnt to attribute greater importance to human capital; similarly we are all agreed—at least rhetorically—to attribute more importance to reduction of poverty than to mere growth of GNP. The trouble is that while we may share in such discoveries, we still differ widely about what conclusions to draw for development policy. We all want to reduce poverty and enable people to live up to their full potential, but that does not lead to any agreement about the policies best designed to achieve these common objectives. Instead, they take their place— alongside mother love and apple pie—as emotional invocations. Thus, the ritual invocation of such common objectives may become a rhetorical mask. The 'human face' may become a face lift for any policies which we advocate; the same may be true in the description of all types of adjustment policies as 'growth-oriented'.

The scenario which is perhaps the most fruitful approach to an understanding of the development story and to drawing proper lessons from it, is the one indicated by the motto from Dr Johnson which precedes the next section: 'Seldom is any splendid story wholly true'. This seems to fit the development story of the last 40 years. Compared with the pre-war and war-time situation, the world of Bretton Woods was indeed a 'splendid story'. The world today would be a worse place without it. Yet the splendid story that emerged was not 'wholly true'; it was incomplete, flawed and carried in its defects the germ of its own destruction. Our problem then is to live up to the scenario of development as a learning process and create a new 'splendid story'. This at any rate is the angle from which we will now look at the story of development.

2.2. The high hopes of Bretton Woods and the worm in the apple

'Seldom is any splendid story wholly true.' (Samuel Johnson)

At the end of the Second World War there was clearly a unique opportunity to reshape the world international system. The old order had been swept away. There was a burning desire to pay heed to the lessons of recent experience and avoid the errors of judgement and policies which were felt to have been among the causes of the disastrous war. The new system created at Bretton

W,oods and in the UN thus reflected the current perceptions of the immediate pre-war and war-time experience. What were these perceptions?

First, there was the perceived need to avoid the disastrous beggar-my-neighbour policies of the 1930s when countries, dominated by traditional and classical doctrines of reliance on 'equilibrating' market mechanisms, got themselves deeper and deeper into competitive devaluations, heavy deflation, rising unemployment, and protectionism, with their terrible social and political consequences. (Perhaps this lesson now needs to be relearned). World trade declined in value between 1929 and 1933 by 65 per cent and in volume during the same period by 25 per cent. The belief in classical policies had been swept away by a new Keynesian consensus on active macro-economic management by governments with full employment set as the primary objective. In the international field, the conclusion drawn was that beggar-my-neighbour nationalist policies must be replaced by international rules of conduct and control by international institutions.

The 1930s had also been accompanied by a disastrous fall in primary commodity prices and the lesson drawn by Keynes and others at the time was the need to stabilize primary commodity prices. For that purpose, it was decided at Bretton Woods that in addition to the IMF and World Bank, a third international organization was needed—the ITO, or International Trade Organization— with the dual purpose of stabilizing primary commodity prices and promoting world trade.

The war-time experience of the industrial countries had demonstrated the potential for macro-economic planning and effective government action to maximize output, mobilize latent resources, achieve full employment, and at the same time control inflation and achieve more equal income distribution. This experience was particularly striking in the case of the UK which, in the person of Keynes, played a dominant intellectual role in the creation of the Bretton Woods system. There was a strong feeling that the same principles of planning, macro-economic management of the economy by governments and mobilization of latent sources based on Keynesian principles, were also applicable to the developing countries' concerns which had become a more important item in world interest as a result of the emergence into independence of the countries of the Indian subcontinent and a shift in colonial policies in Africa towards preparation for independence. For many in the West, it seemed natural to extend the principles of the welfare state from the national to the international sphere, and the idea of international income transfers began to take shape.

Bretton Woods was indeed a 'splendid story'. It was an immense improvement over the situation of the 1930s; it gave us 25 'golden years'—from 1948 until the early 1960s when the Bretton Woods system broke down—as will be presently shown. The success of the new system was not entirely due to its intrinsic value. The Marshall Plan (1948–52) had a great deal to do with creating a period over two decades when the industrial countries, through steady growth at a rate of 5 per cent or more, with full employment, little inflation and balance of payments disequilibria solved first by the Marshall Plan and then by US investment and later by a strong recovery of exports and the emerging balance of payments surpluses of Europe and Japan, also provided a firm foundation for the growth of production and exports in developing countries, enabling them to maintain aggregate growth rates similar to or even higher than those of the industrial countries (although not on a per capita basis). World trade expanded even faster than GNP and protectionist incentives were minimized.

If the Marshall Plan had demonstrated the potential effectiveness of large-scale international income transfers, the response of European countries in presenting joint programmes and moving towards trade liberalization among themselves in the form of the creation of a European Common Market also seemed to demonstrate the possibility of constructive recipient policies and constructive collaboration between donors and recipients. So in the first days of high hopes for the Brave New World, development activists in the UN and elsewhere began to think in terms of multi-annual, large-scale aid of the Marshall type for developing countries, linked to the GNP of the industrial countries and thus increasing at the same steady rate of 5 per cent per annum or more as industrial countries' GNP. A target of 1 per cent of GNP then seemed to be quite modest—the US, under the Marshall Plan had transferred something more like 3 per cent of GNP for 4 years running. While it was recognized and admitted from the beginning that the development problems would be more difficult and longer-term than the reconstruction of Europe and Japan, this was assumed to be offset by the strengthening of donor capacity as the beneficiaries of the Marshall Plan would 'graduate' to large-scale donors. Moreover, the capital transfers could be partly in the form of private investment: the prevailing perception was that there should be plenty of scope for productive investment in developing countries since the marginal productivity of capital must be higher in these capital-scarce countries. However, private investment was assumed to be the junior partner to Marshall Plan-type aid (later, in the first UN Development Decade, quantified as 0.3:0.1).

Where, then, was the worm in the apple? Why did the splendid story not come wholly true? The most obvious defect was that the Bretton Woods system remained *incomplete*. To begin with, the International Trade Organization which Keynes had considered to be an indispensable third pillar of the Bretton Woods system, never came into being. Although it was duly negotiated and agreed at Havana, the 'Havana Charter' was not ratified by the US Congress. This was largely a matter of time lags—by the time the ITO came up for ratification, the climate of opinion in the US had changed: the Roosevelt/Truman era in which 'Freedom from Want' had been proclaimed as a global objective, was beginning to shade into the very different McCarthy era in which the UN and all its works became 'an evil empire'. Another reason why the ITO was not ratified was the fact that commodity prices had temporarily risen, first as a result of world war shortages and then the Korean War, so that intervention by the ITO seemed unnecessary.

Some of the intended functions of the ITO were subsequently shifted to GATT (the General Agreement on Trade and Tariffs); but GATT was a weak version, almost a caricature, of the intended ITO and did not include the vital function of commodity price stabilization. In fact GATT took out the trade policy chapter in the Havana Charter, deleting not only the chapters on commodity agreements, but also those on employment, development and restrictive business practices. GATT became—and to some extent remained—very much a First World institution and initially failed to make allowances for the special problems of developing countries. Nor did the subsequent creation of UNCTAD in 1964 fill the gap left by the failure of the ITO; by that time the shift in economic power and relevance away from the UN was complete and the industrial countries were determined to keep UNCTAD at the level of a talking shop (although some useful initiatives subsequently came from UNCTAD, particularly the acceptance of the

GSP—the Generalized System of Preferences. In fact this initiative was probably more useful to developing countries than all the 'trade liberalizations' under GATT which were largely offset by the growth of restrictions outside the GATT system, including the MFA—Multi Fibre Agreement—and the so-called 'voluntary' export restraints).

The even further reaching plans for commodity stabilization proposed by Keynes never had a real political chance to materialize. Keynes had proposed a world currency to be based not on gold, not on the dollar, not on sterling, not on SDRs, but on 30 primary commodities (including oil and coal); this would automatically have stabilized at least the average price of these 30 commodities. But however ripe the situation at the end of the war was for a Brave New World, this Ultra-new World proposed by Keynes proved to be too radical; at Bretton Woods it sank without trace. Perhaps Keynes would have fought harder for it if he had known that the ITO would not come into existence; but by the time that had become clear, Keynes was dead and in any case, the enthusiasm for a Brave New World had largely evaporated.

The Bretton Woods system was also incomplete in that the UN, which was supposed to be another pillar of the Bretton Woods system, was never brought into action in the way initially expected. This was largely due to the adverse change in the political climate already referred to. The initial hope was that a 'Special Fund' should be set up in the UN to administer large-scale soft aid—more or less on Marshall Plan terms—to developing countries. This proposal, originating in the UN Sub-Commission for Economic Development in 1948, was taken up in more detail in the 1951 Report of the UN Expert Group (which included two subsequent Nobel Prize winners, Arthur Lewis and Ted Schultz) on 'Measures for Economic Development'. Although the process of detailed preparations and negotiations was duly set in motion in the UN system and the statute for a 'UN Fund for Economic Development' was laboriously evolved, under the chairmanship of the subsequent UN Secretary General, U. Thant, the unfortunate initials of this proposed fund, i.e. UNFED, described only too well the fate awaiting this stillbirth. (When it was realized how the initials would be received, the word 'Special' was hastily added in front—but unfortunately the science fiction nature of the new acronym of SUNFED still provided an unfortunately accurate description of the chances of this proposal). The long opposition of the World Bank not only to involving the UN in financial aid but even to the principle of soft aid, also served to prevent this idea materializing. When, with the dawn of the more liberal Kennedy era the chances for soft, multilateral aid became better and the World Bank dropped its opposition to soft aid, it was clear that the Western donor countries would not be willing to channel it through the UN where the developing countries had a major say, but through the World Bank which they controlled. In any case, the new IDA (International Development Association) never reached dimensions remotely comparable with the Marshall Plan. At the same time, the UN received two valuable consolation prizes in the form of being allocated food aid (the World Food Programme) and technical assistance (the UNDP). In fact, the UNDP initially, before its merger with ETAP (the UN Expanded Technical Assistance Programme arising from point IV), still carried in its name of 'Special Fund', a recognition of the aborted SUNFED. But that was meagre consolation compared with the initial hopes. So the Bretton Woods system which was meant to walk on four legs (UN, ITO, IMF and World Bank) was hobbling along on the last two only.

Not only was the Bretton Woods structure incomplete, but it was also distorted. In the original version, which was in line with his high priority of avoiding deflation and recession, Keynes had suggested an IMF which would put adjustment pressure on balance of payments surplus countries rather than deficit countries. This was to be achieved by making it mandatory for surpluses to be held in a World Central Bank and for these deposits of surpluses to carry a negative rate of interest (i.e. to be taxed). Although this vision is still partly reflected in the constitution of the IMF, enjoining it to put equal pressure on deficit and surplus countries, in fact the IMF has proved utterly incapable of pressure on surplus countries, whether Japan and Germany today or OPEC in the 1970s. The pressure is now entirely concentrated on deficit countries which are asked to 'put their house in order'; even among the deficit countries the pressure is selective and there is not significant impact of the IMF on the presently biggest balance of payments deficit country—the USA. The admonition of industrial countries, and specifically the surplus countries, to 'put their house in order' remains entirely at the rhetorical level; there is no question of conditionality or financial sanctions.

There is of course a historical explanation—to some extent an alibi—for this distortion of original intentions. The Keynesian desire to put pressure on surplus countries was based on the undesirability of deflationary pressures in times of unemployment and recession: in such conditions, the surplus country is the enemy of the world economy and should be penalized, while the deficit country is the friend of the world economy and should be supported. During the golden years of full employment, this prescription, of course, was no longer appropriate; pressure on deficit countries was then justified. The trouble is that with the shift in the world situation to slow growth, unemployment and recessions after 1973, the IMF has not returned—or has not been able to return—to the policies originally recommended with the Great Depression of the 1930s in mind, and which now, once again, were appropriate in the light of the economic situation since 1973. In this respect the time lag scenario previously presented would seem applicable: Keynes' proposals were made to cope with the recessionary situation of the 1930s; these proposals were then reversed to deal with the different situation of the 1950s and 1960s, but the reversal was then maintained, and indeed intensified, in a new economic climate when it was no longer appropriate.

There seems little prospect, however, that this process of 'learning but too late' will be continued in the future. In the absence of a world central bank, world currency and global source of liquidity which can be realized or withheld—all these part of the Keynesian proposals—it is difficult to see how even in future the Bretton Woods institutions could put effective pressure on surplus countries. It would certainly require a dramatic reform of the Bretton Woods system in the direction suggested by Keynes. Interestingly enough, there are some faint signs of recognition of what has been lost: for example, in the case of the ITO there is not only the Compensatory Financing Facility, but also the recent addition of commodity prices to the list of IMF indicators—the beginning of a recognition that debt repayment capacity and structural adjustment capabilities are tied to terms of trade.

2.3. The golden years of the 50s and 60s: Were they really solid gold?

The decades of the 1950s and 60s were a period of global expansion of production and trade, one of the longest and most pronounced booms in world history, with full employment and little inflation in the industrial countries. This was a favourable environment for developing countries, including those obtaining independence during that period. This was fully reflected in the statistical and aggregate picture of development, with increases in output, trade, technological capacity, acquisition of planning experience, etc. In many developing countries this period saw the rise of a middle class and the development of entrepreneurship. All the same, the approach to development, based as it was on pre-war and war-time experiences and on the incomplete Bretton Woods system, and to a large extent a reflection of the progress of the industrial countries, showed certain weaknesses which were to become apparent in the course of time and from which some lessons could be drawn. Once again, however, sometimes the actual lessons learnt were lessons based on 'yesterday', i.e. they came too late to be appropriate to newly changed circumstances.

Some of the characteristic approaches to development during the golden years have already been mentioned in the preceding section. To begin with there was a heavy and almost exclusive emphasis on physical capital accumulation. The Keynesian consensus ruled supreme, and the neo-Keynesian development model, embodied in the Harrod-Domar formula, emphasized capital accumulation as the source of growth, with the capital/output ratio in the formula being taken more or less as constant. The emphasis on physical capital accumulation also drew support from Russian planning and its apparent successes. This virtually exclusive emphasis on physical capital accumulation was perhaps most clearly expressed by Maurice Dobb lecturing to the Delhi School of Economics in 1951:

The largest single factor governing productivity in a country is its richness or poorness in capital instruments of production. And I think that we shall not go far wrong if we treat capital accumulation, in the sense of a growth in the stock of capital instruments—a growth that is simultaneously qualitative and quantitative—as the crux of the process of economic development.

This emphasis on capital accumulation was almost universally shared: it was also clearly embodied in the approach of the previously mentioned proposals of the UN experts in 1951. Subsequently, and in the light of experience, it was found that the 'capital/output ratio' can be a very troublesome factor; that it may have an obstinate tendency to remain unfavourable, i.e. high, or even to rise; that it is largely governed by 'human' factors such as education, skill, training, health, nutrition, etc., not explicit in the Harrod-Domar model; that much of the physical capital accumulation, at least in the earlier stages, is of the infrastructure type, with high capital/output ratios and long maturity periods needed for a full return; that contrary to the optimistic belief, based on external economies and the theory of balanced growth, that capital/output ratios would rapidly decline as investment expands, other factors may intervene in the opposite direction: for example, increased investment may outrun the technical and administrative capacity of a country to design, implement and operate efficient development projects, etc. The smaller size and lack of economies of scale could also be a relevant factor in developing countries. So, the initial equation of development with physical capital accumulation led to increasing problems and was increasingly questioned as the golden years went on. A more mature synthesis later emerged in which physical and human capital formation were seen as both necessary and neither sufficient, and emphasis was laid on their interaction. Familiarity with physical capital and its operation will help to develop human skills, just as educated and skilled labour will improve the operation of physical capital and suggest lines of technical progress.

The emphasis on physical capital accumulation was linked with optimism regarding the domestic capacity of developing countries and their governments to mobilize domestic savings and investment and an equally optimistic belief that this might be supplemented by large foreign aid injections on the precedent of the Marshall Plan. Domestic capital accumulation was to be promoted by utilization of surplus labour, especially in agriculture, and utilization of the potential of 'disguised unemployment'. This confidence that domestic savings and investment could be rapidly increased was not entirely misplaced. In actual fact, domestic savings and investment ratios in most developing countries increased quite rapidly and soon reached and exceeded the rather modest initial targets set for them (which in turn were based on optimistic assumptions for capital/output ratios). However, it turned out that quite often the source of the increased domestic savings and investment was not so much the mobilization of latent surplus labour (which would have been a factor making for an egalitarian pattern of development), but rather an emerging inequality of income distribution and a squeezing of the agricultural sector (making for an inegalitarian pattern of development and long-term problems with demand for manufactured goods). As for the hoped-for Marshall type flow of external resources which was supposed to supplement domestic savings and prevent balance of payments difficulties, this failed to materialize. The failure of an attempt at a Marshall Plan under UN auspices, in the name of SUNFED, has already been described. In any case, it is doubtful whether an injection of the Marshall Plan type, whether bilateral or multilateral, would have had the same effect in developing countries as in Europe. The lesson of the Marshall Plan was that such injections are most effective where the recipients come forward with their own proposals and agree in advance on the division and use of the external funds; where the recipients are willing to use the funds as the basis for increased cooperation among themselves; where there is already the human basis in terms of skill, experience and education; and where there is a high degree of technological capacity among the recipients. None of these conditions would have been present in a Marshall Plan for the developing countries during the golden period. Perhaps today the preconditions would be better, but the sad fact is that a Marshall Plan today would not be devoted so much to development as to solving the debt crisis and to damage limitation from the setbacks of the 1980s.

The type of external resources which did, in fact, flow in excess of expectations was private capital. The target for the First Development Decade of the 1960s was for aid to constitute 70 per cent of the total inflow, more than double the private inflow. In fact, the situation was more or less reversed. This substitution of private capital for official aid at concessional terms had obvious implications for future balances of payments: the seeds of the future debt problem were sown. Moreover, insofar as much of this private inflow represented direct investment by multinational corporations, often in the form of subsidiaries, some of the growth of the Golden Years inevitably acquired an exogenous, and often enclave, character rather than representing a truly national capacity. Towards the end of the period, debates developed whether the transfer of technology connected with such direct foreign investment was a valuable bonus of such investment and had national demonstration effects; or whether on the contrary it introduced inappropriate technology, stifled local enterprise and technology and encouraged a brain drain from developing countries. It also meant that some of the rents accruing to protected import-substituting industries were expatriated as profits of foreign subsidiaries, with strain on the balance of payments and nullifying the saving of foreign exchange through import substitution. But the same also applied to more export-oriented types of industrialization. Insofar as the exports came from foreign subsidiaries, the degree of retention of the foreign exchange earned from exports was clearly reduced. The share of foreign subsidiaries in exports of NICs (newly industrialized countries) towards the end of the Golden Era was estimated at 15–30 per cent for South Korea, 40–50 per cent for Brazil, 25–30 per cent for Mexico and 70–85 per cent for Singapore.

Another reason (apart from excessive expectations of aid inflows) why insufficient attention was often paid to possible balance of payments constraints was the fact that at the beginning of the Golden Years, commodity prices were buoyant, with a peak in 1951 at the time of the Korean War; also, many developing countries had accumulated important foreign exchange reserves during the war which could be gradually drawn upon. This happy situation did not last, however: terms of trade and relative prices of primary commodities deteriorated quite sharply during the Golden Years, resuming their declining pre-war trends. This took quite a lot of steam out of the great savings and investment effort; development turned out to be an uphill struggle and the possibility of 'immiserizing growth' began to raise its ugly head. Also, the single-gap neo-Keynesian formula which made growth dependent only on the rate of investment began to be replaced by 'dual gap' theories of development where the balance of payments appeared as a separate and often dominant constraining factor. Thus, for balance of payments reasons, success in raising domestic savings rates could turn sour in that the potential savings capacity could not be fully utilized for lack of foreign exchange. Here, the failure of aid to reach the modest hoped-for targets, let alone the dimensions of a 'Marshall Plan', became increasingly felt as a constraining factor.

Another consequence of the poor experience with primary commodity prices during the period immediately before the war was a certain export pessimism which contrasted sharply with domestic optimism. This export pessimism led to emphasis on industrialization as the most obvious diversification out of primary commodities, not just any kind of industrialization but industrialization with an emphasis on import substitution. As far as reliance on exports of primary commodities was concerned, this pessimism was largely justified by events: in spite of unprecedented expansion in the industrial countries, the terms of trade for primary commodities fell by over 25 per cent between 1951 and 1964 and volume also expanded much less than might have been expected. Where the pessimism, however, proved to be unjustified was in being extended to *all* exports. This was based partly on the pre-war experience of recession in the industrial countries and shrinking world trade, and partly on a belief that exports of manufactures were largely beyond the reach of developing countries. The first assumption turned out to be quite false: far from the pre-war shrinkage of world trade, world trade bounced ahead at rates considerably exceeding even the high growth rates of industrial countries. But the second assumption was largely justified at the time: in the early 50s it was very difficult to visualize the rapid expansion of exports of manufactures from the NICs, India and other developing countries beginning in the 60s. Much of the infrastructure needed for export industries was simply not there; such industries would have lacked the foundation of a domestic market which still had to be created by planning for balanced growth. With the benefit of hindsight and in the light of experience, we can now say that developing countries did not pay sufficient attention during the golden years to the possibilities of *export* substitution rather than *import* substitution, i.e. moving from exports of primary commodities into exports of manufactured goods. As a corollary, not enough attention was paid by many developing countries to the need to keep the import-substituting industries efficient so that they could rapidly develop into export industries. In fact, the methods adopted to establish import-substituting industries were often directly hostile to the development of efficiency as a basis for subsequent exports.

There is a long list of factors now recognized as creating such a danger of inefficient import substitution. This list would include rent seeking rather than efficiency as a basis of profits in protected import-substituting industries; encouragement of foreign penetration of the economy, leading to the elimination of local producers and preventing indigenous learning processes; a tendency to adopt imported capital-intensive technologies; concentration on items of luxury consumption of the type previously imported; absence of sufficient vertical deepening of the import-substituting industries, in particular a failure to develop local capital goods industries. Such a catalogue of sins is fashionable today as a basis for arguing that industrialization should have been more 'export-led' or 'outward-oriented' from the beginning. However, one should be careful before drawing this particular lesson from the experience of the 1950s and 60s. To begin with, when exports of manufactures did start in a promising way in the 1960s, they were often based on industries originally developed as import substitutes, or at any rate for the domestic market; many of the export industries were only possible on the basis of previous infrastructure investment in transport, education, etc. The technological capacity for successful export competition in manufactures had to be built up by industrial experience gained from industrialization for the domestic market.

Moreover, even today it can be shown that 'outward orientation' works better as a recipe for middle-income countries than for low-income countries—and in the 1950s practically all developing countries were still in the category of what are now considered to be low-income countries. There is a clear danger that the lesson of 'outward orientation' will be learned in a less favourable international climate than during the Golden Years and then become counter-productive. But we may accept during the Golden Years, with the strategy of import-substituting industrialization, there was too much emphasis on the first word 'import', and not enough on the second word 'substitution'. The emphasis on industrialization was right (within limits to be discussed) and the emphasis on substitution, i.e. substituting manufactured goods for primary commodities, was also right. But the possibilities of export substitution were underrated. Although this did not prevent a vigorous participation of developing countries as a whole in world trade in manufactures at a later stage, it did mean that when the time came, this participation was concentrated on a relatively small number of developing countries.

Probably the most important weakness of the import substituting industrialization strategy was that it did not *really* substitute for imports. Due to the lack of vertical integration, it shifted imports from finished products to inputs of intermediate and capital goods, saving very little foreign exchange in the process. However, the same objection can also be raised about the later export-led success stories, like South Korea and the other Tigers: the net value added by exports was often only a small fraction of the statistical export value, with a high proportion of the exports being offset by imports of necessary inputs to produce these exports. The chief difference, however, was that whereas import substitution tended to run out of steam when the simpler and final-stage imports had been substituted, in the case of export-led growth, the import content of the exports was steadily reduced in the case of the Tigers and also some of the Latin American countries (as happened before in Japan), so that the net value added represented by a given value of exports was steadily increased. However, it must remain an open question to what extent this difference is due to the superiority of outward orientation over inward orientation, and to what extent it is due to the fact that both import substitution and export promotion were handled with greater efficiency in the case of the successful countries, due to third factors such as standards of education, promotion of indigenous technology, administrative efficiency of the government, entrepreneurial culture, labour discipline, etc. There must be a presumption that these third factors were important because in most of the outward-oriented success stories one will also find that the import-substituting industries developed to a high level of efficiency (many of them become export industries) and that in fact these outward-oriented countries relied heavily on import-substitution in the earlier stages and continued to do so with proper selectivity. Proper selectivity, overall efficiency, proper timing and phasing, the ability to 'pick winners', seemed to be more important elements of successful development than any so-called inward or outward orientation.

The neoclassical 'new orthodoxy' has revived the myth of the passive state. The active developmental state supposedly just retards growth by creating widespread inefficiencies, stifling enterprise and preventing market signals from functioning. Governments should move towards limiting their role to ensuring 'sound money' and 'getting the prices right'. Yet their own examples belie such an interpretation. The East Asian NICs, and especially South Korea, have had extensive state intervention throughout their development in industrial planning, infrastructure, training, finance and labour relations, with subsidization of some industries and protection of others. As Amartya Sen has commented:

If this is the free market, then Walras's auctioneer can surely be seen as going around with a government white paper in one hand and a whip in the other.

This is not to deny the importance of private sector dynamism, but the strategic role of the state was crucial. It is not the size of the state that is the real issue, but rather its roles and effectiveness. In practice this is tacitly acknowledged by many neoclassical economists. One example of this is recent work on the Chilean liberalization experiment, an example par excellence of fully-blown application of free market principles. Revealingly, the growing consensus is that this liberalization was too much too fast. Chile's performance over 1950–85 of −1.1 per cent annual GDP growth was not especially bad by Latin American standards, but could hardly be described as an outstanding success.

In any case, much of the import-substituting and inward-looking nature of the early industrialization was the almost inevitable result of the political situation. This was clearly true in countries like India. The independence struggle had been intimately mixed up with protection against the imports from industrial countries destroying local and traditional industries: Gandhi's spinning wheel and boycott of textile imports from Lancashire are symbolic. The linkage between national independence and inward-looking industrialization was also due to the political perception that national independence and sovereignty are meaningless without a measure of industrialization and self-sufficiency. This perception was to be repeated in the 1960s in the newly independent African countries, with economically even more unsatisfactory results because of the absence of many preconditions for successful industrialization compared with Asia or Latin America. If this process of import-substituting industrialization is looked at as a political necessity, much of the criticism of the process as being economically inferior loses in relevance. The emphasis on physical capital accumulation as the 'crux' of development also led, in due course, to a tolerance of income inequalities and the persistence of poverty. This took the form either of a belief that growth was sooner or later bound to 'trickle down' and spread to the poor, or even more strongly that increased income inequalities were a necessary price to pay for the time being until the luxury of welfare could be afforded from an enlarged cake of production. During this period of the 1950s and 60s the famous 'inverted U-curve' of Kuznets played a big role, which seemed to show that in the earlier stages of development, income inequalities increased until a turning point was reached— presumably at middle-income levels, perhaps after the 'take-off stage' identified by Rostow—when income distribution would become more equal again, and poverty would rapidly melt away under the dual impact of a larger cake and a more equal income distribution. The same idea of a turning point away from inequality towards greater equality and welfare was also inherent in the Arthur Lewis model of development with surplus labour, very influential during this period. As the Golden Years went on however, the existence of such a turning point at a reasonably early development stage became more and more doubtful. There seemed little sign either of trickle down or of a turning point in most of the developing countries. Hence new strategies of 'redistribution with growth' and more directly employment and poverty targeted approaches, came to the fore, as will be described in the next section.

The Arthur Lewis model was also indicative of another weakness in the type of development prevalent during the Golden Years, namely a comparative neglect of agriculture. In this model and much related thinking, the main function of agriculture was to provide rural surplus labour as the cannon fodder of industrialization (reminiscent of what happened in the pioneer days of the Industrial Revolution in Great Britain), to provide a market for industrial goods and to provide the raw materials for processing by the prominent textile, leather and other industries. This passive or negative role ascribed to agriculture was never very convincing: how could agriculture provide a market for industrial goods unless rural incomes were raised? How could agriculture release surplus labour unless productivity was increased? How could growth trickle down to the poor when the great mass of the poor lived in rural areas? These and similar questions were not clearly faced, let alone answered.

This blind spot in the early industrialization drive had several roots: one was the justified pessimism about relative prices of primary and agricultural products, which was perhaps too unthinkingly extended from the international to the domestic arena. There was also a strong belief that technical progress in agriculture would be much slower and more difficult than in industry. This belief has proved largely unjustified, as shown by the tremendous increases in agricultural productivity in North America, Europe and the Far East, where technical progress in agriculture proved to be at least as fast as in industry, as well as the Green Revolution in some parts of the Third World.

Another reason was more political: an 'urban bias' injected into

development policies by the disproportionate political influence of
the urban minority compared with the rural majority. The opposite
'rural bias' in the agricultural policies followed in North America,
Europe and Japan provided yet another reason for comparative
neglect of agriculture: it reduced international food prices, making
imports easier and more tempting. It also made available during
this period massive US food aid enabling governments so inclined
to justify low investment priorities for national food production.
However, all the very large recipients of food aid during the 50s
and early 60s, such as India, South Korea, Israel, Greece, etc.,
eventually managed to use the resources provided by massive aid,
including food aid, to provide the infrastructure investment for
their own Green Revolutions. In this they followed in the footsteps
of Western Europe and Japan, who also very quickly graduated
out of the massive food aid provided by the Marshall Plan into
becoming substantial surplus producers with strong 'rural bias'
policies.

Over-valued exchange rates, often typical of countries engaged
in import-substituting industrialization, work to the disadvantage
not only of export industries but more particularly of agriculture,
by both reducing exports and facilitating competing imports. So in
the total picture of relative neglect of agriculture it was not surprising
that the heavy net agricultural export of developing countries began
to fade as the period went on and net food exports were steadily
converted into net food imports (although the agricultural policies
of the richer countries had as much or more to do with this development than the policies of developing countries).

Yet another phenomenon became apparent towards the second
of the Golden Years decades which served to take some of the gilt
off and was to become a source of great trouble and worry subsequently. This refers to the fact of an increasing cleavage among
developing countries. Growth turned out to be distinctly faster and
easier among the middle-income countries than among the low-
income countries. This remains true even when the circular nature
of this relationship is taken into account, i.e. that faster growth
pushes countries into the middle-income category while slower
growth condemns countries to stay in the low-income category.
Thus, during the last 5 years of the period (1965–70), the per
capita income of middle-income countries, at 3.8 per cent p.a.,
increased almost twice as fast as that of the low-income countries,

at 2.2 per cent. In fact, the middle-income developing countries grew slightly faster than the industrial market economies, even in per capita terms. It was the low-income countries which were beginning to fall sharply behind in GNP growth. Thus the gap opening up during that period was not so much between North and South, but rather between the upper and middle-income countries on the one hand and the low-income countries on the other. The sub-category of what later came to be known as 'least developed countries' began to emerge, and so did a geographical concentration of this sub-category among the then very recently independent countries of sub-Saharan Africa.

Another worrying feature of the Golden Years was the fact that in spite of rapid growth rates, increasing inflationary pressures and an international environment which should have been very favourable to primary commodity prices, they obstinately refused to improve relative to the price of manufactures imported by developing countries. Again, the least developed countries were the worst sufferers since they depended almost entirely on exports of primary products, in the case of many African countries a single primary product. This seemed to reveal a structurally persistent weakness which already then boded ill, in the event of the kind of deterioration in the international climate which was to follow. Also, the suspicion arose, based on the emerging evidence of the 1960s, that even those developing countries which had engaged in successful export substitution of simple manufactures, typically textiles, shoes, processed primary products, etc., for primary exports did not seem to escape the threat of adverse terms of trade. The uneven distribution of gains from international trade was beginning to be seen to be not just a matter of different types of commodities but also of different types of countries, different degrees of technological power and different types of labour markets.

To sum up the experience of the Golden Years: the favourable growth experience, particularly for the middle-income countries, had certainly demonstrated the *possibility* of economic growth. This was more important than it might seem since initially considerable doubt existed among both politicians and economists whether economic growth was not 'naturally' limited to *homo economicus*—economic man as existing in the industrial countries of the temperate zone. Particularly, newly independent countries were viewed rather sceptically as to their growth possibilities. So this demonstration of the Golden Years of growth feasibility was no mean achievement; at any rate, the voices doubting the possibility of growth outside the sacred circle of the North were no longer heard towards the end of the period. Moreover, understanding of development problems had grown considerably during the period: the simple view of the economy as a type of vending machine, suggested by a superficial reading of the Harrod-Domar formula, i.e. you put in more savings and investment and you pull out more growth, had given way to an understanding that even growth, let alone development, is a much more complex process and that in particular it involves factors relating to human rather than physical capital. So in this respect it was particularly important that the Golden Years showed rapid progress, not only in physical investment rates, but also in such indicators of human capital formation as spreading literacy and education, elimination of a number of diseases and reduced mortality rates, including infant mortality rates. This progress in human indicators could be shown to be only tenuously related to GNP growth, illustrating both the limitations of 'trickle-down' and the possibility of development along alternative routes.

But since all this encouraging progress was made in a period of, and to some extent on the back of, steady progress in the industrial countries and a situation in these countries, as a result of full employment and the Keynesian consensus, extremely favourable to trade liberalization, it was not clear during the Golden Years to what extent the growth achieved was dependent on the existence of an 'engine of growth' outside the control of the developing countries themselves. This was to be tested when the favourable international climate was drastically changed in the early years of the following decade of the 1970s, signifying the end of the Golden Years period. It was then that the lack of an internal dynamism in many countries, due often to neglect of agriculture and of indigenous technological capacity, became painfully apparent.

2.4. The 1970s: Growth maintained?
The illusion of debt-led growth

The decade of the 1970s saw the breakdown and disintegration of the Bretton Woods system. The best date to attach to the end of Bretton Woods is probably 15 August 1971 when President Nixon suspended the free convertibility of the US dollar into gold at the fixed rate agreed at Bretton Woods. This ended the era of fixed exchange rates and destroyed the foundations of even the truncated Bretton Woods which had emerged. The breakdown of Bretton Woods was more immediately connected with the emerging payment imbalances between the industrial countries, but also with increasing concern about 'over-heating' of their economies and a consequent displacement of full employment by control of inflation as a priority objective. Thus the engine of growth which had supported the developing countries during the Golden Era began to stutter and then violently change gear. But the event which most imprinted its stamp on the 1970s and gave a disarrayed international system its final ominous push, was the assertion of oil power by OPEC in 1973/74, with the decade suitably ending with the second assertion of oil power in 1979/80. The assertion of oil power provided an opportunity for broader assertion of commodity power and for fundamental shifts in international economic relations; in the event, this opportunity was not realized.

So here again we can speak of 'a splendid story not wholly true'. The splendid part of the story was that if we simply look at growth rates, the developing countries as a whole and even the oil importing developing countries proved quite capable of continuing their growth rates even in the face of reduced growth and serious recessions in the industrial countries. In fact, contrary to what happened during the preceding two decades, the gap in per capita income between the developing countries and the industrial market economies narrowed rather than widened during 1970–81, at least in relative terms.

The maintenance of growth during this period is, however, subject to some qualification. The growth rate of GDP for all developing economies, excepting the high-income oil exporters, receded from the high rate of 6 per cent per annum which it had reached during 1965–70, the last quinquennium of the two Golden Decades, to 5.2 per cent in 1971–80, although this was still higher than the average figure for the two decades. The serious exception was sub-Saharan Africa, where the 1971–80 growth rate not only fell much more heavily (from 4.8 to 3.3 per cent), but was lower than at any period during 1950–70. In per capita terms, growth in sub-Saharan Africa was virtually wiped out; 16 out of 41 of African countries showed absolute declines. The phenomenon of development in reverse, then still confined to half of sub-Saharan Africa, was to become more widespread in the 1980s. In the three worst cases of declines of over 4 per cent per annum (Angola, Chad and Uganda), this reversal was associated with civil wars and could thus still be ascribed to 'extra-economic' causes. At the other extreme, the Middle East and North Africa, benefiting directly or indirectly from high oil prices, achieved new growth records, well beyond the level of the two preceding decades, and the East Asia and Pacific region maintained the very high growth rate of 8 per cent which it had achieved in the preceding quinquennium. But Latin America and South Asia shared the African decline, although less drastically: both these regions, accounting for most of the population of developing countries (outside China), more or less returned to the growth rates of the earlier part of the two Golden Decades. There was also vigorous progress in the competitive position of developing countries in world trade in manufactures. While absolute levels of imports of manufactures by industrial countries were held down by their slower growth and protectionist measures, the share of developing countries in their total markets and in their total imports increased, although from low levels (from 1.7 per cent total market share in 1970 to 3.4 per cent in 1979), with all classes of manufactured goods sharing in the increase. The increase in the share of developing countries in total imports of manufactured goods, from 13.5 per cent in 1970 to 16.5 per cent in 1979, however, entirely concentrated on Far Eastern exporters; Latin America and other regions failed to participate in this increase. Shares both in total markets and in imports are still quite small and should leave room for much expansion in the light of new comparative advantages, always with the important proviso that protectionist measures in the industrialized countries do not prevent this.

Moreover, the maintained growth of GDP—gross domestic product—is subject to some doubt concerning the D for 'domestic', and this applies specifically to the growth of manufactured exports. We had already seen that during the Golden Years the expected preponderance of aid and official development assistance over private investment had in fact been reversed. During the 1970s aid from Western countries continued to stagnate and dwindle, well below the modest UN target, while private capital continued to flow strongly, supported both by the maintained 'credit-worthiness' of developing countries bolstered by commercial bank lending of recycled OPEC surpluses and also by the revolution of communications which made internationalization of operations much easier. As a result, by the mid-seventies in Latin America and Africa typically 40–50 per cent of manufacturing industry was controlled by foreign firms (in some countries 60–70 per cent). In Asia this share was typically lower (India and South Korea 10–15 per cent) although in some Asian countries the 40–50 per cent share was reached or exceeded. In the light of the high share of foreign firms in manufacturing in Latin America and Africa, the conventional warning against an 'enclave' character of foreign investment appears ironical; it was domestic manufacturing control which was beginning to look like an enclave. Equally ironical was the fact that industrialization had been recommended as a way of 'de-linking' from an unequal world economy; in fact, it was becoming a way of firmer integration.

Thus, the cherished aim of industrialization as a means of strengthening national independence had been widely missed. The real growth factor in the 1970s, apart from some oil exporters, had come from neither the industrial nor the developing countries, but from the TNCs (transnational corporations). The typical sales value of the large TNCs had become equal to or higher than the total GDP of even the larger and better-off developing countries. (Excon was equal to Argentina or Nigeria, close to South Korea, more than twice the GDP of Egypt or Pakistan, almost four times that of Chile or Peru). Even the last in ranking of the twenty largest TNCs had sales equal to the GDP of Morocco. To a TNC, investment in a given developing country is usually a small, often marginal, part of its total operations and easily fungible; while to a developing country the operation would be an important, and perhaps technologically indispensable, part of its manufacturing capacity—a situation clearly not making for an equal bargaining position. Competition among TNCs helps to balance the scales, but may be offset, or more than offset, by competition among LDCs for the money and technology of the TNCs. The data for the import purchasing power of total exports by developing countries also seem a 'splendid story', but once again further analysis shows it is not wholly true. In the aggregate, this increased faster between 1970 and 1980 than for industrial countries but (a) 1980 represented a peak for oil export values, and much of this favourable differential had been lost by 1983; for developing countries other than major oil exporters the purchasing power of exports increased more *slowly* than in industrial countries; (b) the aggregate figures do not take into account the more rapid increase in population in developing countries; on a per capita basis the comparison would be less favourable; (c) the least developed countries actually showed an absolute decline in the purchasing power of their exports by over 13 per cent; (d) even among the remaining countries, the favourable differential was entirely confined to exporters of manufactures; the other countries fell behind the industrial countries, in relative terms.

Another apparent achievement of the 1970s was that the successful assertion of producer power in the case of oil interrupted the deteriorating trend in terms of trade of developing countries as a whole for all primary commodities taken as a whole; but of course, the oil-importing countries had a very different story of sharp deterioration to tell. But taking the developing countries as a whole, the improvement in terms of trade through high oil prices shifted financial surpluses and financial power strongly in the direction of the Third World. This raised great hopes of using this newly-found power for the establishment of a New International Economic Order (NIEO). It also raised the possibility of creating an indigenous dynamic of development within the Third World itself, and a prospect of using the new financial power for the creation of indigenous technological capacity. The sad part of the story is that this opportunity was lost, and the NIEO ran into the sands. Worse, the way the oil surpluses were recycled through Euro-dollars and the commercial banks of the industrial countries, as well as the new non-Keynesian deflationary response of the industrial countries together ensured that the net outcome would be adverse to the Third World. Not only was the opportunity lost, but it turned into a trap: the term 'debt trap' which became current in the 1980s is an apt description of what happened.

But we are here concerned not with the history of this decade but with the lessons of experience that were drawn for development policy and for development thinking during this decade. In the first place, there was a growing disillusionment with growth as a necessary and sufficient development objective. This was not in any way due to a slowing of actual growth in the course of the Golden Years. Quite on the contrary, the growth rate of developing countries speeded up from 4.2 per cent in 1950–60, to 5.1 per cent in 1960–65 and to 6.0 per cent in 1965–70. Even the growth rate of the low-income countries taken as a whole speeded up during the period, although less than in the middle-income countries as well as starting from a lower level so that the gap between the two groups widened throughout the two decades. Rather, the disillusionment was due to the increasing evidence that rapid growth of GNP could be combined with increasing unemployment and underemployment, increasing poverty and often also increasing inequality of income distribution. At the same time the industrial countries also became disillusioned with growth although for rather different reasons, since in their experience growth led to inflationary pressures and balance-of-payments trouble. For the developing countries the shift in objectives from simple growth initially took two forms: one was the establishment of employment as a major and over-riding objective; the other was a shift to redistribution.

The shift to employment was based on the evidence of increasing unemployment and under-employment both in urban and rural areas; the social and political tensions and pressures thus created were seen to undermine the foundations of continued growth so that there was need for a new approach. Although there was much talk at that time of a 'dethronement of GNP', this is not in fact a very good description of what happened. Growth continued to be considered as a necessary condition for development but was no longer accepted as a sufficient condition. Employment creation was not seen as an alternative to growth but as a proper instrument of growth which would produce not only growth but also a pattern of growth conducive to more equal income distribution, less poverty, more social contentment and less political unrest. In development analysis this shift to employment objectives was typified by the shift from the Arthur Lewis model in which the surplus labour released from agriculture was assumed to be more or less fully absorbed by the growing urban industries, to the Harris-Todaro model. Under the Harris-Todaro model the drift to the towns would be far in excess of available employment opportunities; the gap between rural subsistence incomes and wages in the modern industrial urban sector would attract job seekers from the rural areas in a multiple ratio equal to the income gap. If urban modern sector wages are three times rural incomes, one-third of the chance of a job would be sufficient to attract a migrant from the rural areas; hence there would be three job seekers for each available job; two-thirds of them would remain unemployed or condemned to make a living as well as they could in the informal sector. This model seemed to correspond much better to reality than the Arthur Lewis model. The shift to employment as a major objective was quite logically accompanied by particular emphasis on the need for employment-intensive technologies; so this became also the era of a search for and emphasis on 'appropriate' technologies. Moreover, since small-scale production normally is more employment-intensive than large-scale production, it also became the era of 'small is beautiful'. Equally logically, with employment moving to the centre as the crux of development, such 'human capital' aspects as training, skills, health and other factors in productivity were now given increased weight, compared with physical capital accumulation.

In institutional terms, the emphasis on employment naturally placed the International Labour Organization (ILO) in the centre of development policy, particularly through its newly-organized World Employment Programme. In particular the ILO employment missions, with 'pilot missions' first to Colombia, Sri Lanka and Kenya and subsequently many other countries, had a considerable impact on policy and thinking. This was true in particular of the Kenya Employment Mission which also marked the transition from an emphasis on employment to emphasis on the need for a more direct attack on poverty, by pointing out that the so-called unemployment or under-employment in developing countries was a misnomer. In fact, most of the so-called unemployed or under-employed were working quite hard to earn a living; the real problem was their low income levels. They were the 'working poor' rather than the 'unemployed'. The Kenya Mission also drew attention to the potential of the informal sector as a source for the labour-intensive and appropriate technology needed, rather than an undesirable residual as it appeared in the Harris-Todaro model. The new 'employment-oriented strategy' had some obvious limitations. The idea of labour-intensive small-scale appropriate technology conflicted with the desire for industrialization and modernization; the creation of 'appropriate technology' required a technological capacity in some ways even greater than that required for the earlier growth-oriented investment pattern. The latter could to a large extent be imported or imitated, whereas the appropriate technology would have to be newly created. Ironically, under the Harris-Todaro model, the creation of more employment would only intensify the urban unemployment problem since for every new job there would be several migrants as long as rural surplus labour was available. Reliance on employment-oriented strategy also conflicted with the increasing role of direct foreign investors and multinational corporations. Also, employment could not deal with the poverty groups not capable of employment, those too old to work, too ill, crippled, broken families, orphaned children, etc.; employment to provide an income does not solve the problem of access to health, to education, to clean water, to sanitation, etc.—all services which relate to public action rather than private employment.

Yet in spite of such limitations, the employment orientation had a valid and lasting impact. It emphasized not only the contribution to production which more productive employment could provide, but also the sense of participation and self-respect which improved earning capacity from employment could bring: the issue of human rights as a development objective emerged at this stage. Employment emphasis was especially useful in the agricultural sector where the basis for an appropriate technology largely existed and it became increasingly apparent that in fact the small-scale farmer was more productive in terms of output per acre than the large farmer, and also was quite capable of responding to economic incentives. Employment creation in the agricultural sector also became the key to agricultural improvement through public works schemes, particularly during the slack agricultural seasons, and in times of drought or other emergencies. It was discovered that not only emergencies but also persistent poverty were due not so much to lack of food available, but rather to breakdown in the 'entitlement' mechanism for obtaining access to food and other essentials of life; employment either for an income or directly paid in food was perhaps the most obvious method to create such entitlements.

An employment-oriented development policy also provided an essential bridge between the growth-oriented strategy emphasizing 'productive' investment, and a subsequent poverty orientation which could be accused of shifting to 'unproductive' activities such as redistribution, provision of social services and direct income support. Employment creation was at the same time clearly productive and yet naturally targeted so as to achieve greater equality of income distribution and produce a better trickle-down effect on the poor than mere growth itself. Nobody could accuse an employment-oriented strategy of playing 'zero-sum games'.

Where employment creation seemed most successful, as in the East Asian 'tigers', it was because it was nurtured both by a high degree of literacy, education, skill and willingness to train in the labour force, and a rapid development of general technological capacity (rather than a specific 'appropriate technology') which enabled them to remain internationally competitive in labour-intensive lines of exports even with rising real wages, and to maintain equal income distribution. It was such factors rather than concentration on employment creation as such which made for expansion of employment—in other words, employment was more of a result than an objective or guide to policy.

The other shift in development strategies during the earlier part of the 1970s, apart from the shift to employment objectives, was greater concern with income distribution. The symbolic slogan or strategy emerging in this period was 'Redistribution With Growth' (RWG). This was, of course, linked to employment-oriented strategies: an increase in employment would normally also improve the equality of income distribution, particularly if it related to agriculture, the informal sector and was based on labour-intensive technologies, as proposed. So it is not surprising that the RWG strategy also emerged from the Kenya Employment Mission Report which in fact contained a chapter entitled 'Redistribution *From* Growth'. The subtle shift from redistribution *from* growth to redistribution *with* growth added an important new element. Redistribution from growth put growth first and then suggested the use of the resources created by growth for deliberate distribution measures rather than waiting for 'trickle down'. This policy which could be described as 'incremental income distribution' was put forward as having the great advantage of making redistribution politically more acceptable since it would come out of additional resources and nobody would be absolutely worse-off. This aspect of growth first and redistribution next from the resources created by growth was always a worrying weakness since it disregarded the possibility, perhaps likelihood, that the policies needed to promote growth might be incompatible with redistributive policies (and vice versa), and hence the one might undermine the other. The shift to redistribution *with* growth emphasized the simultaneity and complementarity of redistribution and growth: it was part of the greater emphasis on human capital, with a denial of a trade-off between distribution and growth, and instead an assertion of the compatibility and complementarity of the two. A number of development analysts were going one step further and were advocating redistribution *before* growth. An important argument was that, for example, the growth in Japan and Korea owed both its intensity and its egalitarian character to the fact that through land reform, heavy investment in education and health, etc., capital assets were fairly equally distributed before the growth process started; it was argued that in this way growth did not only have a more solid and sustainable foundation, but also would assume a pattern which was favourable for sustained equality.

The shift in thinking away from growth towards employment and redistribution in the early 70s found a particularly ready echo in the World Bank which at that time had a liberal phase (liberal in the sense of Keynesian/progressive) during the McNamara period, in sharp contrast to its subsequent domination by monetarist and neoliberal views (this time in the Chicago sense). The World Bank became a lead agency in advocating RWG strategies, emphasizing the importance of human capital investment and helping to promote directly poverty-oriented 'basic needs strategies'. One indication of the compatibility of these strategies with growth is that the World Bank's rate of return on its projects did not suffer in this period. This shift also had implications for approaches to development planning. The original concept of GNP growth focuses attention on macro-economic planning, which indeed was developed in close parallel with implementing GNP targets. This is less true of employment targets. Clearly there is no single homogeneous employment problem; the problem of the unemployed school leaver, for example, is a rather different problem from that of the small farmer without access to water. So the employment emphasis paves the way for a less aggregated and more dispersed view of planning. This is even more true of poverty-removal and basic-needs objectives. The character of the different poverty groups is even more diverse and heterogeneous than is the case for different employment problems. Moreover, the nature of poverty problems may differ even among neighbouring villages, or among urban households living close to each other in the same town. Thus poverty-oriented planning and the provision of basic requirements for population groups now lacking them are by their very nature and almost by definition a highly decentralized affair. Local planning as well as local participation, particularly on the part of those directly affected by the lack of basic requirements, is naturally moving into the foreground of the picture. Community development rather than central planning seems the natural principal tool for a basic-needs-oriented development strategy.

Perhaps ironically, this particular implication of RWG/basic needs strategies in moving away from the centralized macro-economic planning associated with GNP growth to looser and more decentralized forms of policy was to fit in well with criticism of centralized planning coming from quite a different direction during the tide of neoliberal counter-revolution characteristic of the 1980s.

The lower growth rate and the re-emergence of unemployment in the industrial countries almost inevitably meant an increase in their protectionism. The attempts by GATT to reduce tariffs and liberalize trade were more than offset by increased non-tariff barriers, 'voluntary' export restraints, further tightening up of agricultural policies with inevitable protectionist consequences and other ways of evading the spirit if not the letter of GATT (or what could have been the letter of the vanished ITO). These non-tariff barriers applied with greater severity to developing countries than to North-North trade, and affected about a quarter of their total exports. The protectionist measures already introduced against the export thrust from a limited number of developing countries gives some indication of the industrialized countries' possible response if a more widespread competitive export expansion was attempted.

In addition to rising protectionism, the abandonment of fixed, or at any rate stable, exchange rates in favour of floating rates, introduced new elements of uncertainty into the international trade prospects of developing countries. Under normal circumstances such uncertainty would have been an argument for greater inward orientation, reliance on import substitution and expansion of trade of developing countries among themselves. If this did not happen to any significant degree, it was largely because the pressure on import capacity deriving from industrial countries' protectionism and from trade uncertainties were swamped by the readiness, indeed the passionate keenness, of commercial banks in the big financial centres to offer loans, initially at low or negative real rates of interest. This made it relatively easy to maintain imports, even in the face of more precarious export prospects and uncertainties. The temptation for developing countries to avoid timely adjustment to the less favourable climate of the 1970s by relying on 'easy money' from the commercial banks, offered not only readily but without conditionality, proved to be too much to resist. This overall picture did not apply equally to all developing countries; the four East Asian tigers, for example, showed their remarkable capacity for adjustment by absorbing high oil prices, increasing protectionist barriers for their exports and exchange rate uncertainties by increasing productivity, keeping real wages low and a strong planning capacity in successfully picking winners; moreover, they did this with less reliance on commercial bank loans than the Latin American countries.

Another factor which maintained the growth of countries like South Korea but also a number of other developing countries was a spill-over effect of OPEC surpluses. There was a development of OPEC aid and investment programmes, although aid was highly concentrated in Middle Eastern countries and investment often channelled through financial institutions of industrial countries; but additional exports of oil exporters, the export of labour to these countries resulting in often significant remittances back to the developing countries, as well as the procurement of construction and other contracts in oil-rich countries all helped to maintain growth. Although this was a more solid basis than borrowing from commercial banks, in that it did not result in an increased debt burden, it also turned out to be a somewhat precarious and temporary source of development finance, dependent on the continuance of the large OPEC surpluses. It was still a 'dependent development' although from the point of view of the Third World as a whole it could be considered as a better approach to self-reliance. But in the event, the OPEC engine of growth proved as temporary as the Keynesian growth of the industrial countries during the Golden Years had been, and the opportunities it offered were not taken. Instead of laying new foundations for sustainable growth in the 1980s, the OPEC engine merely served to replace the other failing engine and postpone the impact of its failure. The nature of the 1970s as a period of illusionary debt-led growth raises a number of issues which contain important lessons for the future. The initial collapse of the Bretton Woods system in 1971 and the subsequent failure of the industrial countries to coordinate their own exchange rate and other policies, together with the shock in 1973/74 of the first major rise in oil prices, clearly led to quite different perceptions on the part of the industrial and developing countries respectively. The industrial countries at first assumed that the crisis was merely a temporary phenomenon, no doubt a serious hiccup in the progress of the two previous decades but one that could be dealt with through existing institutions, largely by way of normal lending operations of their own commercial banks recycling OPEC surpluses. Meanwhile, the rapid growth with full employment of the Golden Years might have to be abandoned in favour of slower growth, unemployment and recessionary periods; but at a time when prevailing politics and ideologies were beginning to swing to the right and the fight against inflation became a major objective, this price seemed to be worth paying. All this seemed justified at the time, and in the event the basic assumption that the shift in financial power relations towards developing countries, or at least towards OPEC countries, could be counteracted by the industrial countries turned out to be justified. This perception on the part of the industrial countries further implied that any later debt repayment phase could be easily handled in traditional ways through the resumed growth in the 1980s which was confidently expected, and/or through continued lending and capital transfers. It took the second big rise in oil prices in 1979/80 at the very end of the decade to shake this perception. On the part of the developing countries there was a different perception, i.e. that the shift in financial power and the successful assertion of commodity power represented a permanent and fundamental break with the past, both necessitating and making possible a New International Economic Order. The developing countries felt strong enough to confront the industrial countries with programmes and demands for such an NIEO. They may have underestimated the confidence of the industrial countries to absorb the shocks of the early 1970s within the framework of the existing order and existing institutions, and also their readiness to abandon the Keynesian full employment consensus of the 1950s and 60s. The lesson of the past had been that it took a very major crisis of the dimensions of the recession of the 1930s and the World War to create the preconditions for a completely new international order, and even then (as we have seen) there was in the end hesitation and difficulty in adopting wholly new and radical ideas. The developing countries assumed that the upheavals of 1971 and 1973/74 constituted a similar crisis offering a similar opportunity.

In the event, the breakdown of Bretton Woods in 1971 and the assertion of oil power in 1973/74 constituted a crisis sufficient to terminate the progress of the Golden Years, but not sufficient to create a consensus for an NIEO. By the time the second big oil shock came at the end of the decade, the world system had become adjusted to running at a slower rate, and the industrial countries had brought into play their technological capacity in reducing the impact of high oil prices. Thus, although the recession following the second oil shock was at least as severe as the one after the first oil shock, it once again failed to reach the dimensions required for a consensus on a need for fundamental changes. With the benefit of hindsight, the developing countries, rather than relying on a perceived fundamental shift in power and confronting the industrial countries with a programme for NIEO, could have chosen two other strategies. One would have been to use their new financial power for the creation of a separate international system, at the same time additional to, and partially delinked from, North-South relations; this was, of course, the route of extended South-South cooperation (ECDC) for which there was in any case plenty of economic scope and justification. Another strategy could have been to use the power shift which had undoubtedly occurred in the early 1970s to press for more piecemeal concessions and modifications of the battered Bretton Woods system—perhaps restoring some of the missing pieces discussed above—in the hope of inducing the industrial countries to return to the Keynesian consensus of high growth rates and full employment which had stood the developing countries in good stead.

The lesson of events of the 1970s for the developing countries was that assertion of commodity power without control of financial institutions, and not backed up by technological power, is empty and temporary. The same failure was also demonstrated for the assertion of power by individual countries or groups of producers without a system of full collaboration within the Third World as a whole.

2.5. The 1980s: A lost decade—development in reverse?

The description of the 1980s as a decade 'lost' for development could be described as 'a sad story not wholly true'. It is not wholly true most obviously in the geographical sense: the decade may be 'lost' for Latin America, Africa and also the oil exporters (at least compared with their position achieved in the 1970s) but it is not true of Asia. Given the demographic and economic importance of Asia, it is not clear which is the exception and which is the rule! But for the other three categories mentioned, to speak of a 'lost' decade may be an understatement; for sub-Saharan Africa, in particular, the 1980s became a disastrous decade and this subcontinent rapidly acquired the character of a marginalized Fourth World, increasingly recognized as requiring special criteria. The other true part of this sad story is that the decade was 'lost' to development in the sense that attention shifted to debt settlement, stabilization, adjustment, structural change, liberalization, etc.—often at the expense of everything that had previously been understood as development, whether growth, employment redistribution, basic needs or reduction of poverty. This shift was associated with the ascent of neoliberal ideologies, a shift in decision-making on development strategy to creditors, donors and international financial institutions, and within the Bretton Woods system from the World Bank which had traditionally stood for development to the IMF which had traditionally come to stand for 'stabilization'. Perhaps the most symbolic development was the shift of the World Bank out of exclusive project lending—which had previously been put forward as the soundest form of development assistance—to balance of payments support in the form of structural adjustment lending and the establishment of a largely IMF-determined 'cross-conditionality' for World Bank action.

The geographical separation between Asia where development continued, and the rest of the developing world where it was 'lost', had already been foreshadowed in the 1970s. In that period (1969–78), the export volume of Asia (without the Middle East) had increased faster than import volume (10.8 per cent p.a. against 8.6 per cent), thus simultaneously constraining debt accumulation and strengthening repayment capacity, while the sub-Saharan Africa and Latin America export volumes increased much slower than import volumes, with the opposite effect. In sub-Saharan Africa, export volume increased by only 1.4 per cent p.a., less than the rate of population increase; even the increase in import volume, although three times higher at 4.1 per cent, was barely sufficient to maintain per capita imports. In Latin America also, import volume grew over three times more than export volume (6.4 per cent against 1.7 per cent). Roots of a debt crisis were thus clearly planted in Latin America and Africa, rather than Asia.

For these countries, the 1980s proved a time of rude awakening from the illusionary growth of the 1970s. Over the five years 1982–86 the cumulative percentage falls in per capita GNP totalled 16.5 per cent for sub-Saharan Africa, 9.7 per cent for the highly indebted countries and 11.5 per cent for oil exporters. For all these categories of developing countries this amounted to a major reversal of development, not just a 'lost decade'. The share of industry in GDP in developing countries which had increased during 1965–80 and had exceeded that of the industrial market economies, fell back and by 1986 was again below that of the industrial countries; it was the developing, not the industrial economies which 'de-industrialized'. In sub-Saharan Africa, de-industrialization was precipitous and brought the share of industry below what it had been in 1970; industrial output declined absolutely by 2.3 per cent p.a. during the first half of the decade. There were also absolute declines in the highly indebted countries and the high-income oil exporters. Investment ratios generally declined for practically all categories of developing countries; in the aggregate, the fall from 26.9 per cent of GDP in 1980 to 23.5 per cent in 1986 brought the ratio below the 1973 level; again the cuts in the ratio were sharpest in sub-Saharan Africa (by 36 per cent) and in the highly indebted countries (by 31 per cent); again the focus of development reversal emerges clearly. The terms of trade of developing countries as a whole deteriorated during 1981–86 by a cumulative percentage of 13.9 per cent (but 34.1 per cent for sub-Saharan Africa and 17.3 per cent for the highly indebted countries). The only thing that seemed to be vigorously increasing for many categories of developing countries was the outstanding debt, with debt service reaching 4.3 per cent of GNP and absorbing 19.7 per cent of exports (as much as 29.6 per cent in sub-Saharan Africa and 27.8 per cent in the highly indebted countries). External debts in 1987 exceeded three years' exports both for sub-Saharan Africa and the 15 heavily indebted countries. The major exception of Asia must be re-emphasized. The category of low-income countries was held up by the remarkable progress of China and India which dominate this category; and the exporters of manufactures were held up by the success stories of East and South-East Asian NICs. Predictably, during the decade much debate centred around the lessons from

Asian successes and the ways in which they could be transplanted to Africa, debtors and other developing countries.

The 1980s opened with a strong recession which represented a culminating point of the contest between commodity power on the one hand, and technological and financial power on the other hand. Commodity power was represented by the second quadrupling of oil prices in 1978/80, while the technological and financial power of the industrial countries was represented by their capacity to reduce the oil content of production, to step up oil exploration and substitution for oil and to reduce the demand for oil further by accepting or even welcoming a recession which would reduce inflation as well as the demand for oil. In this contest, technological/financial power proved to be stronger than commodity power, all the more so since the industrial countries had had the change of adjusting to higher oil prices seven years earlier, with the first quadrupling of 1973/74.

For the oil-importing developing countries the constellation of circumstances could not have been worse: reduced import volumes by the developing countries with both recession and protectionism interacting in the same direction; highly unfavourable terms of trade, both as a result of high oil prices and a deterioration of other commodity prices in relation to the their manufactured imports from industrial countries (the latter increased by high cost of energy); a reduction and later virtual cessation of commercial bank lending and a rise in real interest rates so that debt burdens increased through both lower export earnings and higher service payments simultaneously, as well as a strong appreciation of the dollar in the early years of the decade resulting from the high rates of interest; spreading 'aid fatigue' among industrial countries due to both the recession and the spread of monetarist neoliberal ideologies. The shortcomings of the Bretton Woods system in providing no mechanism for the industrial countries and the balance of payments surplus countries to 'get their act together' made themselves strongly felt. All these circumstances conspired to make the 1980s a lost decade for development. It was a sign of the times that even in such circumstances it could be seriously debated whether the internal policies of developing countries rather than external circumstances were responsible for their difficulties.

It was perhaps ironical that just at a time when the international climate became so disastrously hostile to development the bastions of financial power in the industrial countries and in the leading financial institutions were captured by a neoliberal ideology which preached all-out 'outward orientation' and 'market orientation' as the secret of successful development. If the 1950s and 60s could be said to have displayed a time-lagged misplaced trade pessimism based on pre-war experience, so it could be said of the 1980s that they were dominated by a doctrinal and time-lagged trade optimism based on the trade expansion of the 1950s and 60s and the subsequent illusionary maintenance of developing country imports in the 1970s. The crucial difference, however, was that the inward-oriented industrialization policies of the 50s and 60s were almost certainly justified as a necessary foundation for a subsequent successful outward-orientation in a favourable economic climate; whereas the policies now impressed on developing countries under the name of outward orientation had their justification not in laying the foundations of subsequent sustainable growth (although that was their supposed purpose) but rather to permit payment of their debts.

Here again we have a tragic time-lag situation. Adjustment and restructuring for the purpose of repaying debts, or rather of keeping debts within more manageable limits, would have been the appropriate requirement for the 1970s. The maintenance of import capacity at the expense of balance of payments deficits and increasing indebtedness could have been justified only if policies of developing countries had then been firmly directed towards using the borrowed capital to build up a firm position in tradables so as to create a reasonable balance of payments position permitting a discharge of debt service. Given the inability of industrial countries to prevent the slowed-down growth and sporadic recessions of the 1970s, or even their willingness to employ such recessions and promote unemployment as part of their fight against inflation and OPEC power, such policies during the 1970s would have had to rely as much or more on import substitution than export promotion. That at least would be an overall judgment, without excluding the possibility of specific countries finding their place in a pattern of a gradual increase in the capacity of a number of developing countries for manufactured exports of a genuinely national character, i.e. other than as a result of relocation and internationalization of production on the part of the transnational corporations. To the extent that this did not happen, there is an element of truth in holding the domestic policies of developing countries responsible for some of the troubles of the 1980s. This, however, is subject to some major qualifications: at the time, in the 1970s, when exhortations to restructure in preparation for debt settlement would have been appropriate, not much was heard in this direction from those now in a position not only to advise but to impose such policies. Instead, at the time, the developing countries were urged and indeed pressed to borrow without conditionality or much control of the use of the borrowed resources. Moreover, the type of internal policy that would have been needed in the 1970s was not the type of policy restructuring advocated in the 1980s. There is no evidence that the rise in real interest rates and the severe global recession of the early 1980s was foreseen at the time of low or negative rates in the 1970s.

The policies now impressed upon developing countries under the signs of restructuring, adjustment, retrenchment, stabilization, etc., are justified on the grounds that they are necessary to 'lay the foundations of subsequent sustainable growth'. Leaving aside the question of symmetrical adjustment required from industrial, creditor and balance of payments surplus countries, this approach disregards one of the basic insights of the early development period of the 1950s. Much thinking prevalent then had been based on a view of development and growth as a process of 'cumulative causation', or a system of beneficial or vicious circles or spirals. The vicious circle of poverty, for example, was well established: poor people are poor because they are undernourished or illiterate, and they are undernourished and illiterate because they are poor. In the same way, poor countries are poor because they have low savings and investment and they have low savings and investment because they are poor. In the strategy of balanced growth, the vicious circle took the form of treating the failure of section A to grow as due to the failure of other sectors B, C, D, etc. to grow and supply both the inputs and demand for sector A; the same is true of sector B who fails to grow because sector A fails to grow. In the 'stages of growth' paradigm developed by Rostow this took the form of saying that the earlier stages of assembling the preconditions of growth are very difficult, but once the various elements have been assembled and can mutually complement each other, everything will fall into place and the economy can take off. The present doctrine of neoliberal adjustment is in danger of disregarding all this. It holds that one can temporarily deflate, arrest growth, reduce government expenditures, reduce expenditures on physical and human investments, etc., while at the same time gathering strength for a new and hopefully more sustainable period of growth and development. This disregards the possibility that each cutback may make it more difficult to resume future growth from such a weakened basis. The picture of a 'slippery slope' may be more appropriate than the picture of 'reculer pour mieux sauter' (stepping back to gain room for a forward jump) which underlies the neoliberal approach to adjustment. Yet this possibility is not sufficiently considered or guarded against in the climate of the 1980s.

All this is not to say that the neoliberal critics of earlier development policies do not deserve to be seriously listened to. It had become apparent to the developing countries themselves that a regime of over-valued exchange rates carried dangers of inefficient allocation, rent seeking, capital flight, etc.; that prices and markets have a role to play in the efficient allocation of resources and are often better instruments than administrative regulation or controls; that over-expansion of the government sector might conceivably suppress latent entrepreneurial sources in the private sector which could be released by less regulation; that planning machinery can easily become over-centralized at the expense of local initiative and popular participation; that trade liberalization can be to the advantage of developing countries themselves; that proper price incentives to farmers can be a useful tool of stimulating domestic food production when that can be combined with other measures of a more structural character which are also needed; that industrialization which is at the expense of agriculture can be self-defeating and should be replaced by a type of development in which agricultural development and industrialization can mutually support each other; that policies should not be excessively 'urban biased'; that subsidies and other measures targeted at lower income groups often have a way of failing to reach the poorest and sometimes benefit the better-off instead; that public services no less than the private sector should be governed by principles of efficiency and low-cost services, etc. All this long list of insight (which could easily be further extended) had already emerged from previous developments, and there is no need to create a neoliberal counter-revolution for discovering them. All the same, in so far as the critics of previous strategies have kept on hammering away at these and other shortcomings, they have rendered a useful service. But they have rendered no service by combining these insights with an abandonment of development objectives for the sake of adjustment; by being indifferent, in fact if not rhetorically, to the social impact or 'human face' aspects of the policies they propose; by a failure to put equivalent pressure on surplus countries as well as deficit countries, or on high income deficit countries as well as poorer deficit countries; by applying doctrines developed in different circumstances on the value of free markets to other circumstances where the assumed conditions simply do not exist; by elevating discharge of debt service to an ultimate objective and allowing it to displace in fact the old consensus objectives of growth, employment, redistribution and basic needs.

The insistence on structural adjustment as a pre-condition for new development is justified on the grounds that it is not a policy imposed by the international financial institutions and major industrial governments, but rather an inescapable necessity, given the 'Facts of Life'—the 'Facts of Life' being slower growth in the industrial countries, failure of industrial countries to coordinate balance of payments and exchange rate policies, the overhanging debt burden, weakness of commodity prices, etc. This is an argument which is obviously true as far as it goes. Given an international climate so unfavourable to development, the developing countries have no choice but in one way or another to adjust themselves to it and if necessary cut back their ambitions, and they must try as much as possible to make a virtue of necessity. However, the argument leaves scope for two substantial doubts. First, in the spirit of Bretton Woods and numerous UN resolutions and other proclamations as well as under their own constitutions, it should be the duty of the international financial institutions as well as major governments not simply to accept the unfavourable international climate and expect the developing countries to adjust to it, but rather to change and improve it. Secondly, even if the unfavourable climate is taken as given, it does not follow that the only or even the best form of adjustment is in the nature of 'stabilization', which tends to become a code word for retrenchment. Are there not more expansionary forms of adjustment available? In particular, adjustment through intensified trade and other forms of economic cooperation of developing countries with each other is not included in the adjustment packages now presented. Moreover, the country-by-country approach in which individual, although in essence very similar, packages are imposed country-by-country seems designed, by its very nature, to set developing countries against each other, for example in trying to expand exports simultaneously; this can be self-defeating due to the fallacy of composition and the possibility of immiserizing growth. The route through increased cooperation among developing countries would often seem more hopeful but it is not taken up in the dominant neoliberal approach. The potential for trade between developing countries remains largely untapped. Expanded South-South trade can be treated as a partial delinking from the slowed-down rate of growth of the industrial countries no longer acting as an efficient engine of growth, as Arthur Lewis did in his Nobel Prize lecture in 1980. Alternatively, expanded South-South trade can also be supported by those in favour of closer international integration as a stepping stone towards fuller integration on more equal terms. This debate is as fruitless or inconclusive as to debate whether a half-filled glass of water is 'half full' or 'half empty'! South-South trade is not the only method open to developing countries to maintain their own growth in a less favourable international climate: other methods would include the export-led route in securing a greater share of domestic markets in industrial countries; or successful import substitution; or the development of internal dynamism based on increased technological capacity so as to create a domestic engine of growth to replace the faltering external engine. The latter would almost certainly be required in any case, even for a successful implementation of the other methods of export promotion, import substitution or increased South-South trade. South-South trade in turn can be helpful in creating techno-logical dynamism, and also in providing a basis for improved exports to industrial countries as well as efficient import substitution.

At present only around a quarter of LDC exports go to other developing countries. Thus a given fall in exports to industrial countries would require a three-fold proportionate increase in South-South trade to compensate. However, the heavy taxation of normal export proceeds for debt payment puts a strong premium on expansion of unorthodox methods of trade through barter trade, counter trade, etc.; South-South trade could play an especially important role in promoting such unorthodox methods of trade expansion.

What is striking is the self-assurance and disregard of institutional specificities with which the neoliberal recipe is applied by its adherents, in the face of much previous experience, much professional doubt and obvious economic, social and political realities. In this respect, it resembles more a brand of religious fundamentalism than a school of thought. Perhaps this also explains the surprising ease with which this counter-revolution has captured the commanding heights in the dominant countries and institutions. The severe depression of the early eighties was sufficient to produce fundamental changes, if not in the actual international order then at least in thinking about development. But it is difficult to believe that this shift in thinking will be more lasting than some of the earlier shifts described. Like the other changes in thinking which come and go, and yet leave some of their insights behind, the 'adjustment' period to the neoliberal religion may have passed its peak in the mid-eighties. There has been an increasingly visible wish at the end of the eighties to return to the business of development which remains a global priority. There is more doubt about the social, political and environmental consequences of adjustment policies; less self-confidence in the neoliberal conditionality as against the judgement of LDC governments and many practitioners; less assertion of the doctrine that development is constrained by domestic mismanagement rather than external factors.

Both physical investment and human capital formation have received serious set-backs during this phase when concern with development and growth has been largely displaced by adjustment and stabilization. The decline in investment in low-income economies other than China and India and among major debtor countries and oil exporters has been described at the beginning of this section. Similarly, human capital has been run down alarmingly. As documented by the UNICEF studies on 'Adjustment With a Human Face' and 'The Impact of the World Recession on Children', the cuts in government expenditures have affected the welfare of poorer people and particularly women and children disproportionately; the measures taken under the neoliberal prescription for adjustment, such as abolition of food subsidies, devaluation, trade liberalization, privatization, etc., have contributed to greater inequalities of income distribution, with the well-to-do in a better position to protect their interests. The resulting falling indicators of child nutrition, child health and schooling, as well as the rise in

the ultimate indicator of child mortality, are particularly ominous since their impact on development is bound to be felt for at
least a generation. It is difficult so see how this can possibly be
described as 'laying' the foundations for subsequent sustainable
growth'.

It is not only growth which has gone into reverse, at least in
Africa and Latin America, but also the basic needs strategies of
the late 1970s, redistribution (with or without growth) together
with the increase in the savings and investment ratio. Thus it may
be said that all the previous approaches and recipes for development have been submerged in the new orthodoxy of primacy of
coming to terms with the debt crisis, and of conforming to the
deterioration of the international climate since the early 1970s. As
the decade of the 1980s drew to a close and broad decline of investment, physical and human, and widespread reversal of development
became apparent, resistance to the neoliberal counter-revolution
increased. Increasingly it is now accepted that in the first half of the
decade adjustment was not sufficiently 'growth oriented'; that it
must be given a more 'human face'; that more external resources
are needed to smooth the process of adjustment and make it politically possible; that adjustment must be made less harsh and stretched
out over a longer period; that some element of debt relief is inevitable as part of the adjustment process; that the reverse transfers of
capital from developing to industrial countries, including even to
the international financial institutions, are counterproductive and
perverse as well as reverse; that the neoliberal recipe is of doubtful
validity in an unfavourable economic climate and when applied to
low-income countries with difficult structural problems; that a
common ideology (neoliberal in this case) results in adjustment
programmes which are much too similar—in fact almost identical—
between different countries and which fail to take sufficient account
of country-specific features; that adjustment must become more
symmetrical between debtor and creditor countries, surplus and
deficit countries and also between LDC deficit/debtor countries and
key currency deficit/debtor countries like the USA.

The adjustment problems with which many of the developing
countries have been faced in the 1980s are in fact unique in their
abruptness and cumulative impact. The problem is at least three-
fold: first, to adjust to a growth rate of industrial countries which
has now been set for 15 years at a 'good year' standard of 3 per

cent per annum instead of 5–6 per cent of the Golden Years, and this with interruptions by recessions, without any apparent sign of a return to former growth rates. Second, the steep deterioration in terms of trade for the primary commodity exporters (now also including the oil exporters) which brought commodity prices in 1987 to their lowest real level since the 1930s; since then there has been a partial recovery, but still leaving a major cumulative deterioration by some 30–35 per cent in terms of trade since 1979. Thirdly, there is the cessation of capital inflows and their replacement by a reverse transfer of capital (some of this represented by the capital flight almost inevitably connected with the adjustment plight of developing countries and representing one way in which the well-to-do can protect themselves).

To put this in concrete and broad quantitative terms: export earnings of developing countries are by now perhaps 25–30 per cent lower than they would be if the industrial countries had maintained the earlier growth rates and continued trade liberalization. A further tax of perhaps another 30 per cent is put on export earnings as a result of deteriorating terms of trade reducing the import capacity represented by export earnings. Yet another 30 per cent or so represents a tax on export earnings as a result of debt service commitments. For the large number of developing countries simultaneously affected by all these three factors, the cumulative tax on export earnings and import capacity represented would be of the total order of perhaps 60–70 per cent, amounting to a real collapse of export earnings available for the financing of developmental imports.

Admittedly, not all countries are simultaneously and equally affected by all these three factors; the 25–30 per cent tax on export earnings for debt service in particular is often in fact unsustainable and leads to rescheduling and increasingly also measures of debt relief. It is difficult to translate this into terms of the Golden Years metaphor of the 'take off'; the more appropriate metaphor now would often be that of the aborted take off with heavy damage to the machine which may take quite some time to repair, or even of a crash landing. For those parts of the developing world for whom development has been reversed in the 1980s, perhaps the decade of the 1990s will have to be a 'decade of rehabilitation', hopefully aided by a better international climate and a truly international structural adjustment in global relations.

Summing up the experience of the last two decades, we can now see that in some senses those involved acted in their own interests: the OPEC members in raising the price of oil, the international banks in lending the deposited receipts to the fastest growing economies of the day—the very term 'newly industrializing countries' suggests the potential for rapid growth. For the developing countries, the chance to borrow funds at low or negative real rates of interest, without conditionality, was too good to miss.

The lack of any appropriate international institutions prevented any coordination of this process. Any desire amongst OPEC members to channel their resources into development projects was heavily circumscribed by the lack of appropriate development agencies. Depositing the funds with international banks ensured that they went almost exclusively to the middle-income developing countries. Furthermore this meant that they flowed in a haphazard way determined by short-term outlooks, rather than a longer-term assessment of LDCs' needs and capacities that an effective international institution might have provided. The failings of this process are now all too apparent; in its own way it is a striking example of the severe shortcomings of leaving the distribution of development funds to the free market. But at just the time when the institutions— and the projected institutions—of Bretton Woods were needed, they were actually disintegrating and surrendered to an ideology which made them agents of retrenchment rather than development— a new policy of NRNG (neither redistribution nor growth), of adjustment without a human face. The 'decade of rehabilitation' will also have to apply to the international system and to international institutions. Some of this rehabilitation will have to consist of retrieving earlier insights and initiatives which we have lost; another part of this will have to consist of new insights and new initiatives. Fortunately, the signs are that the need for this rehabilitation is now too obvious to be disregarded. The road of the 1990s may lead us away from NRNG through AWHF (adjustment with a human face) to resumed RWG (redistribution with growth) and on to a real Bretton Woods—which is where we came in.

2.6. Postscript

I have been aware, even before listening to Sukhamoy Chakravarty's comments, that this paper is as incomplete as the Bretton Woods system. I had always intended to develop it further and the comments by Professor Chakravarty will provide me with guidance in that planned future expansion. In particular, I hope to take to heart his admonition to create a better balance between my two teachers by adding a dash of Schumpeter to the description of the ideas of Keynes. I believe some of the things which Sukhamoy Chakravarty suggests are in fact contained in my paper, albeit in embryonic form, but others are omitted from the present version. My paper also has more on development experience in the sense of actual events rather than development thinking, and Professor Chakravarty to some extent restores the balance between the two. I am glad to think that the reader of this volume will be able to read his contribution as well as my own. Taken together, I believe the two come closer to the complete picture, which still awaits full realization—and, perhaps more important, to an outline of the 'cooperative world order' which both of us want.

3   A Reaction to Lessons of Post-War Development Experience

3.1. Introduction

Professor Hans W. Singer is rightly regarded as one of the foremost contributors to the post-war literature on development in matters relating to the formulation of development policy. His continuous work at the United Nations Secretariat along with the role he has played as adviser to numerous developing countries in very different parts of the world has been an important contributing factor to the shaping of his views on the so-called 'development problématique'. Thus, he is not an armchair theorist, giving his advice on the basis of arbitrary intellectual constructions arrived at from preconceived assumptions or from mere ideological predilections.

It is, therefore, a rare privilege to have been asked to comment on Professor Singer's paper on 'Lessons of Post-war Development Experience, 1945–88', chapter 2 of this volume. Professor Singer's analysis is comprehensive, judicious and clear. I share largely Professor Singer's basic perceptions regarding the 'limited character' of the Bretton Woods institutions, such as the IMF and the World Bank, in terms of their scope, priorities and effectiveness, his regret at the abandonment of the proposal for ITO, the limited role of the GATT, especially as far as the developing countries are concerned, and the flawed nature of the international market mechanisms in terms of the distribution of gains from trade and investment. In particular, Professor Singer is entirely justified in his critique of the asymmetric nature of the surveillance exercised by the IMF in regard to 'surplus' and 'deficit' countries. As he rightly points out, even amongst 'deficit' countries, the IMF pressure is selective and there is no significant impact of the IMF on the presently biggest balance of payments deficit country—the USA. In sum, Professor Singer's review of the 'distorted character' of the Bretton Woods structure is both extremely pertinent and important.

I would also broadly agree with Professor Singer's periodization of forty years' experience which has not been a homogeneous episode in history, although I may have some different perception about the relative influences of different causal forces shaping the contours of the 'golden age' stretching over the period 1945–70. In particular, I do not feel quite sure as to how effective Keynesian demand management policies during this period would have been in the absence of certain supply side opportunities which opened up during this period, particularly the availability of cheap Middle East oil or commercialization of inventions/discoveries made during the Second World War.

There are several ways in which I could hope to supplement Professor Singer's rich and comprehensive presentation. Of these alternative approaches, which can be described as historical, institutional and conceptual, I would prefer to concentrate on the conceptual side.

Professor Singer presents a retrospective view of the development literature that emerged in the nineteen-fifties. In particular, he points out that developing countries did not pay enough attention during the 'golden years' to possibilities of 'export substitution' as distinct from 'import substitution'. However, he is not so dogmatically critical about import substitution as many authors tend to be, especially after the neoclassical resurgence of the late seventies and early eighties. He also rightly points out that the idea of import substitution is not a foreign transplant, at least in the case of India, as the idea was emphasized by eminent leaders such as Mahatma Gandhi and Jawaharlal Nehru. While not disagreeing with the general thrust of Professor Singer's review of import substituting industrialization, it is possible to maintain that the main limitations of development strategy that emerged during the fifties and have largely continued thereafter in many countries of the Third World, go somewhat deeper. I may mention here three major limitations: (a) adoption of a highly mechanistic approach to the development process; (b) overwhelming, and sometimes exclusive reliance on quantity adjustments as against price adjustments for ensuring growth with stability; (c) a conceptually flawed approach to the theory of 'capital' and technological choice. I will elaborate on these three limitations somewhat further presently.

3.2. The mechanistic approach to the development process

On the first limitation mentioned above, it is worthwhile to stress that the mechanistic approach ignored the *qualitative* changes which generally accompany the growth process and are, in fact, an integral part of sustained growth processes over time.

As an illustration, I mention Arthur Lewis' famous dictum that if a country could only raise its savings rate from five per cent to twelve per cent, it will have satisfied the principal requirements of sustained and satisfactory growth thereafter. The underlying logic behind this argument was a simple growth equation involving one crucial parameter, e.g. the capital-output ratio and an assumption relating to the rate of population growth. The fact of the matter was that there was no firm analytical basis for extrapolating these magnitudes from the observed historical data, as currently developed countries had gone through their so-called 'take off' phase under different technological and historical régimes. One needed to allow for the emergence of new factors, products, processes as well as different sociological responses especially in situations where development was largely a 'foreign transplant'. As a result we find that there are countries which have exceeded the above critical ratio, yet it may be maintained that they have to go a great deal further in sustaining structural transformation before large masses of people could hope to see a substantial improvement in their lives. India is one such country which has succeeded in raising its savings rate above the cut-off line and that too without any revolution, in contrast with what Lewis had expected. Without playing down India's achievement in this regard, an issue that I have discussed in my recent book *Development Planning: The Indian Experience*,[1] I would like to emphasize that in order to bring about a more substantial occupational redistribution of labour amongst productive pursuits, which is a prerequisite to reducing current 'dualism' between 'rural' and 'urban' areas, far more needs to be done not only in the area of financial resource mobilization but also in the upgradation of quality and skill composition of its labour. At the same time, natural resources as a constraint on growth process which largely disappeared from economic consideration before the 'oil shock' have emerged as a predominant factor

[1] S. Chakravarty, *Development Planning: The Indian Experience*, Oxford University Press., Oxford, Delhi, etc., 1987.

in shaping the possible contours of development policy especially in India and China.

Perhaps the habit of mechanistic reliance on numerically tractable growth models coupled with an inadequate data base had something to do with the neglect of sociological dimensions of the development process. This is illustrated in our next discussion of the second limitation.

3.3. Quantitative adjustments and price adjustments

What I want to stress in continuation with the former point, is that in a changing world of technology and tastes, one must properly emphasize the need for building up adequate 'transformation capacity'. This is a Schumpeterian concept rather than a Keynesian one. I believe that early development economics relied too much on Keynes in emphasizing quantity adjustments. Thereby it, implicitly or explicitly, ignored some very important lessons that Schumpeter taught us which involve changes in price relationships based on innovations, broadly interpreted. Professor Singer was a student of both Schumpeter and Keynes. While he has written numerous articles on the importance of Keynes for development theory, perhaps some day he will address himself to the Schumpeterian insights into development process, a point I do not want to elaborate here.[2]

Some may recall here that the early post-war years when development theory was emerging as a sub-discipline within economics were not lacking in controversy. This is understandable as the focus of the development problem was shifted considerably from the pre-war years. Broadly speaking, pre-war development literature emphasized limitations arising from lack of motivation and initiative on the part of the so called 'backward areas'. Boeke was a foremost authority on this problem in Holland, but there were others as well. As distinguished from this, there was the tradition initiated by F. List already in the 19th century which was regarded as conceptually flawed by most mainstream economists, although Marshall was more perceptive. When in the forties, thanks to the pioneering work done by Rosenstein-Rodan, Mandelbaum, Prof.

---

[2] I may be permitted, however, to refer here to my R. C. Dutt Lectures: *Alternative Approaches to a Theory of Economic Growth—Marx, Marshall, Schumpeter*, Orient Longman Ltd., Calcutta, 1982.

Singer and others, a new approach to development problems of hitherto 'backward countries' emerged, there was widespread enthusiasm that the key to a process of accelerated growth had at last been found. This soon generated a counter response. Jacob Viner, Sydney Frankel and Peter Bauer, to mention only three prominent writers, wrote critically about the newly found consensus on development issues. However, none of them stressed the Schumpeterian dimension, which I consider to be important, which centres around the concept of 'creative' rather than 'adaptive' response. Nevertheless, on re-reading the literature, I find in Viner's criticisms more value than was assigned to them by policy-makers in many developing countries, at least during the fifties and early sixties. To cite two examples, Viner pointed out how distributional issues could be missed out altogether in the search for maximizing the rate of growth of gross domestic product or even of product per capita, or how for countries which had not gone through a period of 'agricultural revolution' attempts to speed up the industrialization process could not go far without causing serious distortions to the economic structure, especially the balance of payment.[3]

In my own country, the urge to industrialize was strongly emphasized by the planners and policy-makers at a time when the level of food productivity per hectare was way below what it was in countries like Taiwan or the Korean peninsula. In contemporary discussions on the success story of the NICs, while the role of labour-intensive manufactures is repeated ad nauseam, very few care to point out the critical importance of their initial start in land augmenting technical change in agriculture which was ironically enough carried out under   Japanese auspices— in order to supplement the Japanese diet of rice, a political need especially after the 'rice riots' in Japan in the 1920s. Land reform under the occupation authorities after World War II, also did much to promote further growth of land productivity as well as to widen the home market. I believe that land reforms could have been carried out in the early fifties in India, and in some other countries, and more effectively than the present ruling political coalition could permit. This has imposed serious distortions on the efficiency of resource use, let alone in the area of equity.

[3] See J. Viner, *International Trade and Economic Development*, Oxford: Clarendon Press, 1953, pp. 99–100.

I think that Professor Singer's well known analysis of the structurally flawed nature of the distribution of gains from trade and investment in favour of rich developed countries is fundamentally correct despite many criticisms which had been voiced from orthodox quarters. But it is doubtful whether most developing countries understood the full import of the critique of neoclassical trade theory which he presented, which was clearly connected with the lack of integration of the markets within the domestic economies of less developed countries. Without adequate mobility of resources and in the presence of considerable divergences in the value productivity of resources across sectors, neoclassical prescriptions do not hold in an actual welfare improving sense but neither does indiscriminate protection to industrial activities. I believe that this latter point was not adequately grasped by many policy-makers in shaping their policy framework, which has led to serious problems through accentuating dualism.

I believe that Arthur Lewis provided a useful explanation of the tendency of the terms of trade to deteriorate for cash crop exporting countries in the Wicksell lectures which were delivered during the mid-sixties.[4] Without denying the importance of various causal factors stressed by Prebisch and Singer, it would be unwise for developing countries to ignore the main message of Lewis's three-sector model of trade, which found the essence of this problem of deterioration to lie in the large *stagnant* levels of food productivity in the tropics.

3.4. 'Capital' and technological choice

In one of his earlier papers called 'Dualism Revisited',[5] Professor Singer has rightly stressed the importance of international technological dualism and 'internal dualism', but I wonder whether we are in sight of an answer to this most profoundly disquieting problem. The problem is especially difficult to tackle as it exceeds the purely economic instrumentalities that a government can command. I have in mind here the role of 'demonstration effect', both nationally as well as internationally. When the consumption

---

[4] See W. A. Lewis, *Aspects of Tropical Trade, 1883–1965*, Stockholm, Almquist and Wiksell, 1969.

[5] H. W. Singer, 'Dualism Revisited', in A. Cairncross (Ed.), *The Strategy of International Development*, Macmillan, London, 1974.

basket modernizes much more quickly than the production basket, the economic role of many traditional consumer goods shrinks, leading to a shift towards 'imported' consumer goods implying correspondingly a great deal of pressure on the 'balance of payments', apart from creating substantial underemployment. This is a form of 'deindustrialization' which has some analogues in more advanced industrialized countries as well. I am not sure that the so-called 'appropriate technology' school provides an answer to this question. This is because supporters of 'intermediate technology' still operate within the same conceptual mould as the neoclassical capital theorists. What is needed, I think, is to re-examine basic concepts such as capital and technological choice (and transfer).

On this set of issues, some very penetrating observations were made by Veblen[6] a long time ago which are no less relevant today. Unfortunately, Veblen is known to most students of economics as an 'institutionalist', who had little ability or willingness to theorize on the fundamentals of economic theory. While expressions such as 'leisure class' or 'conspicuous consumption' have entered our contemporary vocabulary, expressions first coined by Veblen, it is a sad fact that apart from Duesenberry's work on the consumption function, modern economists have done little to develop his corpus of thought. Yet I believe that Veblen has very major lessons to offer to the sub-discipline of 'development economics'. I am not referring in this context to his analysis of the German industrialization experience, an analysis which was also highlighted by Gerschenkron, but to his very perceptive articles on the nature of capital or to his critique of Professor Clark's economics. In particular, I refer to the distinction that he draws between 'tangible assets' and 'intangible assets', defined as 'immaterial industrial expedients', which are 'necessarily a product of the community, the immaterial residue of the community's experience, past and present, which has no existence apart from the community's life and can be transmitted only in the keeping of the community at large'.[7] Elsewhere, he says that 'the loss of these objects—tangible assets—would entail a transient inconvenience. But the accumulated habitual knowledge of the ways and means in the production and use of these appliances is the outcome of long experience and experimentation'.

[6] See e.g. T. Veblen, *The Place of Science in Modern Civilization*, New York, Atheneum, 1966 (First published in 1919), pp. 348–50.

[7] See T. Veblen, op. cit., pp. 185–6.

What Veblen is getting at is no small matter when we come to issues which involve technology transfer and generation of productive knowledge, which can cope with changes in economic and environmental circumstances of developing economies. I believe that the sustained growth of population accompanied by piecemeal introduction of modern technology along with a highly consumerist orientation emanating from the mass media in the West have left many low-income countries less competent to look after their *basic needs* than they were in a position to do forty years ago. As one example, dependence on processed foods has notoriously increased, despite UN advice to the contrary. This had led in many cases to technological regression in village communities, where old knowledge and skills have died out to the disadvantage of the poor. I also think that the mere expression 'human capital' does not adequately capture Veblen's insight, which consists in the common possession by a specific human group of a body of knowledge and thought processes which are of a problem-solving variety.

One of the reasons, and I emphasize the point that I am not offering a complete explanation, as to why the capital-output ratio associated with new technology tends often to be much higher in developing countries than in its native country of origin, is that it operates in developing countries by creating a violent rupture between the way things have been traditionally done and the plethora of instructions given in the most recent manuals, which require for their comprehension the existence of a relatively educated labour force. I am not suggesting that the phenomenon has gone unnoticed in the literature. What has been very inadequately realized in the development literature, however, is that the problem is incapable of being treated by merely stepping up investment in material and human capital when gains are to be only individually appropriated. Developing countries do suffer from limited 'absorption capacities', if what is given out to them for absorption consists of ready-to-be-consumed material products, originating wholly in the very different cultural environment of highly developed countries.

What I am suggesting here is not that developing countries would not benefit from international capital transfers on suitable terms and conditions, but the point that in the long run the solution may lie in the area of internal innovations in terms of both technology and institutions, especially institutions that operate in the domain of generation of relevant knowledge and experience.

3.5. State and market

There is a body of thought that would suggest that the major
institutional reform that is needed is to allow for a more free play
of market forces in the developing countries with emphasis on
privatization. It is clear that neither Professor Singer nor I would
agree with such a conclusion, although we may both see merits in
moving away from unnecessary bureaucratic intervention. Our
argument on this point would be the same as those given by classic
theorists of market failure. Externalities and returns to scale, both
static and dynamic, are too important to be left to be handled by
privately motivated behaviour. There is correspondingly a clear
case for collective action. However, there are clearly different
ways in which collective modes of action can be organized. To deal
with problems of international externalities, we need to adapt the
institutional mechanisms which govern trade and investment
amongst nations as Professor Singer has pointed out. Similarly,
there could be problems of organizing irrigation waters for crop
diversification which may require collective action much lower
down the scale within a given national economy.[8]

During the fifties and sixties, nation states were treated as pre-
eminent collective actors. This was both understandable and to a
certain degree very appropriate. Understandable because decolonization was too recent an experience not to leave a mark on
people's perceptions; appropriate to a considerable extent, because
the agenda of the post-colonialist state was perceived in a developmentalist mode. Furthermore, the so-called Bretton Woods
institutions had been set up with some expectations that they
would play a major role in ironing out international inequalities
and not merely fluctuations.

Forty years of experience have taught us that the 'developmentalist
state' may not always perform up to our expectations, while the post-
war institutional mechanisms devised in the late forties to coordinate problems of growth and stability amongst nations have largely

---

[8] Relevant action here can imply the need for suitable redefinition of property
rights on functional lines as argued by several authors including myself. I may refer
to my article, 'Theory of Development Planning: An Appraisal', in *Economic
Structure and Development*, in the Tinbergen Festschrift, edited by H. C. Bos, H.
Linnemann and P. de Wolff, North Holland Publishing Company, Amsterdam,
1973.

broken down under the growing pressure of their internal contradictions and major changes in financial and technological spheres.

3.6. Some lessons

What lessons do we draw from this stark picture? My first conclusion
would be that the developmental role of the state has to be recast
but cannot be abandoned. Why I say that it has to be recast and
not abandoned stems from my understanding of the price system
in its *four-fold* capacity:

1. prices as a system of exchange relationships serving as allocative
   devices;
2. prices as determining a system of distribution of incomes;
3. prices as a way of encouraging technological innovations; and
   finally,
4. prices as a system of power relationships.

We know that, excepting for situations of severe shortages, prices
may do a better job in allocating *given amounts* of scarce resources
amongst competing uses, than most states can do given the infrastructural and informational limitations. This is doubtless a change
in perception born out of experience especially from that of cen-
trally planned economies. Similarly, we also know that in certain
areas of production, proper prices may stimulate economy of
resource use as well as stimulate new discoveries involving substitute
products and processes. I believe that this second point was inadequately realized in the earlier development literature. However,
when we come to questions involving distribution of incomes,
there is little evidence to suggest that price determined outcomes
bear any systematic relationship to society's notion of 'fairness', a
notion which is vital to the healthy functioning of any polity.
Similarly, unrestricted sway of the price mechanism builds up
positions of power through monopolies or oligopolies, domestic
and transnational, which can prevent many desirable changes in
political and economic spheres. Furthermore, even when they
promote innovations, they may do so only at a high price. A good
example is provided by publicly funded research in agriculture as
distinguished from research carried out by transnationals.

I, therefore, believe that if we take the totality of our experience,
what has been demonstrated is the need for strategic planning and

selective state intervention. Professor Tinbergen has long sought an optimum economic order. The task remains incomplete. Perhaps the time has come to take a fresh look at this whole range of issues taking into account dimensions which are not always fully quantifiable.[9]

Secondly, our understanding of sources of development must be broadened so as to include both cultural and sociological dimensions, along with a better understanding of *organizational behaviour*. The latter includes a study of different methods of labour compensation, such as profit sharing as well as different modes of exercising intra-firm control.

Thirdly, we need to evolve new rules of the game involving major collective actors, i.e. the so-called nation states, which may create new economic space within which the developing countries may have more elbow room for structural transformation with equity.

On this last set of questions, there are obviously some who are inclined to believe that we may somehow muddle through, till something hopeful turns up. At the other extreme, we have economists who advocate 'delinking' on the part of the Third World as the only viable option left.

This is not the place to enter into a detailed evaluation of these different strands of argument, as the arguments are both complex and conjectural. As far as I can judge, countries in Africa, south of Sahara, despite their considerable natural resources, are the ones which are likely to suffer most from the present policy of muddling through, although South Asia will not be far behind in terms of human suffering. Countries which are likely to do reasonably well on the basis of the present scenario are countries of East Asia. Latin America remains an open question especially as long as the debt issue persists and so does China in my opinion for very different reasons. That would imply that a large majority of mankind may not have much to look forward to in the nineties. Whether such a world is viable is, in my opinion, an open question. My doubts increase when growing rivalries amongst developed

[9] See J. Tinbergen, 'Some Suggestions on a Modern Theory of the Optimum Regime', in C. H. Feinstein (Ed.), *Socialism, Capitalism and Economic Growth*, (Essays presented to Maurice Dobb), The University Press, Cambridge, 1967. See also L. H. Klaassen, L. M. Koyck and H. J. Witteveen, (Eds.), *Jan Tinbergen: Selected Papers*, North Holland, Amsterdam, 1959.

countries are taken into account, including the expenditure on arms and also the growing sway of protectionist opinion.

Theoretical blueprints are not difficult to suggest which, when suitably implemented, are likely to improve the lot of many. But whether the political will for implementing a more cooperative world order, such as the world witnessed for a brief while when the Bretton Woods institutions were devised even with their limitations, is more than I can confidently talk about. But I dare say, there are bold spirits who will try to improve things and not become victims of myopia. It is the job of development economists to provide them with analytically rigorous and historically well grounded formulations of different scenarios. Professor Singer's paper is a step in that direction.

PART 2

The Newly Industrializing Countries

4   The NICs in the World Economy: Towards an Open World Economy in the Mid-1990s

COLIN I. BRADFORD, JR

4.1. Introduction

This paper was prepared as a keynote lecture commemorating the twentieth anniversary of the Centre for Development Planning at Erasmus University in Rotterdam. It is also the initial outcome of work I began in 1988 as part of the research programme of the new strategic planning unit at the World Bank. The charge of strategic planning at the Bank is to think about the evolution of the world economy and the World Bank within it in a longer term perspective. The focus of my effort has been on developing alternative scenarios of the world trade environment in the mid-1990s.

The paper provides a first report of the effort thus far made to model the world trade environment in a way that is useful for understanding alternative configurations which might occur in the medium-term future. The perspective out of which the modelling work has been done is informed by my research over the last decade on the newly industrializing countries. The first part of this paper will discuss briefly the importance of the newly industrializing countries (NICs) in shaping the trends, patterns and structure of the world economy over the last twenty years and the issues their emergence and prominence pose for the future.[1] The second section of the paper will describe the general contours of the world trade model I have developed and how it works. The third section will spell out the macro-economic and trade strategies that serve as inputs (exogenous assumptions) to generate sets of alternative scenarios of the world economy in the mid-1990s. The last section

[1] The statistical work and computer programming for the trade model in this paper was done by Carlos Herran, whose outstanding work is gratefully acknowledged.

will analyse the results of the simulations and their possible implications for the world economy and the role of the NICs in the
future.

4.2. The Emergence of the NICs and their role in the world economy: issues for the future

Clearly, as the papers by Professor Tinbergen and Professor Singer
will undoubtedly have pointed out, one of the most significant
developments in the world economy in the last twenty years has
been the emergence of a select group of rapidly industrializing,
highly dynamic exporters of manufactured goods. These countries
have become a new class in the world economy, neither Third
World nor First World, neither developing nor developed but
rather transitional economies that have come into their own as
actors on the global economic stage.

One issue of some consequence in the analysis of this phenomenon
has been the identification of what constitutes an NIC. Ideally, as
William Branson has pointed out, it would be best to specify some
ex ante criteria for identifying NICs and apply a clustering algorithm
to a data set for a large number of developing countries that would
differentiate countries into groups according to their measured
similarities with each other and their measured dissimilarity with
others (Bradford and Branson [1987:6–7]). This would provide a
means of distinguishing NICs from non-NICs based on detached
empirical analysis rather than ex post tautologies that in effect
assert that high performance countries are countries that have
done well or that associate presumed policy reforms with positive
results in high growth countries.

This analysis has yet to be done. An experimental beginning was
undertaken under my direction by a Yale undergraduate in his
Senior Essay in which he compiled data on twenty NICs and
applied the clustering algorithm to them to establish four clusters
of NICs (Wozencraft [1987]). The average annual growth rates of
four variables between 1965 and 1980 were used as criteria: growth
of GDP, manufactured output, value added in manufacturing and
manufactured exports. The criteria suggest that NICs are defined
as dynamic, rapidly industrializing exporters of manufactures. The
clustering algorithm applied to twenty countries selected as potential NICs yield four groups or tiers of NICs based on these four

criteria. Averages for three of the four criteria are also obtained for 28 middle-income countries. This is not a satisfactory procedure to achieve Branson's original intent but it does provide some interesting results shown in Table 4.1.

First, Korea, Singapore and Taiwan, not surprisingly, constitute the first tier NICs based on these criteria. Second, somewhat surprisingly, three of the four South-East Asian ASEAN countries

TABLE 4.1: *Average Annual Growth Rates, (1965–80)*

	GDP	Manufactured Output	Value Added in manuf.	Manufactured exports
First Tier				
Korea	9.2	17.4	19	39.7
Singapore	10.4	13.8	11.4	25.7
Taiwan	9.6	12.3	n.a.	37.9
Mean Growth Rates	9.7	14.5	15.2	34.4
Second Tier				
Hong Kong	9.1	11.5	6.1	21.4
Indonesia	7.6	11.6	10.2	22.0
Malaysia	7.3	11.4	8.1	26.2
Thailand	7.7	10.7	8.0	31.8
Brazil	8.4	9.3	9.5	31.1
Mean Growth Rates	8.0	10.9	8.3	26.5
Third Tier				
Mexico	7.1	8.4	7.1	24.1
Turkey	5.6	7.0	6.6	32.9
Greece	5.5	8.0	7.0	30.7
Philippines	5.8	7.4	5.5	29.8
Spain	4.6	7.3	6.8	27.7
Colombia	5.9	6.3	6.4	23.2
Mean Growth Rates	5.7	7.4	6.5	28.0
Fourth Tier				
Yugoslavia	5.9	5.6	6.9	17.1
Portugal	5.2	6.3	7.2	16.1
Egypt	5.7	6.8	4.7	6.7
Pakistan	5.5	5.6	3.0	13.6
India	3.7	4.0	2.6	12.1
Argentina	3.1	2.5	3.1	23.0
Mean Growth Rates	4.8	5.1	4.5	14.7
Middle-income countries				
Mean Growth Rates	4.8	—	6.7	19.7

Source: Wozencraft [1987]

that are normally thought of as NICs of the future (Indonesia, Malaysia, and Thailand) are solidly in the second tier based on the 1965 to 1980 data, and the fourth country normally associated with them (the Philippines) is in the middle of the third tier. As a result, these four countries are clearly an important group in the world economy and are designated 'next tier Asia' in our world trade model to distinguish them from the four NICs in East Asia, Korea, Singapore, Taiwan and Hong Kong, Hong Kong being in the second tier of the clustering results. Third, Brazil and Mexico are clearly NICs by these criteria while Argentina's status is very questionable except for its growth rates of manufactured exports. Nonetheless, we include Argentina in the big three Latin American group in the world trade model because of its GDP size and the significance of its exports in both growth and magnitude. Fourth, in Southern Europe, Spain, Greece, and Turkey are solidly within the third tier while Portugal and Yugoslavia are not in the same class. Industrialization in these countries really preceded that of the Asian and Latin American NICs with the spurt occurring in the 1950s and 1960s (Bradford, in Bradford and Branson [1987:192]) but they remain important exporters of manufactures today. In the trade model, we create two groups of Southern (Mediterranean) European NICs, Spain, Portugal and Greece (ECMed), the new entrants into the enlarged European Community (EC), and Yugoslavia, Turkey, Egypt and Israel (NonECMed), an eclectic group of fast growing, industrializing exporters of manufactures.

These five groups of NICs [the East Asian gang of four (NIC4), the ASEAN 4 or next tier Asia (NTA), the Latin American three (LAT), the three new EC entrants (ECM) and the other four Mediterranean economies (NECM)] have become important new participants in world trade based on exceptionally high rates of growth of their manufactured exports, dynamic GDP growth and still faster rates of growth in the industrial sector, implying an increasing share of the manufacturing sector in the economy. As a result, of course, the share of world exports accounted for by these countries has increased (Chart 1), as have also the export shares of the socialist countries (Eastern Europe, the Soviet Union and China) (Chart 2). The combination of these trends with a relative decline of the EC and the US in world trade and the rise in the Japanese share in world exports yields a near doubling in the shares of world exports accounted for by the three socialist blocs and the four NIC blocs taken together from roughly 10 per cent in 1966 to roughly 20 per cent in 1985 (Chart 3). The NICs and the oil exporting countries also have played a major role in the 1970s and 1980s in global economic adjustment on the import side offsetting contractions in import demand in industrial countries after the oil shock (Chart 4 and Bradford, Ch. 11 in Turner and McMullen [1982]). Through the 1970s imports as a share of GDP rose commensurately with the rapidly rising export-GDP share in the NICs to provide an important stimulus to global growth.

This significant change in the structure of world trade arises due to the dynamic growth rates of these new blocs, their increased openness to trade and their exceptionally rapid rates of export growth. The consequence of these trends is that, led by the NICs, the share of world GNP generated by the developing countries had increased to nearly 15 per cent by 1980 compared to 11 per cent in 1960 (Kennedy [1987:436]). These trends raise the issue of the importance of these new players and patterns for the future of the world economy. What will be the structure of trade and world GNP in the future? Will the industrial countries continue to dominate the world economy as slow growth occurs elsewhere? Or do the new powers represent new sources of growth and dynamism for the world economy providing an alternative to exclusive reliance on the industrial countries for global stimulus for growth? Instead of focusing only on economic policy coordination among the United States, Germany and Japan, are there alternative strategies involving the NICs and other trading blocs such as the socialist economies that can lead to positive outcomes for both world trade and world economic growth? The structural change generated by the NICs in the last two decades provokes new questions for the future that go beyond the traditional frameworks of intra-OECD interactions and North-South relations to a global economic perspective potentially involving broader and more complex dynamics.

Another major way in which the NICs pose issues for the future is more qualitative. The rise of the NICs has spawned a debate about the trade policy regime that has led to their successful development. What is interesting in that debate is the fact that different interpretations seem to follow from different paradigms. Economists have by and large seen the success of the NICs as a vindication of open market policies of trade and financial liberalization removing distortions and making markets work yielding greater efficiency and competitiveness (for example, Balassa [1981]). Political scientists have by and large seen the state as critical in the success of the NICs (for example, Deyo [1987]). My own interpretation has been that the highly dynamic economies we identify as NICs have generally followed what might be called strategy-led paths to rapid development which have been characterized by export push, investment drives, and structural change rather than by open markets, competitive prices, and demand responsiveness (Bradford [1987]). My interpretation as it turns out is quite similar to that of colleagues at another school of management who also give predominant weight to national strategy and national ideology as explanatory variables in dynamic development performance (Scott and Lodge [1985] and Lodge and Vogel [1987]). Trade theory has benefited from incorporation of some insights from industrial organization theory regarding the benefits of scale economies, learning curves and imperfect competition to formulate a new strategic trade theory emphasizing the role of bargaining and strategic moves in determining growth and market share outcomes (Krugman [1986]).

The strategy-led interpretation of the NIC success stories is consistent with a more historical view offered by Richard Rosecrance. Rosecrance sees the potential transformation of international relations from the predominance of interactions of military-security states over issues of territory giving way to the rise of trading states competing over economic issues (Rosecrance [1986]). It is also consistent with a somewhat revisionist view offered by David Baldwin of economic statecraft as being economic policy in the service of foreign policy objectives irrespective of the degree or kind of government intervention in the economy (Baldwin [1985:77]). From this perspective, both economic liberalism and mercantilism are forms of economic statecraft which join economic means to political ends. Traditionally, liberalism has been conceived of as economic measures for economic ends and hence somehow void of political content. Mercantilism, on the other hand, is traditionally construed as being more politically driven and hence a less legitimate form of economic statecraft. Baldwin's analysis makes clear that all states have foreign economic strategies that join economic means to political ends. It follows that international debate and negotiations should focus on the content of those strategies rather than the legitimacy of having strategies or not.

Parallel with this line of intellectual argument, the NIC experience constitutes clear testimony to the relevance of trade strategies to the future patterns of interaction among trading states and the main trends defining the world economy in the future.

The NICs also represent a model for the future of managed openness. (They fit Bryant's category of 'intermediate interdependence', rather than nearly closed, small, open, or supernational. Bryant [1980] Chapter 10.) The East Asian NICs in particular have brought their economies into a new and highly interactive relationship with the world economy that in their case has been quiet, stable and sustainable. The Mediterranean Europe experiences have been less dramatic and the Latin American experience has been more volatile due to the relatively greater role of debt in the opening to trade. But the NICs in general have brought an innovative mix of public and private sector dynamics to bear on the transition process towards greater openness and interdependence with the world economy that characterizes these economies as a class unto themselves. They perhaps represent a model for other global economic transitions in the future, such as the movement of the US and Japan toward greater economic balance, the opening of the Soviet Union, Eastern Europe and China to the world economy, the opening of the European Community to the rest of the world as it achieves internal integration in the early 1990s, the renewed opening of Latin America and other highly indebted countries to trade while managing major debt flows, the continued openness of the NICs in the face of protectionist pressures, and the emergence of next tier NICs as major exporters of manufactures.

Too often in the past there has been a false dichotomy between outward orientation and trade liberalization on the one hand and inward-looking orientation and intervention on the other. What the NIC experience offers us, in my view, is a fusion of these dichotomies in which clearly formulated trade strategies have led to public sector–private sector collaboration toward a successfully managed transition to open economy interactions with the world economy (Gilpin [1987] Chs. 5 & 10 passim). (By 'open economy', I mean high trade-GDP shares, not trade liberalization as frequently associated with the term in the literature. For more on these distinctions, see Bradford and Branson [1987] Ch. 1.)

To summarize, the NIC experiences then provide us with a window to the future. They highlight the potential role of the new trading states in stimulating growth, the salience of trade strategies in determining global outcomes and the relevance of the NIC model of managed openness for economic transitions of major countries and blocs in the future. This optic on the world economy derived from the NIC experience of the last two decades is a particularly apt one to take from a strategic planning perspective. It also seems fitting that the first public discussion of this approach should occur at a conference honouring the research efforts of a prominent research centre concerned with development planning. Trade, of course, is determined by a variety of forces, not the least of which is the power of markets. The approach in this paper does not deny or ignore that basic fact of economic life. But, perhaps especially in recent years, there has been something of an under-appreciation of the important positive role that governments play in promoting trade. I hope that this approach, by highlighting the role that trade strategies can play and by stimulating possible world economic outcomes, may provide interesting insights into the future and implications for economic planning.

4.3. Modelling future patterns of world trade

From this brief review of the international economic issues for the future posed by the performance of the NICs in the recent past, we hypothesize a new global economy no longer predominantly deter-mined by intra-OECD interactions but one which is also composed of the new trading states or NICs from the developing world and those actual or potential trading economies from the socialist bloc. The trade model used here consists of 12 blocs consisting together of 36 economies with trade as a high share of GDP. As far as possible, these 12 blocs were grouped so that they would have geopolitical meaning so that one could reasonably talk about trade strategies and economic policies with some sense of homogeneity within groups although quite obviously in the end every nation is unique and certainly is sovereign. These 12 blocs are composed of countries which by and large are sufficiently dynamic that they have some autonomy in policy-making. They are the core economies of the new global economy which are capable of proactive policy or strategic trade policy behaviour and which together largely determine the overall trends in the world economy.

These 12 blocs consist of the industrial economies—the United

States, Japan and the European Community 7 (namely, the United Kingdom, France, Germany, Italy, the Netherlands, Belgium and Luxemburg)—NIC blocs discussed in section 3.2. above, namely ECMed (Spain, Portugal, Greece), NonECMed (Yugoslavia, Turkey, Egypt, and Israel), the three major Latin American economies (Brazil, Mexico, and Argentina), East Asian NIC4 (Korea, Taiwan, Singapore, and Hong Kong), next tier Asia4 (Malaysia, Thailand, Indonesia and the Philippines), and the Eastern European 6 (East Germany, Czechoslovakia, Poland, Hungary, Romania, and Bulgaria), and three large closed economies, namely the Soviet Union, China and India. The two bar charts (charts 5 and 6) show that trade among these 12 blocs constitutes 70 per cent or more of their total exports in 1985 for all 36 countries with the exception of the US and the UK (in part because Canada, Australia and New Zealand are not included) and accounts for 65 per cent or more of their total imports in 1985 for all 36 countries with the exception of the US, Japan, and Brazil. These percentages are even more impressive for trade in manufactures, especially on the import side where for most countries more than 80 per cent of their imports are exports from other core countries (Charts 7 and 8). The resulting trade matrix of imports and exports among the 12 blocs captures 74 per cent of total world trade and 84 per cent of world trade in manufactures.

The rest of the developing world was divided into three blocs to represent groups of countries of major interest to the World Bank. The first of these blocs consists of 17 highly indebted countries now known as the HICs. These countries are: Argentina, Bolivia, Brazil, Chile, Colombia, Costa Rica, Ivory Coast, Ecuador, Jamaica, Mexico, Morocco, Nigeria, Peru, the Philippines, Uruguay, Venezuela, and Yugoslavia. The HIC bloc in this trade model contains the 12 countries from this group that are left once the five countries that belong to one of the core blocs have been eliminated. The second bloc consists of the oil exporting countries (OPEC) once overlapping countries have been dropped. This strips this bloc of some major oil exporters but duplication is not logical and the integrity of the other blocs was deemed more important for the purposes of this model than the integrity of the OPEC bloc. As a result, we have a proxy OPEC group. The third bloc is the World Bank category of low income countries (LICs) that consists of the 38 countries in this category after China and India have been removed.

This model involves making policy assumptions or strategy decisions for the 12 core blocs that generate results within the 12 blocs themselves as well as in the three developing country blocs. The three developing country blocs are treated as passive blocs which are impacted on by the strategies and resultant patterns of the 12 core blocs. Left out of this model are the following industrial countries: Canada, Australia and New Zealand, the Scandinavian countries, Ireland, Austria and Switzerland. Of the World Bank's category of 23 upper-middle-income countries only Panama, Uruguay and South Africa are excluded. The most numerous exclusion is 17 of the 33 lower-middle-income countries that are mostly in Central America, the Caribbean, Africa and the Middle East. (The list is: Liberia, Yemen (PDR), Yemen (Arab Republic), Zimbabwe, the Dominican Republic, Papua New Guinea, Honduras, Nicaragua, El Salvador, Guatemala, Botswana, Jamaica, Paraguay, Tunisia, Mauritius, Jordan and Lebanon.)

The model is built around the trade matrix composed of columns containing the demand for imports by the 15 blocs and rows consisting of the supply of exports by each bloc to every other bloc. The diagonal shows intra-bloc trade. The model is intended to be and is in fact simple and transparent. The idea is that one should be able to trace outcomes back to the inputs generating them. There are no behavioural dynamics that inexplicably drive the results.

There are several restrictive features and assumptions in this model. First, it is a real side set of relations with financial variables, for the moment at least, excluded. There are no monetary variables domestically and no capital account transactions internationally. These dimensions are being incorporated in further work. The model generates trade balances but not current account balances. The trade balance results obviously imply changes in domestic macroeconomic variables. If there is an increase in net exports as a percentage of GDP, clearly investment, consumption, or government spending as a percentage of GDP must decline to make room for the improvement in the trade balance. Conversely, if net exports decline, domestic absorption can increase. The data sets developed along with the trade model contain the domestic macro-economic variables consistent with the trade matrix but at this stage there has not been time to relate them analytically. Given some of the sizeable changes envisaged in trade patterns in some scenarios, the macro-economic counterparts will provide a crucial check on the consistency, feasibility and desirability of trade outcomes.

The important point here is that the modelling effort manipulates trade outcomes first and then, at a later stage, will derive the macro-economic adjustment required to obtain the trade results rather than making macro-assumptions in order to generate trade outcomes. Obviously, in practice the macro-economic policy inputs would constitute the instrument variables that would yield the trade balance results but for the moment the model is intended to treat trade as the target variable and then develop the macro-economic implications later.

A second characteristic is that this model is demand driven. Each bloc's demand for imports is the key driving force generating the outcomes. These import demand projections induce export growth in the rest of the world in the same way that final demand in an input-output matrix generates intermediate production and hence gross output results. The endogenous variable in this model is exports. As a result, the model assumes the absence of supply bottlenecks in both magnitude and composition of production for export. In effect, it assumes that Eastern Europe would in fact be able to achieve a specified level of exports to the East Asian NICs and that the composition of exports would fit with the productive structure of Eastern Europe or the demand pattern of East Asia.

There are three exogenous variables in this model. First, the rate of GDP growth anticipated for each of the 15 blocs for the 1985 to 1995 period is assumed rather than induced. The growth rates for this period contained in the World Bank's 1988 World Development Report base case were taken as points of departure but it was necessary to alter these as various simulations were worked through. This projected rate of GDP growth generates a set of GDP numbers for 1995 for each bloc. The second exogenous variable is the target import share of GDP in 1995 for each of the blocs. The import-GDP shares can be set under varying assumptions about the policy environment anticipated. If sluggish economic growth is anticipated between now and the mid-1990s, lower import-GDP shares would be expected compared to a more dynamic global economic context both as cause and effect. Simultaneously with specifying the import-GDP shares, assumptions are made about the export-GDP share that should be consistent with the growth and import share assumptions. The export-GDP share is an estimated target of what the results would be given all the other assumptions being made rather than a control variable as is the import-GDP share. Given 1995 GDP numbers and 1995 import-GDP shares, 1995 import numbers (M_j) are derived for each bloc. These are the demand variables for the trade matrix.

The third exogenous variable is the import strategy of each bloc. The columns in the trade matrix show the percentage share of total imports by each bloc from each bloc. This model supposes that countries have trade strategies that are on the margin directed toward certain countries or regions as sources of imports and markets for exports. The United States, for example, might decide that increasing imports from the Soviet Union would be in the broader security interest of the United States as a means of integrating the Soviet economy into the world economy. The Koreans are reportedly interested in developing export markets in Eastern Europe. The Latin Americans are interested in geographically diversifying their export markets, especially as the US increasingly needs to adjust its trade balance. Countries send trade missions abroad with the idea of promoting exports in regions where larger gains are anticipated than it is expected will be achieved by the operation of market forces alone. And so on. Hence, the manipulation of the coefficients in the columns of the trade matrix represent the anticipated results of the combination of shifts in import sourcing strategies on the part of each bloc and the shifts in export marketing strategies. For example, if we assume that the share of total US imports from the Soviet Union in 1995 will be double that in 1985, we are assuming a degree of complicity between the superpowers to achieve this result and do not know what proportion of this result is due to a shift in the US import strategy and what proportion is due to a shift in the Soviet export marketing strategy. This model allows us to exogenously determine the import coefficient for each bloc and to derive the export coefficients (exports to each bloc as a percentage of total exports by each bloc). Import sourcing strategies are being set explicitly whereas export market strategies are being set implicitly. In the end, it takes two to tango.

These three sets of instrument variables—GDP growth rates, imports as a share of GDP and import coefficients—generate a new matrix of imports and exports in 1995 and a new set of import and export coefficients, or to put it in a more interesting way, a new structure of world trade. The principal endogenous variable is exports. Summing across the rows of the 1995 trade matrix yields total exports in 1995 for each bloc which divided by the projected 1995 GDP gives us the induced export-GDP share in 1995.

Algebraically, the model is as follows:

$$Y_{1995(j)}^{1980\$} = Y_{1985(j)}^{1980\$} \times \triangle Y^*/Y_{1985-95(j)}$$

$$M_{1995(j)}^{1980\$} = Y_{1995(j)}^{1980\$} \times (M^*/Y)_{1995(j)}$$

Where: Y is GDP for each country or bloc (j), the subscript is the year and the superscript is the currency in which the variable is measured.

M is imports (goods and nonfactor services)

M/Y is the imports-GDP share, imports as a percentage of GDP

$\triangle Y/Y$ is the real average annual growth rate of GDP

*   indicates an exogenous or projected variable

These data are all taken from or based on the Andrex data system of the World Bank.

The United Nations Trade Matrix for 1985 has been reconfigured to correspond to the 15 blocs specified in our trade model with an additional bloc for the rest of the world. This matrix consists of M_{ij}s and X_{ij}s where

$M_{ij} =$ imports by country j from country i where i represents the rows and j the columns of the matrix;

$X_{ij} =$ exports by country i to country j.

Therefore, for any given set of importing (j) and exporting (i) blocs:

$X_{ij} \equiv M_{ij}$ by definition the exports of country i to country j equal the imports of country j from country i.

$\sum\limits_{i=1}^{16} M_{ij} = M_j^{tot}$ The sum of the M_{ij}s in each column equals the total imports of each importing country of bloc (j).

$$\sum_{j=1}^{16} M_{ij} = \sum_{j=1}^{16} X_{ij} = X_i^{\text{tot}}$$

The sum of the M_{ij}s in each row equals the total exports of each exporting country or bloc (i).

Then:

$$\frac{[M_{ij}]}{[M_j^{\text{tot}}]} = [m_{ij}]$$

The vector of M_{ij}s in each column divided by the vector of corresponding total imports generates a matrix of import coefficients of m_{ij}s where

$m_{ij} =$ the imports by bloc j from bloc i as a percentage of total imports by bloc j.

Similarly:

$$\frac{[X_{ij}]}{[X_i^{\text{tot}}]} = [x_{ij}]$$

The vector of X_{ij}s in each row divided by the vector of corresponding total exports generates a matrix of export coefficients of x_{ij}s where

$x_{ij} =$ the exports of bloc i to bloc j as a percentage of total exports by bloc i.

The matrix of import coefficients for the 16 blocs for 1985 or some exogenously determined variant of it (*) is joined with the import vector for 1995 to generate a new trade matrix of imports and exports in 1995, as follows:

$$\begin{array}{cccccc}
1980\$ & & 1985^* & & 1980\$ & & 1980\$ \\
[M_j^{\text{tot}}] & \times & [m_{ij}] & = & [M_{ij}] & = & [X_{ij}] \\
1995 & & & & 1995 & & 1995
\end{array}$$

Because the relative growth rates of the 16 blocs are different from each other and the import-GDP shares have changed from 1985, the matrix of induced exports is going to be different in structure (i.e. $[x_{ij}]^{1995}$ is going to be different from $[x_{ij}]^{1985}$) even if we do not change the matrix of import coefficients $[m_{ij}]^{1985}$

Induced exports in 1995 are the endogenous variable of primary interest in this model. The incremental change in exports since 1985, the rate of growth of exports between 1985 and 1995, and the export-GDP share in 1995 are all of major consequence.

$$\Delta X_{1985-1995(i)}^{1980\$} = X_{1995(i)}^{1980\$} - X_{1985(i)}^{1980\$} \qquad \text{incremented exports}$$

$$\sqrt[10]{\frac{X_{1995(i)}^{1980\$}}{X_{1985(i)}^{1980\$}}} - 1 = r_{x(i)} \qquad \text{rate of growth of exports}$$

$$X_{1995(i)}^{1980\$} / Y_{1995}^{1980\$} \qquad \text{exports-GDP share}$$

If the induced export-GDP share overshoots the target export-GDP share, several possibilities exist. One is that the combination of growth rates, import share changes and shifts in import coefficients of the trade partners of the overshooting bloc are more powerful than anticipated in generating exports. Hence, some downward adjustment is necessary in the instrument variables of the trade partners or some upward adjustment in the GDP growth of the overshooting bloc must be made to account for the stimulus to growth of the incremental demand for its exports. This latter adjustment would appropriately drive down the export-GDP share by increasing the GDP of the overshooting country. Conversely, a smaller than anticipated export-GDP share implies that the world economy as postulated in that scenario is not structured in such a way as to be able to generate the level of exports anticipated or pari passu that the rate of growth of GDP projected for the under-shooting bloc is too high to be consistent with the projected dynamics and needs to be adjusted downward. These examples illustrate one of the ways in which the model is a closed circuit providing a consistency check on the results.

A second check is the potential spillover of exports to the 'rest of the world'. In exogenously reconfiguring the import coefficients, the share of imports from the rest of the world has been held constant so that all the change in the structure of imports occurs within the 15 blocs. On the other hand, since the export projections are induced, the percentage of exports to the rest of the world in 1995 may exceed or fall short of that percentage in 1985. Since this is a residual term, if the 1995 export share to the rest of the world exceeds the 1985 share for a given bloc, the combination of growth rates, openness to imports and import strategies of its trade partners are not sufficient to induce the same share of bloc exports to the other fifteen as in 1985. Conversely, if the 1995 export share to the rest of the world falls short of the 1985 share, it implies that growth, openness, and import strategy assumptions of its trade partners have been over-specified and need to be more modest to be consistent.

Finally, attached to the model is a method of decomposing the export results by bloc to each bloc according to the proportion of incremental exports in each cell of the matrix in 1995 generated by the GDP growth rate of each importing country, changes in the import share of each importing country, and changes in the import coefficient of each country. This provides a trace on the results to enable us to locate the existence of disproportionate contributions to them once the other two consistency checks have highlighted a problem. This methodology also provides an average for each exporting country of the contribution of each of the three exogenous variables to the total incremental exports between 1985 and 1995.

The result of this relatively simple and transparent modelling is a computer program with over 660,000 data bytes. The decomposition tracing exercise itself is 15 exporting blocs times 15 importing blocs times 3 exogenous variables which yields 675 indicators to examine. Nonetheless, it is not an overwhelming task to use this model to simulate scenarios with relatively few general policy inputs so that alternative results can be examined comparatively as following in a rather straightforward way from alternative sets of macro-economic and trade strategies which taken together constitute different global strategies. We now turn to the policy content of the analysis.

4.4. Macro-economic and trade strategies of the major blocs

4.4.1. *Major issues for the 1990s*

The model constructed in this way allows us to stimulate the impact on the world economy of alternative policy assumptions in each of the major blocs. As a result, the model permits us to address major issues in the world economy as they might evolve over the next several years. Those addressed here are the working out of major imbalances between the United States and Japan, the implications for Europe and for the rest of the world of the completion of the European common market in 1992, the potential opening of the Soviet Union, Eastern Europe and China to the market economies, and finally the reduction in the patterns of increasing regionalization of trade. These major issues are addressed through alternative assumptions about growth patterns, degrees of openness, and the import strategies of the major blocs in dealing with these issues.

The degree of regionalization in trade patterns is illustrated by patterns of trade shown in the trade matrix of trade flows in 1985. This year provides a structure of world trade at the peak of the strong dollar and as a result amplifies the importance of the US import stimulus to the world economy characteristic of that year. The matrix provides a clear profile of the degree of regionalization of the world economy (see Table 4.2). In 1985 42 per cent of Latin America's imports came from the US and 44 per cent of Latin American exports went to the US. This is after 'a progressive disentanglement of Latin America from the North American economy in trade in the recent past' (Bitar [1987:8]).

The patterns of regionalization in Europe are not surprising. Fully half of EC7 trade (both imports and exports) is within the EC7 group. The EC7 is also the dominant export market for the ECMed3 and the NonECMed4 with 51 per cent of ECMed exports and 34 per cent of NonECMed exports going to the EC7 compared with interactions between and among the ECMed and NonECMed countries ranging between 1 and 4 per cent of imports and exports. Despite the fact that between 43 and 37 per cent, respectively, of ECMed and NonECMed imports come from the EC7, this only amounts to 6 per cent of EC7 exports.

The Soviet Union and Eastern Europe are as highly interdependent in trade as the EC7. The Soviet Union exports half its total exports to the six Eastern European countries and imports half its total imports from them. The EE6 import half their total imports from the Soviet Union and export 40 per cent of their exports to the Soviet Union. The EC7 accounts for 13 per cent of Soviet imports and 12 per cent of EE6 imports but this trade only amounts

TABLE 4.2: *World trade matrix*
STRUCTURE OF IMPORT SOURCES (1985)
(Percentage of Total Block Imports)

	USA	JAPAN	EC	ECMED	NECMED	LAT3	NICs	N.T.ASIA	E.EUR	USSR	CHINA	INDIA	HICs	OPEC	LICs	Rest
USA		0.210	0.080	0.080	0.160	0.420	0.150	0.144	0.009	0.040	0.130	0.103	0.170	0.200	0.104	0.235
JAPAN	0.180		0.030	0.030	0.034	0.050	0.220	0.204	0.007	0.040	0.380	0.102	0.063	0.120	0.095	0.075
EC	0.180	0.060	0.510	0.430	0.374	0.120	0.100	0.120	0.120	0.130	0.130	0.264	0.304	0.320	0.260	0.331
ECMED	0.010	0.004	0.030	0.020	0.030	0.010	0.005	0.004	0.006	0.010	0.010	0.010	0.025	0.025	0.008	0.015
NECMED	0.010	0.004	0.020	0.010	0.025	0.002	0.005	0.002	0.030	0.050	0.003	0.003	0.007	0.030	0.007	0.009
LAT3	0.080	0.030	0.020	0.060	0.020	0.050	0.008	0.009	0.010	0.020	0.030	0.020	0.062	0.030	0.010	0.014
NICs	0.110	0.094	0.020	0.020	0.010	0.006	0.080	0.230	0.001	0.004	0.130	0.071	0.063	0.049	0.070	0.038
N.T. ASIA	0.030	0.130	0.010	0.003	0.006	0.006	0.110	0.054	0.002	0.006	0.010	0.010	0.014	0.009	0.030	0.009
E.EUR	0.005	0.003	0.020	0.020	0.070	0.020	0.001	0.006	0.210	0.480	0.040	0.020	0.040	0.030	0.020	0.029
USSR	0.001	0.010	0.026	0.020	0.020	0.005	0.002	0.003	0.490		0.030	0.090	0.015	0.010	0.090	0.046
CHINA	0.007	0.050	0.004	0.002	0.007	0.010	0.080	0.030	0.010	0.020		0.003	0.010	0.007	0.030	0.009
INDIA	0.005	0.010	0.003	0.004	0.003	0.000	0.002	0.003	0.002	0.015	0.001		0.001	0.007	0.010	0.002
HICs	0.040	0.010	0.020	0.040	0.008	0.060	0.020	0.003	0.020	0.003	0.009	0.020	0.040	0.010	0.006	0.025
OPEC	0.020	0.210	0.050	0.160	0.120	0.170	0.130	0.100	0.020	0.005	0.003	0.200	0.107	0.040	0.120	0.030
LICs	0.002	0.005	0.005	0.004	0.004	0.001	0.004	0.004	0.002	0.003	0.003	0.010	0.004	0.008	0.030	0.003
Rest	0.295	0.165	0.154	0.104	0.110	0.070	0.088	0.086	0.062	0.176	0.097	0.079	0.102	0.099	0.108	0.132
SUBTOT	0.705	0.835	0.846	0.896	0.890	0.930	0.912	0.914	0.938	0.824	0.903	0.921	0.898	0.901	0.892	0.868
	0.710	0.830	0.848	0.903	0.891	0.930	0.915	0.916	0.939	0.826	0.909	0.926	0.898	0.895	0.890	0.869

Table 4.2: (*Contd.*) STRUCTURE OF EXPORT MARKETS (1985)
(Percentage of Total Block Exports)

	USA	JAPAN	EC	ECMED	NECMED	LAT3	NICs	N.T. ASIA	E.EUR	USSR	CHINA	INDIA	HICs	OPEC	LICs	Rest
USA		0.110	0.200	0.020	0.030	0.080	0.070	0.020	0.004	0.010	0.020	0.008	0.025	0.040	0.009	0.354
JAPAN	0.380		0.100	0.008	0.008	0.010	0.130	0.040	0.003	0.020	0.080	0.009	0.010	0.060	0.010	0.132
EC	0.100	0.010	0.490	0.030	0.030	0.008	0.020	0.007	0.020	0.015	0.008	0.007	0.010	0.060	0.008	0.177
ECMED	0.100	0.010	0.510	0.030	0.030	0.010	0.010	0.005	0.010	0.020	0.020	0.005	0.030	0.060	0.004	0.146
NECMED	0.110	0.010	0.340	0.020	0.040	0.003	0.020	0.002	0.090	0.130	0.003	0.002	0.040	0.120	0.004	0.096
LAT3	0.440	0.060	0.160	0.050	0.040	0.030	0.010	0.005	0.010	0.030	0.020	0.005	0.010	0.050	0.003	0.077
NICs	0.370	0.110	0.100	0.007	0.006	0.002	0.080	0.080	0.001	0.003	0.050	0.010	0.010	0.040	0.010	0.121
N.T. ASIA	0.180	0.310	0.110	0.003	0.005	0.005	0.230	0.040	0.004	0.008	0.010	0.003	0.003	0.020	0.010	0.059
E.EUR	0.020	0.004	0.140	0.010	0.030	0.008	0.001	0.002	0.210	0.390	0.020	0.003	0.005	0.040	0.004	0.113
USSR	0.005	0.010	0.180	0.010	0.010	0.003	0.002	0.001	0.520		0.010	0.020	0.005	0.010	0.020	0.194
CHINA	0.085	0.220	0.077	0.003	0.010	0.017	0.316	0.040	0.40	0.040		0.002	0.003	0.020	0.020	0.107
INDIA	0.230	0.130	0.210	0.020	0.010	0.001	0.030	0.010	0.020	0.130	0.002		0.003	0.100	0.003	0.084
HICs	0.250	0.040	0.270	0.030	0.030	0.040	0.030	0.005	0.040	0.080	0.005	0.006	0.030	0.020	0.010	0.162
OPEC	0.190	0.180	0.220	0.050	0.020	0.040	0.090	0.020	0.010	0.003	0.001	0.020	0.014	0.025	0.110	0.097
LICs	0.100	0.070	0.330	0.020	0.020	0.004	0.050	0.020	0.020	0.030	0.010	0.020	0.014	0.110		0.112
Rest	0.320	0.063	0.283	0.016	0.015	0.009	0.030	0.010	0.017	0.040	0.012	0.004	0.010	0.027	0.007	0.139

Source: United Nations (Comtrade)

Methodology: Figures represent Total Value of Trade to and from countries grouped into blocks. The original figures are in current dollars.

to a total of 4 per cent of total EC7 exports. To summarize, the main channels for trade in Europe are among the EC7 and between the Soviet Union and the EE6 with considerable trade (20 per cent) among the EE6. The spill-over effects from these main channels does not appear to be large based on the 1985 trade matrix.

Much attention has been focused recently on the dynamism of the Pacific Basin. The matrix of trade interactions within the Pacific Basin shows that the East Asian NICs, Next Tier Asia, and China receive 65 per cent of their total imports from each other and the United States and Japan combined (Table 4.3). Japan, the NICs, NTA and China export between 63 and 77 per cent of their total exports within the region. Japan receives only half (48 per cent) of its imports from within the Pacific Basin. (20 per cent of Japanese imports are from OPEC whereas only 8 per cent of Japanese imports come from EC7, ECM, NECM, EE and the Soviet Union combined.) The United States receives 36 per cent of its imports from Pacific Basin countries while only 22 per cent of US exports go to the region. With the exception of the United States and Japanese oil imports from OPEC, roughly two-thirds of Pacific Basin trade occurs within the region. This is at once a powerful and relatively self-contained source of economic growth.

TABLE 4.3: *Pacific Basin*

From	Imports by				
	USA	Japan	NIC	NTA	China
USA	--	21	15	14	13
Japan	21	--	22	20	38
NIC	11	9	8	23	13
NTA	3	13	11	5	1
China	1	5	8	3	--
Total	36	48	64	65	65

From	Exports to				
	USA	Japan	NIC	NTA	China	Total
USA	--	11	7	2	2	22
Japan	38	--	13	4	8	63
NIC	37	11	8	8	5	69
NTA	18	31	23	4	1	77
China	9	22	32	4	--	67

The 1985 trade matrix manifests a broad pattern of regionalization in world trade. The dominant flows are within the European Community, between the Soviet Union and Eastern Europe, within the Pacific Basin, and between Latin America and the United States. One major question facing the world community is whether the trade and economic growth possibilities that follow from these regionalized patterns are as beneficial for the world economy as a more globalized pattern of world trade. The trade model put forward in this paper allows us to explore those alternative scenarios for the world economy.

Sets of three alternative scenarios are presented here. The middle or base case scenario in each set assumes that the structure of world trade remains static through 1995. The regionalized patterns just discussed would continue into the mid-1990s under this base case scenario. Furthermore, import-GDP shares for 1985 are assumed to prevail into the mid-1990s as well so that present imbalances would be expected to continue into the future. For the US and Japan, at least, some detailed work at the World Bank suggests the extension of the 'current policy' scenarios in each country is highly likely (Watkins [1988] and Park [1988]). Of the three exogenous variables that drive the trade model, only GDP growth rates are varied in the base case scenario. Our base case is developed with reference to the World Bank Base Case for 1987–95 in the 1988 World Development Report. One set of scenarios uses it explicitly to estimate the 1985–95 growth rates for our base case, while a second set of scenarios is more pessimistic. The World Bank Base Case growth rate projections for 1987–95 are as follows:

	1987–95
Industrial Countries	2.3
Exporters of Manufactures	5.0
Highly Indebted Countries	3.2
Oil Exporters	2.7
Low-Income Countries	5.4

On either side of the base case scenario, there are two alternatives: a lower growth, more closed economy scenario in which import-GDP shares decline in all blocs relative to their 1985 level but the structure of trade remains the same as in 1985; and a higher growth, more open economy scenario in which import-GDP shares increase relative to the base case and in addition the structure of trade changes becomes less regionalized. These scenarios permit a comparison of a static moderate growth trajectory (the base case) with a more closed, less trade, lower growth path (lo-closed) with a more open, higher growth, more globalized trade pattern (hi-open). The elements of these strategies go hand in hand. If, for example, the United States is only able to achieve trade balance by reducing its import-GDP share to its export-GDP share, this would entail a reduction in the US import-GDP share from 13 per cent of GDP in 1985 to 8 per cent of GDP in 1995. Since 38 per cent of Japanese exports went to the US in 1985, a reduction in the US import-GDP share would be expected to bring down Japanese exports which might also bring with it a proportionate reduction in the import-GDP share as well. European integration increases intra-European trade as a share of total EC7 and ECMed trade but the fortress Europe concept in a slower growth world economy lowers slightly total import-GDP shares in the three European blocs in this scenario. Less import demand by the US, Japan, and Europe would slow the growth and hence import demand in their trading partners causing import-GDP shares to drop in the other blocs and GDP growth rates to decline worldwide. (See Table 4.4

TABLE 4.4   *Import-GDP Shares; Alternative scenarios*

	lo-closed	base case 1985	hi-open	Export-GDP share 1985
USA	8	13	13	8
JAPAN	11	13	17	17
EC	28	30	35	32
ECMED	20	22	26	23
NECMED	23	25	27	23
LAT3	5	7	10	14
NICs	45	49	54	54
N.T.ASIA	24	26	30	29
E.EUR	15	18*	20	--
USSR	5	7*	10	--
CHINA	7	12	12	8
INDIA	7	10	12	6
HICs	16	16	16	20
OPEC	18	18	20	--
LICs	22	22	22	15

* CEPII (Chelem)
Source: Andrex (GDP Shares in 1980$)

with the import-GDP shares for the three scenarios and the export-GDP shares for 1985 to match the base case import-GDP shares.)

In the hi-open scenario, for example, the US attempts closing its trade deficit by 1995 by increasing its export-GDP share toward its import-GDP share of 13 per cent. A major question is under what set of assumptions about degrees of openness, growth, and changes in trading patterns will such an outcome be feasible for the United States economy. (Experimental simulations showed that increasing the import-GDP share to 15 per cent left the US trade deficit at 4 per cent of GDP.) The commonplace solution to the US policy problem is to advocate a further opening of the Japanese economy to imports and a coordinated stimulus package of growth policies in Japan and Germany to spur US exports. In the hi-open case, the import-GDP share for Japan in 1995 is raised to the level of its export-GDP share in 1985 (17 per cent) providing a four percentage point GDP share increase in its import share. In this scenario, European integration is expected to increase substantially EC7 GDP growth and to enable the import-GDP share to rise. Most studies in the last several years have found the gains from US-Japan-German coordination to lack sufficient growth and trade gains to warrant or compel governments to actually coordinate their monetary and fiscal policies for growth objectives.

This dead-end suggests trying to integrate the working out of the US trade imbalance with other structural changes in non-OECD blocs to see to what extent these shifts might generate patterns of trade and growth that would ameliorate the US imbalance but provide gains for other blocs, regions and countries as well. The opening of the socialist bloc to trade with the rest of the world, the maintenance of openness in Latin America despite the debt problem and in East Asia despite the threat of protectionism, and the globalization of trade patterns through deliberate strategies to seek export markets and import sources outside the normal regional channels taken together with the OECD adjustments already postulated could provide a set of mutually beneficial global growth and trade gains.

The import demand of the East Asian NICs, Next Tier Asia, the Latin America three, ECMed and NonECMed, Eastern Europe, the Soviet Union, China, and India taken together accounted for 26 per cent of US exports, 31 per cent of Japanese exports, and 16 per cent of EC7 exports in 1985. These new players or potential trade powers (NICs in the broadest sense) have a possible global stimulus role to play through their size, growth, openness, trade promotion policies and import sourcing strategies. The hi-open scenario combines OECD adjustment patterns with the increased openness in non-OECD blocs (what the OECD Secretariat calls MDEs, major developing economies) with globalization strategies in all blocs. The assumptions about the degree of openness for each bloc are shown in Table 4.4. It remains to specify the trade strategies of each bloc.

4.4.2. *Trade strategies*

As previously indicated, countries have trade strategies for a variety of economic and political reasons. Import sourcing decisions and export marketing programmes are targeted on certain countries or regions where the greatest overall gain is anticipated. Size, dynamism, stability, and the long-term outlook all play a role. The potential of gaining an investment presence or export penetration in a market can influence import sourcing strategies, and vice versa. Security considerations, macro-economic interactions, and political relations influence trade policies. Whereas monetary and fiscal policies, exchange rate dynamics, and other economic variables would be expected to heavily influence the trade balance, trade policies would be expected to also have a geographic dimension. It is that dimension that is explored heuristically in what follows.

The trade strategy for the United States hypothesized in the hi-open scenario is one in which the US is trying to rectify its trade balance globally through export expansion rather than import contraction and at the same time trying to reduce its import dependence on Japan, the East Asian NICs, and the EC7 (50 per of US imports in 1985). To do this 12 percentage points of total US imports are exogenously allocated away from Japan (− 6%pt), the EC7 (− 4%pt) and the NICs (− 2%pt) and redirected toward the large closed economies (the Soviet Union (+ 2%pt), China (+ 1%pt) and India (+ 0.5%pt)), toward other NIC blocs (Latin America (+ 2%pt), Next Tier Asia (+ 2%pt), and Eastern Europe (+ 1.5%pt)) and toward the highly indebted countries (HICs) (+ 2%pt). This amounts to an opening of the US toward the socialist bloc on the import side, an attempt to alleviate the trade-debt conundrum in Latin America and the HICs, and to increase trade with India and Next Tier Asia. In some measure, these shifts anticipate the likelihood that the US will lose some of its share of the EC7 and ECMed markets as these economies make room for more trade between themselves and that the US will need to develop stronger trade relations elsewhere to compensate for weaker links with Europe.

The trade strategy for Japan is to increase its import-GDP share to the level of its export-GDP share by opening its market relatively more to imports from the US, Latin America, the HICs and China. The strategy is meant to ease the US trade imbalance with Japan, alleviate the world debt problem, and spur export growth in important Japanese markets so that trade balance adjustment in Japan can occur with continued high export-GDP shares for Japan rather than through import contraction. This trade strategy is also an attempt to anticipate a loss of Japanese market share in the enlarged European market and to globalize Japanese trade links beyond the Pacific Basin. To do this, import coefficients for Japan are reconfigured to increase the proportion of Japanese imports from the US (+ 4%pt), Latin America (+ 1%pt), the HICs (+ 2%pt) and China (+ 2%pt) and to decrease the proportion from the EC7 (− 2%pt), the NICs (− 3.4%pt) and Next Tier Asia (− 3%pt) in the hi-open scenario.

The trade strategy for the European Community entails an increase in intra-EC7 trade from 51 to 53 per cent, an increase in EC7 imports from ECMed from 3 to 5 per cent, in EC7 imports from NonECMed from 2 to 3 per cent, and an increase in EC7 imports from EE6 from 2 to 3 per cent. This combined shift in import coefficients of 6 percentage points of total EC7 imports is offset by a reduction in the percentage of imports from the US (− 3%pt), Japan (− 1%pt), Latin America (− 1%pt), the NICs (− 1%pt) and the HICs (− 1%pt). The further integration of the European Community in the early 1990s is hypothesized to have a major effect on the share of import by Spain, Portugal and Greece from the EC7 economies. The ECMed import coefficient with the EC7 increases from 43 to 50 per cent to correspond to the level of intra-EC7 trade in 1985. This leads to a reduction in the ECMed import coefficients with the US (− 2%pt), Japan (− 1%pt), Latin America (− 3%pt) and the HICs (− 1%pt). The import sourcing structure of the NonECMed economies is projected to shift toward the EC7, increasing from 37.4 per cent to 40 per cent, and toward the ECMed, increasing from 3 to 4 per cent. These increases would be offset by declines in NonECMed import coefficients with the US (− 2%pt), Japan (− 1.4%pt) and Latin America (− 0.5%pt).

The combined effect of these shifts by the three European blocs is to weaken the traditional trilateral linkages between the US, the EC and Japan and to reduce imports from Latin America as trade ties within the broad European region are strengthened through further integration. This includes some opening by the EC7 to imports from the Eastern European NICs at the cost of imports from the East Asian NICs which themselves are developing trade ties with the EE6. (*New York Times*, 29 September 1988)

The trade strategy for Latin America is to export sufficiently not only to service external debt but to maintain imports at a high enough level to sustain investment and internal stability. The hi-open scenario envisages the import-GDP share of LAT rising from 7 per cent in 1985 to 10 per cent in 1995 with the expectation that the scenario will induce a LAT export-GDP share of 14 per cent or so in 1995. The major Latin American economies will continue to be major forces in world trade. The hi-open scenario hypothesizes Latin America looking for trade relations in the Pacific Basin and in Europe as a way of deregionalizing its dominant trade patterns with the US. A draconian shift away from the US is projected with the LAT import coefficient with the US dropping from 42 per cent to 30 per cent. This shift is offset by increases in imports from Japan (+ 3%pt), from EC7 (+ 3%pt), in intra-LAT trade (+ 3%pt), from NICs and NTA (+ 2%pt) and OPEC (+ 1%pt).

The trade strategy of the East Asian NICs is to open more to imports (the import-GDP share is projected to rise from 49 per cent in 1985 to 54 per cent in 1995 which is equal to the export-GDP share in the base year) to achieve less of a trade surplus in the 1990s as a means of easing the general trade imbalances of East Asia with the United States. The EANICs are projected to increase trade relations in the Western hemisphere and to open to greater trade with the socialist bloc while importing relatively less from the Asia Pacific region itself. The import coefficients are increased with the US (+ 3%pt), LAT (+ 1.4%pt), Soviet Union (SU) (+ 1%pt), EE6 (+ 1%pt) and China (+ 2%pt) while import coefficients are decreased with Japan (− 4%pt), NTA (− 2%pt), intra-NIC trade (− 1%pt) and the EC7 (− 2%pt).

The trade strategy of Next Tier Asia is very similar to the EANICs. Imports as a share of GDP are projected to increase by 1995 to 30 per cent from 26 per cent in 1985 to ease the East Asian trade surplus with the rest of the world. Import coefficients are increased with the US (+ 2.6%pt), LAT (+ 1%pt), EE6 (+ 1.4%pt), SU (+ 1.7%pt), and the HICs (+ 1.7%pt) while import coefficients are reduced with Japan (− 3.4%pt), EC7 (− 2%pt), NICs (− 2%pt), and NTA (− 1.4%pt). Under this scenario, Next Tier Asia is deregionalizing, opening to the socialist bloc (except China), and shifting import demand toward the US and Latin America while importing relatively less from Europe. These geographic shifts complement its macro-policy effort to contribute to greater global balance.

The trade strategy imagined (perhaps an appropriate word) for Eastern Europe contemplates a major shift in intra-CMEA (Council of Mutual Economic Assistance, i.e. the Soviet Union and Eastern Europe) from 70 per cent of total EE6 imports to 50 per cent. The import coefficient of intra-EE6 trade is reduced from 21 to 15 per cent and the EE6 import coefficient with the Soviet Union is reduced from 49 to 35 per cent. East Europe increases its trade with the rest of the world by increasing its import coefficients with the US (+ 4%pt), Japan (+ 4%pt), EC7 (+ 3%pt), LAT (+ 2%pt), NICs (+ 1%pt), China (+ 1%pt), India (+ 1%pt), and the HICs (+ 2%pt). The trade pattern envisaged for Eastern Europe in this scenario is a shift from inward-looking trade relations within the region and dependence on the Soviet Union to a major opening of trade relations with the rest of the world. The orders of magnitude in this rendering probably considerably overstate the extent of this shift that is likely to occur by 1995. In this sense, it is a maximalist dimensioning of a global strategy by the EE6.

The trade strategy for the Soviet Union is quite similar to that of Eastern Europe and complements it. The Soviet Union reduces its import coefficients with the EE6 from 48 per cent of Soviet imports to 35 per cent in 1995 with a small reduction of two percentage points in the coefficient with NonECMed, especially Yugoslavia and Turkey. The Soviet Union embarks on a global export strategy hoping to raise both the export-GDP and import-GDP shares by 1995 to around 10 per cent from about 7 per cent in 1985 (CEPII data) and hence, to achieve bilateral balance, shifts its import sourcing strategy toward the rest of the world, hoping to improve its access to technology in the process. As a result, Soviet import coefficients are increased in this scenario with the United States by 4 percentage points, and with Japan and Europe by 2 percentage points each. Other increases are with the NICs (+ 1.6%pt), NTA (+ 1.4%pt), China (+ 2%pt), India (+ 1.5%pt) and the HICs (+ 0.7%pt). These shifts are reciprocated by the opening of the US, the NICs, NTA, and OPEC to imports from the Soviet Union but, in this scenario, there is no increase in the opening of Europe, Japan, China, or India to the Soviet economy. Alternatives can be explored subsequently.

The trade strategy for China attempts to enable the country to return to an import-GDP share that peaked in 1985 at 12 per cent without incurring such a massive trade deficit as to trigger an immediate closing of the economy in subsequent years. Imports as a share of GDP declined to 8 per cent in 1987. China's strategy in this scenario is to obtain its manufactured goods imports from the US and Eastern Europe (rather than the EANICs and Japan) and to obtain its raw material imports from Latin America and Next Tier Asia. Other alternatives could be imagined. This scenario follows the pattern of other blocs in reaching outside the region to less traditional sources of imports. As a result, the import coefficient with the US increases by 5 percentage points while that with Japan declines by 8 percentage points (this is clearly excessive) and that with the EC7 decreases by 3 percentage points of China's total imports. The import coefficient with LAT, NTA, and EE6 increase by 2 percentage points each.

The trade strategies for India, the HICs and the LICs remains unchanged in their import sourcing dimension. Import coefficients for these three blocs remain constant for all three scenarios. India opens its economy in the hi-open scenario pushing its import-GDP share to 12 per cent. Except for the EC7, China, and the HICs, the import coefficients for all the other blocs with the LICs double between 1985 and 1995, though these are all 1 per cent or below in 1985 which itself is a measure of the weak pull the world economy exerts on the poorest countries. The trade strategy of OPEC is to derive more of its imports from the Latin American, East Asian and East European NICs as well as the large socialist economies while reducing its import shares with the OECD economies. As a result, the import coefficients with the US, Japan and the EC decline by 2 percentage points each. The OPEC import coefficients with LAT, NICs, EE6, the Soviet Union, China and the LICs increase by 1 percentage point of OPEC imports each.

The import coefficients for each of the major blocs for each of the three scenarios are given in Table 4.9 in the next section. Recall that the coefficients are the same in the lo-closed scenario as in the base case. The trade strategies discussed above are embodied in the changes in the import coefficient vectors for the hi-open scenario as compared to the import coefficient vectors for the base case. (See Tables 4.8, 4.9 and 4.10.)

4.5. The induced pattern of trade, export growth and world GDP

4.5.1. *Lo-closed versus Hi-open scenarios*

The principal results, differentiated by each scenario, are the level of GDP, the level of total exports, the rate of growth of exports between 1985 and 1995, and the export-GDP share in 1995. The export-GDP share in 1995 induced by each scenario can be juxtaposed to the import-GDP share target in 1995 to derive balance of trade (BOT) as a percentage of GDP for each bloc in 1995. These trade balance results can tell us which countries or blocs are correcting their imbalances and which countries are bearing the burden of trade deficits to spur world trade and economic growth.

Table 4.5 shows the exogenously determined GDP growth rates and the endogenously determined export growth rates for the three scenarios. The basic pattern in the relations of these two sets of growth rates is that the export growth rate lags behind the GDP growth rate in the lo-closed scenario, is roughly equivalent to it in the base case, and exceeds the GDP growth rates in the hi-open scenario. This makes intuitive sense, given the assumptions. These relations hold for 11 of the 15 blocs; the exceptions are the US, Japan, the East Asian NICs, and Next Tier Asia. Export growth rates in Pacific Asia are lower in the hi-open scenario because the deregionalization of trade patterns embodied in this scenario drain the region of some of its growth stimulus. With this exception, however, export growth rates are quite robust in this scenario.

In the lo-closed scenario, however, world export growth rates are dismal. Given the fact that modest GDP growth rate and import-GDP share assumptions generate export growth rates that are roughly equal to GDP growth rates in the base case, it is clear from the results in the lo-closed case that world trade will suffer

TABLE 4.5: *Export and GDP growth rates*
1985–95 (Average annual real rates of growth)

		Lo-closed	Base case	Hi-open
USA	Export	2.1	3.6	5.8
	GDP	2.0	2.3	3.0
JAPAN	Export	0.5	3.5	3.5
	GDP	3.0	3.4	3.8
EC	Export	1.9	3.3	5.8
	GDP	3.0	3.4	4.4
ECMED	Export	1.8	3.3	9.1
	GDP	3.0	3.4	4.4
NECMED	Export	1.3	3.1	7.0
	GDP	3.0	3.4	4.4
LAT3	Export	0.3	3.0	5.6
	GDP	3.0	4.0	4.5
NICs	Export		3.5	4.0
	GDP		6.0	7.0
N.T.ASIA	Export	1.4	3.8	6.4
	GDP	5.0	6.0	7.0
E.EUR	Export	0.3	2.9	5.6
	GDP	1.4	2.0	3.0
USSR	Export	1.0	2.8	5.0
	GDP	2.3	2.8	3.3
CHINA	Export	1.7	4.0	10.2
	GDP	3.0	4.0	5.0
INDIA	Export	0.9	3.2	9.2
	GDP	4.0	5.0	6.0
HICs	Export	0.9	3.2	6.0
	GDP	3.0	3.2	5.0
OPEC	Export	1.9	3.7	6.6
	GDP	2.7	2.7	3.7
LICs	Export	1.9	3.6	9.8
	GDP	3.0	5.4	6.0

severe setbacks if import-GDP shares fall as projected in that
scenario. In fact, the GDP growth assumptions in the lo-closed
case are not dramatically less than the base case, while the trade
growth results are decidedly worse. The only other causal variable
to change is the set of import-GDP shares. These decrease in
general by only 2 percentage points of GDP except for the US, the

NICs, and China. (See Table 4.4.) The policy conclusion suggested
by this scenario is that sustaining import capacity in the 36 countries
in the major trading blocs is crucial to sustaining world trade
growth.

The 1995 export-GDP shares induced by each of these scenarios
are shown in Table 4.6. In the lo-closed scenario, the 1995 export-
GDP share drops in all blocs compared to the 1985 levels, except
for the United States which maintains its 1985 level of only 8 per
cent. The big declines are in the NICs and Next Tier Asia, with 4
percentage point decreases in Japan and the EC and 3 percentage
point declines in Latin America and the HICs.

Under this scenario, the United States does indeed achieve
trade balance by reducing the export-GDP share precisely to the
import-GDP share level. Japan continues to run a trade surplus,
but down to 2 percentage points of GDP from 4 in 1985. Exports
as a share of GDP in Japan drop 4 percentage points, from 17 to 13
per cent. This is not the preferred path for economic adjustment
for either economy, quite apart from the negative spill-over effects

TABLE 4.6: *Lo-closed scenario 1995*
              Percentage of GDP

	M/Y* Lo-closed	X/Y 1985 Actual	X/Y Lo-closed	BOT Lo-closed %pt of GDP Surplus	Deficit
USA	8	8	8	0	
JAPAN	11	17	13	2	
EC	28	32	28	0	
ECMED	20	23	21	1	
NECMED	23	23	20		−3
LAT 3	5	14	11	6	
NICs	45	54	39		−6
N.T. ASIA	24	29	20		−4
E.EUR	15	17	15	0	
USSR	5	7	6	1	
CHINA	7	8	7	0	
INDIA	7	6	4		−3
HICs	16	20	17	1	
OPEC	18	n.a.	17		−1
LICs	22	15	13		−8

this pattern for the economic superpowers would have on the world economy as a whole.

Given balance in the US and the EC and a surplus in Japan, the blocs running trade deficits in this scenario are the East Asian NICs and Next Tier Asia as well as the world's poorest countries, the LICs and India. All three socialist bloc entities, the Soviet Union, Eastern Europe and China, achieve trade balance but with very low trade GDP shares and quite low GDP growth rates. Latin America and the HICs run trade surpluses but very low import-GDP shares in LAT and very low GDP growth rates (3.2 per cent) in the HICs.

The induced export-GDP shares and resulting trade balances for the hi-open scenario are shown in Table 4.7. The export-GDP shares of all blocs except for Japan and the EANICs gain from the open scenario over the base case. The blocs that reap the largest GDP share increase over the base case (and over the 1985 actual shares) are ECMed, China and the LICs, with lesser but still substantial gains by Eastern Europe, NonECMed, India, NTA

TABLE 4.7: *Hi-open scenario 1995*
Percentage of GDP

	M/Y* Hi-open	X/Y Base case	X/Y Hi-open	BOT Hi-open %pt of GDP	
				Surplus	Deficit
USA	13	10	11		−2
JAPAN	17	17	17	0	
EC	35	32	36	1	
ECMED	26	23	36	10	
NECMED	27	22	30	3	
LAT 3	10	13	15	5	
NICs	54	42	41		−13
N.T. ASIA	30	24	27		−3
E.EUR	20	19	22	2	
USSR	10	7	8		−2
CHINA	12	8	14	2	
INDIA	12	5	8		−4
HICs	16	20	22	6	
OPEC	20	20	24	4	
LICs	22	13	21		−1

and to a lesser extent LAT. Compared to the lo-closed scenario, these results constitute major gains for all blocs on both the import and the export side.

The US continues to run a trade deficit of 2 percentage points of GDP while Japan achieves balance with the import share rising to the export share of 1985, a share which is actually achieved in 1995. This scenario generates a strong demand for Eastern European and Chinese exports resulting in trade surpluses in 1995. The further integration of the European Community and its enlargement yields significant trade gains for the EC7 but especially for Spain, Portugal and Greece and to a lesser extent for the NonECMed bloc. Latin America, the HICs and OPEC also run trade surpluses with strong export performance in both growth and share terms. The main trade deficit blocs in this scenario are the NICs, NTA and India.

Further dimensions of the differences between these three scenarios are seen in Table 4.8 which shows the world totals for exports and GDP in 1995 under each scenario and the structure of world exports and world GDP by bloc in 1995. The hi-open scenario generates $2.3 trillion more world GDP in 1995 than the lo-closed scenario and $1.3 trillion more exports. Compared to the base case, the hi-open scenario induces $1.5 trillion more GDP and $860 billion more exports.

The structure of world GDP by blocs does not change very much perhaps because the GDP growth rates by bloc are within a reasonably close range. But the structure of world exports by blocs does show some significant change with the OECD losing 3.3 percentage points of world exports in the hi-open scenario compared to the lo-closed scenario. ECMed and China make the biggest gains while the LICs, EE6, LAT, and India also make substantial gains in the share of world exports in the hi versus the lo scenario. The NICs and the Soviet Union lose world export market share while Non-ECMed, NTA, the HICs and OPEC make small gains.

4.5.2. Pacific Basin growth

As a result of the attempt to decentralize the patterns of world trade, in the hi-open scenario, perhaps an excessive proportion of import demand has been shifted away from Japan and the East Asian NICs. This scenario, in fact, deflects nearly 18 percentage points of total import demand of other blocs away from Japan. The NICs experience an adverse shift of 6 percentage points of

TABLE 4.8: 1995 World trade scenarios ($ millions, %)

	LO-CLOSED CASE				WDR BASE CASE				HI-OPEN CASE			
	X	GDP	X/TX	GDP/GDP	X	GDP	X/TX	GDP/GDP	X	GDP	X/TX	GDP/GDP
USA	320739	3793425	12.1	22.2	371444	3906485	11.6	21.8	458945	4182174	11.3	21.6
JAPAN	230371	1721073	8.7	10.1	308318	1789091	9.7	10.0	310116	1859519	7.7	9.6
EC 7	1120110	3949042	42.2	23.2	1294913	4105111	40.6	22.9	1646449	4519855	40.7	23.3
ECMED	81964	397787	3.1	2.3	94526	413508	3.0	2.3	163293	455285	4.0	2.4
NECMED	53830	274811	2.0	1.6	64174	285671	2.0	1.6	93239	314533	2.3	1.6
LAT 3	74938	706313	2.8	4.1	97666	777962	3.1	4.3	125654	816183	3.1	4.2
NICs	114543	291312	4.3	1.7	149323	352439	4.7	2.0	157184	387135	3.9	2.0
N.T. ASIA	67189	328838	2.5	1.9	85394	361533	2.7	2.0	109114	397125	2.7	2.1
CHINA	46819	625449	1.8	3.7	58429	688895	1.8	3.9	104092	758076	2.6	3.9
INDIA	14093	333239	0.5	2.0	17589	366703	0.6	2.0	30969	403163	0.9	2.1
USSR	125147	2123646	4.7	12.5	150529	2240681	4.7	12.5	186113	2352080	4.6	12.1
E.EUR	113750	742772	4.3	4.4	146971	787912	4.6	4.4	191177	868656	4.7	4.5
HICs	86517	516351	3.3	3.0	107609	526466	3.4	2.9	140520	625844	3.5	3.2
OPEC	178218	1074087	6.7	6.3	213493	1074087	6.7	6.0	280589	1183375	6.9	6.1
LICs	23911	178976	0.9	1.0	28189	225335	0.9	1.3	50652	238496	1.3	1.2
TOTAL	2652139	17057121	100	100	3188567	17901879	100	100	4048106	19361499	100	100

TABLE 4.9: *Import Coefficients*

USA

Trade Partners	M* source (closed)	M source (85 base)	M* source (open)
USA			
JAPAN	0.210	0.210	0.150
EC	0.180	0.180	0.140
ECMED	0.010	0.010	0.010
NECMED	0.010	0.010	0.010
LAT3	0.080	0.080	0.100
NICs	0.110	0.011	0.090
N.T. ASIA	0.030	0.030	0.050
E.EUR	0.005	0.005	0.020
USSR	0.001	0.001	0.020
CHINA	0.007	0.007	0.020
INDIA	0.005	0.005	0.010
HICs	0.040	0.040	0.060
OPEC	0.020	0.020	0.020
LICs	0.002	0.002	0.004
Rest	0.295	0.295	0.295

EC7

Trade Partners	M* source (closed)	M source (85 base)	M* source (open)
USA	0.080	0.080	0.050
JAPAN	0.030	0.030	0.020
EC	0.510	0.510	0.530
ECEMD	0.030	0.030	0.050
NECMED	0.020	0.020	0.030
LAT3	0.020	0.020	0.010
NICs	0.020	0.020	0.010
N.T. ASIA	0.010	0.010	0.010
E.EUR	0.020	0.020	0.030
USSR	0.026	0.026	0.030
CHINA	0.004	0.004	0.004
INDIA	0.003	0.003	0.003
HICs	0.020	0.020	0.010
OPEC	0.050	0.050	0.055
LICs	0.005	0.005	0.005
Rest	0.154	0.154	0.154

JAPAN

Trade Partners	M* source (closed)	M source (85 base)	M* source (open)
USA	0.210	0.210	0.250
JAPAN			
EC	0.060	0.060	0.040
ECMED	0.004	0.004	0.004
NECMED	0.004	0.004	0.003
LAT3	0.030	0.030	0.040
NICs	0.094	0.094	0.060
N.T. ASIA	0.130	0.130	0.100
E.EUR	0.003	0.003	0.003
USSR	0.010	0.010	0.010
CHINA	0.050	0.050	0.070
INDIA	0.010	0.010	0.010
HICs	0.010	0.010	0.030
OPEC	0.210	0.210	0.210
LICs	0.005	0.005	0.010
Rest	0.165	0.165	0.165

NECMED

Trade Partners	M* source (closed)	M source (85 base)	M* source (open)
USA	0.160	0.160	0.140
JAPAN	0.034	0.034	0.020
EC	0.374	0.374	0.400
ECEMD	0.030	0.030	0.040
NECMED	0.025	0.025	0.020
LAT3	0.020	0.020	0.020
NICs	0.010	0.010	0.010
N.T. ASIA	0.006	0.006	0.006
E.EUR	0.070	0.070	0.070
USSR	0.020	0.020	0.020
CHINA	0.007	0.007	0.007
INDIA	0.003	0.003	0.003
HICs	0.008	0.008	0.008
OPEC	0.120	0.120	0.120
LICs	0.004	0.004	0.008
Rest	0.110	0.110	0.110

Table 4.9 (*Contd.*)

ECMED

Trade Partners	M* source (closed)	M source (85 base)	M* source (open)
USA	0.080	0.080	0.060
JAPAN	0.030	0.030	0.020
EC	0.430	0.430	0.500
ECMED	0.020	0.020	0.020
NECMED	0.010	0.010	0.010
LAT3	0.060	0.060	0.030
NICs	0.020	0.020	0.020
N.T. ASIA	0.003	0.003	0.003
E.EUR	0.020	0.020	0.020
USSR	0.020	0.020	0.020
CHINA	0.002	0.002	0.002
INDIA	0.004	0.004	0.004
HICs	0.040	0.040	0.020
OPEC	0.160	0.160	0.160
LICs	0.004	0.004	0.008
Rest	0.104	0.104	0.104

NICs

Trade Partners	M* source (closed)	M source (85 base)	M* source (open)
USA	0.150	0.150	0.180
JAPAN	0.220	0.220	0.180
EC	0.100	0.100	0.080
ECEMD	0.005	0.005	0.004
NECMED	0.005	0.005	0.005
LAT3	0.006	0.006	0.020
NICs	0.080	0.080	0.070
N.T. ASIA	0.110	0.110	0.090
E.EUR	0.001	0.001	0.010
USSR	0.002	0.002	0.010
CHINA	0.080	0.080	0.100
INDIA	0.002	0.002	0.002
HICs	0.020	0.020	0.020
OPEC	0.130	0.130	0.130
LICs	0.004	0.004	0.008
Rest	0.088	0.088	0.880

LAT3

Trade Partners	M* source (closed)	M source (85 base)	M* source (open)
USA	0.420	0.420	0.300
JAPAN	0.050	0.050	0.080
EC	0.120	0.120	0.150
ECMED	0.010	0.010	0.010
NECMED	0.002	0.002	0.002
LAT3	0.050	0.050	0.080
NICs	0.006	0.006	0.020
N.T. ASIA	0.006	0.006	0.010
E.EUR	0.020	0.020	0.020
USSR	0.005	0.005	0.005
CHINA	0.010	0.010	0.010
INDIA	0.000	0.000	0.000
HICs	0.060	0.060	0.060
OPEC	0.170	0.170	0.180
LICs	0.001	0.001	0.002
Rest	0.070	0.070	0.070

N.T. ASIA

Trade Partners	M* source (closed)	M source (85 base)	M* source (open)
USA	0.144	0.144	0.170
JAPAN	0.204	0.204	0.170
EC	0.120	0.120	0.100
ECEMD	0.004	0.004	0.004
NECMED	0.002	0.002	0.002
LAT3	0.009	0.009	0.020
NICs	0.230	0.230	0.210
N.T. ASIA	0.054	0.054	0.040
E.EUR	0.006	0.006	0.020
USSR	0.003	0.003	0.020
CHINA	0.030	0.030	0.030
INDIA	0.003	0.003	0.003
HICs	0.003	0.003	0.020
OPEC	0.100	0.100	0.100
LICs	0.004	0.004	0.008
Rest	0.086	0.086	0.086

Table 4.9 (*Contd.*)
E.EUR   CHINA

Trade Partners	M* source (closed)	M source (85 base)	M* source (open)	Trade Partners	M* source (closed)	M source (85 base)	M* source (open)
USA	0.009	0.009	0.050	USA	0.130	0.130	0.180
JAPAN	0.007	0.007	0.050	JAPAN	0.380	0.380	0.300
EC	0.120	0.120	0.150	EC	0.130	0.130	0.100
ECMED	0.006	0.006	0.006	ECEMD	0.010	0.010	0.010
NECMED	0.030	0.030	0.030	NECMED	0.003	0.003	0.003
LAT3	0.010	0.010	0.030	LAT3	0.030	0.030	0.050
NICs	0.001	0.001	0.020	NICs	0.130	0.130	0.130
N.T. ASIA	0.002	0.002	0.010	N.T. ASIA	0.010	0.010	0.030
E.EUR	0.210	0.210	0.150	E.EUR	0.040	0.040	0.060
USSR	0.490	0.490	0.350	USSR	0.030	0.030	0.030
CHINA	0.010	0.010	0.020	CHINA			
INDIA	0.002	0.002	0.010	INDIA	0.001	0.001	0.001
HICs	0.020	0.020	0.040	HICs	0.009	0.009	0.009
OPEC	0.020	0.020	0.020	OPEC	0.003	0.003	0.003
LICs	0.002	0.002	0.004	LICs	0.003	0.003	0.003
Rest	0.062	0.062	0.062	Rest	0.097	0.097	0.097

USSR   INDIA

Trade Partners	M* source (closed)	M source (85 base)	M* source (open)	Trade Partners	M* source (closed)	M source (85 base)	M* source (open)
USA	0.040	0.040	0.080	USA	0.103	0.103	0.100
JAPAN	0.040	0.040	0.060	JAPAN	0.102	0.102	0.100
EC	0.130	0.130	0.150	EC	0.264	0.264	0.260
ECMED	0.010	0.010	0.010	ECEMD	0.010	0.010	0.010
NECMED	0.050	0.050	0.030	NECMED	0.003	0.003	0.003
LAT3	0.020	0.020	0.020	LAT3	0.020	0.020	0.020
NICs	0.004	0.004	0.020	NICs	0.071	0.071	0.070
N.T. ASIA	0.006	0.006	0.020	N.T. ASIA	0.010	0.010	0.009
E.EUR	0.480	0.480	0.350	E.EUR	0.020	0.020	0.020
USSR				USSR	0.090	0.090	0.090
CHINA	0.020	0.020	0.040	CHINA	0.003	0.003	0.003
INDIA	0.015	0.015	0.030	INDIA			
HICs	0.003	0.003	0.010	HICs	0.020	0.020	0.020
OPEC	0.005	0.005	0.005	OPEC	0.200	0.200	0.200
LICs	0.003	0.003	0.006	LICs	0.010	0.010	0.020
Rest	0.176	0.176	0.176	Rest	0.079	0.079	0.079

Table 4.9 (*Contd.*)

HICs				LICs			
Trade Partners	M* source (closed)	M source (85 base)	M* source (open)	Trade Partners	M* source (closed)	M source (85 base)	M* source (open)
USA	0.170	0.170	0.070	USA	0.104	0.104	0.100
JAPAN	0.063	0.063	0.060	JAPAN	0.095	0.095	0.090
EC	0.304	0.304	0.300	EC	0.260	0.260	0.260
ECMED	0.025	0.025	0.030	ECMED	0.008	0.008	0.008
NECMED	0.007	0.007	0.007	NECMED	0.007	0.007	0.007
LAT3	0.062	0.062	0.060	LAT3	0.010	0.010	0.009
NICs	0.036	0.036	0.040	NICs	0.070	0.070	0.070
N.T. ASIA	0.014	0.014	0.014	N.T. ASIA	0.030	0.030	0.030
E.EUR	0.040	0.040	0.040	E.EUR	0.020	0.020	0.019
USSR	0.015	0.015	0.015	USSR	0.090	0.090	0.088
CHINA	0.010	0.010	0.010	CHINA	0.030	0.030	0.029
INDIA	0.001	0.001	0.001	INDIA	0.010	0.010	0.009
HICs	0.040	0.040	0.040	HICs	0.006	0.006	0.008
OPEC	0.107	0.107	0.100	OPEC	0.120	0.120	0.130
LICs	0.004	0.004	0.004	LICs	0.030	0.030	0.030
Rest	0.102	0.102	0.102	Rest	0.108	0.108	0.108

OPEC

Trade Partners	M* source (closed)	M source (85 base)	M* source (open)
USA	0.200	0.200	0.180
JAPAN	0.120	0.120	0.100
EC	0.320	0.320	0.300
ECMED	0.025	0.025	0.025
NECMED	0.030	0.030	0.030
LAT3	0.030	0.030	0.040
NICs	0.049	0.049	0.060
N.T. ASIA	0.009	0.009	0.009
E.EUR	0.030	0.030	0.040
USSR	0.010	0.010	0.020
CHINA	0.007	0.007	0.020
INDIA	0.007	0.007	0.007
HICs	0.010	0.010	0.010
OPEC	0.040	0.040	0.040
LICs	0.008	0.008	0.020
Rest	0.999	0.099	0.099

OECD import demand. As a result of these assumptions (and the fact that the trade-GDP shares of the NICs are extremely high, M/Y equals 49 per cent and X/Y equals 54 per cent on 1985), export growth rates and export-GDP shares in 1995 are not what one would expect from these dynamic economies. By changing the import coefficient of the trading partners of Japan and the NICs to restore 14 percentage points of import demand to Japan and 6 percentage points to the NICs, the model generates more favourable results for both blocs. Japan's export growth rate for the decade improves by a full percentage point, from 3.5 to 4.5 per cent, and its export share rises to 17 per cent. In the NICs, export growth moves up from 4.1 to 4.9 per cent while its export-GDP share jumps from 41 to 44 per cent. The cost of the improvement in the Pacific Basin outlook is a drop of 2 percentage points in the export-GDP share for both the HICs and the LICs. The export growth rate for the decade for the HICs drops from 5.9 to 5.0 per cent and for the LICs from 9.9 to 8.8 per cent.

If the growth rates and import-GDP shares from the hi-open scenario for all blocs are used with no changes in the trade matrix, the export-GDP shares for Japan and NICs improve by 3 and 6 percentage points respectively over the hi-open scenario with import coefficient changes. This shows the degree to which the current structure of world trade favours these Pacific Basin blocs. But five other blocs experience major declines in export-GDP shares: ECM from 36 to 26 per cent; NECM from 30 to 26 per cent; China from 14 to 10 per cent; India from 8 to 6 per cent; and the LICs from 21 to 15 per cent. The world economy does not yield benefits without costs.

4.5.3. *European integration*

The absence of EC integration and the increases in import-GDP shares that accompany it have a negative effect on export growth rates in seven of the 12 blocs outside of Europe, no effect on US and Japan export growth rates compared to the hi-open case and positive effects on export growth rates in LAT, HICs, and the EANICs.

If somehow Europe were able to maintain the higher import-GDP shares of the hi-open case without the geographic reallocation of import coefficients within the three European blocs and between them and the rest of the world, then US and Japanese export

TABLE 4.10:   *Export-GDP shares and Export growth rates*

	Export-GDP shares		Export growth rates	
	Hi-open	without SU/EE	Hi-open	without SU/EE
USA	11	11	5.9	5.5
JAPAN	16	15	3.5	3.0
EC	36	36	5.9	5.7
ECMED	36	36	9.1	9.0
NECMED	30	29	9.0	6.6
LAT	15	15	5.7	5.3
NICs	41	39	4.1	3.7
NTA	28	27	6.6	6.1
E. EUR	22	24	5.6	5.5
USSR	8	9	5.0	5.5
CHINA	14	13	10.4	9.4
INDIA	8	6	9.3	6.6
HICs	22	21	5.9	5.3
OPEC	24	24	6.8	6.7
LICs	21	21	9.9	9.7

Note: Scenario without USSR and East Europe is the hi-open scenario for all other blocks with base case assumptions in the USSR and EE6 blocks, for GDP growth, import-GDP shares and import coefficients.

growth would be enhanced considerably over the hi-open case as would LAT, HIC, and WIC export growth. Export-GDP shares behave in commensurate fashion (See Table 4.10).

4.5.4. *The opening of the Soviet bloc*

There is a question of what difference the opening of SU and EE to the market economies makes to the other blocs. If we lower the GDP growth rates to levels in the base case for the Soviet Union (3.3 to 2.8) and for EE (3.0 to 2.0), reduce the import-GDP shares to the base case for the SU (10 to 7 per cent) and EE (20 to 18 per cent), and change their import coefficients back to the base case (i.e. highly regionalized trade) but leave the assumptions of the hi-open case for all other blocs in place, the model will generate results which allow a rough understanding of the impact of the opening of the SU and EE on the world economy. Given their small trade with the rest of the world, we would expect these export growth losses in other blocs to be relatively small. These results also measure the impact of a unilateral opening of other blocs to the Soviet Union and the EE6 on these two socialist blocs.

The results show that the US, Japan, NECM, LA, NICs, NTA, and the HICs lose between 0.4 and 0.6 percentage points on their average annual real growth of exports for the 1985 to 1995 period. China loses 1 percentage point and India loses 2.7 percentage points of export growth. The only blocs not to experience an export growth-rate loss are the EC7, ECM, OPEC and the LICs. The export-GDP share drops slightly in seven of the 13 blocs. (Table 4.11.)

Another interesting result is that the unilateral opening of the other blocs toward the SU and EE6 as hypothesized in the hi-open scenario actually increases the export growth of the SU over the result in the hi-open reciprocal opening case from 5.0 to 5.5 per cent. This is due to the fact that the SU is getting the benefit of the openness of EE to SU in current patterns along with the new opening of the other blocs to it embodied in the hi-open scenario. The other EE6, on the other hand, experience a slight loss in export growth because of the large increase over the hi-open scenario in the SU import coefficient with EE (from 35 to 48 per cent), and the slow growth of the Soviet economy.

The results provide an indication that the rest of the world has some stake in the opening of the SU and EE to the world economy in terms of expanded export demand, and that the SU and the EE6 stand to make significant gains by an opening of other major trading states to them.

4.5.5. *The fate of the LICs*

The hi-open scenario is quite optimistic for the lower-income countries, too. The 5.4 per cent GDP growth in the WDR base case projections for the LICs presumes the inclusion of China and India. More reasonable assumptions would be 3.0 per cent GDP growth in the lo-closed scenario, 3.5 in the base case and 4.0 in the hi-open scenario. Isolating the lowering of the hi-open GDP growth rate for the LICs by one-third, from 6 to 4 per cent, has only a slight impact on export growth rates in other blocs. Only the EC7, India, OPEC and the LICs themselves experience a 0.1 per cent decline in their export growth prospects for the decade. This shows the negligible effect of the LICs on the world economy.

The hi-open scenario also assumes a doubling of the import

TABLE 4.11: *Regression Equations for Household Demand for Money (Real)*

	Export growth rates			Export-GDP shares		
	with EC	without EC M/Y = base case	without EC M_{ij} = hi-open	with EC	without EC M/Y = base case	without EC M_{ij} = hi-open
USA	5.9	5.9	6.8	11	11	12
JAPAN	3.5	3.5	4.1	16	16	16
EC	5.9	4.3	5.6	36	32	35
ECMED	9.1	4.6	5.8	36	24	26
NECMED	7.0	4.1	5.0	30	22	24
LAT	5.7	6.5	7.0	15	17	18
NICs	4.1	4.4	4.9	41	42	44
NTA	6.6	6.3	6.6	28	27	28
E.EUR	5.6	4.4	4.9	22	20	21
USSR	5.0	4.0	4.7	8	7	8
CHINA	10.4	10.1	10.4	14	14	14
INDIA	9.3	8.9	9.3	8	7	8
HICs	5.9	6.7	7.5	22	24	26
OPEC	6.8	5.8	6.5	24	22	23
LICs	9.9	9.3	9.9	21	20	21

coefficient of most other blocs in the model with the LICs. To test the sensitivities of the outlook for the LICs to the other changes embodied in a hi-open scenario, the doubling of import coefficients is removed. This along with the lower GDP growth rate for the LICs, yields an export-GDP share of 18 per cent for the LICs instead of 21 per cent, implying a trade deficit of 4 per cent of GDP in this hi-open scenario. Their export growth rate falls from 9.8 per cent in the original hi-open scenario to 5.8 per cent in this scenario. This is some improvement over the base case (15 per cent import-GDP share and 3.6 per cent export growth) but is still far short of needs of these countries. A real improvement in the economic prospects of the LICs require major changes in world economic conditions and a massive increase in demand for their exports over the next decade embodied in the hi-open scenario.

Chart 1:   **EXPORT SHARES: Groups of LDCs; (1966-1986)**
(Percentages of Total World Exports)

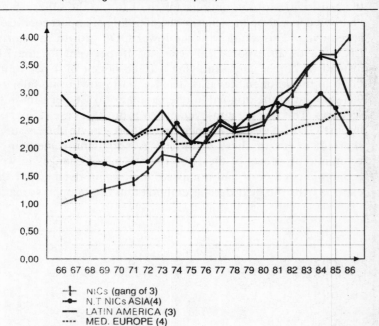

- ─┼─ NICs (gang of 3)
- ─●─ N.T NICs ASIA(4)
- ─── LATIN AMERICA (3)
- •••• MED. EUROPE (4)

Chart 2:   **EXPORT SHARES: Socialist Countries; (1966-1986)**
(Percentages of Total World Exports)

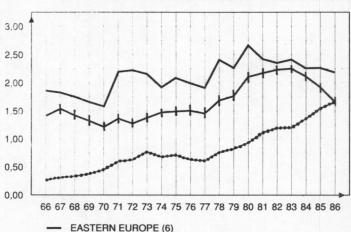

- ─── EASTERN EUROPE (6)
- ─── USSR
- •••• CHINA

Chart 3:

Structure of World Exports: (1966-1986)
(Selected Countries)

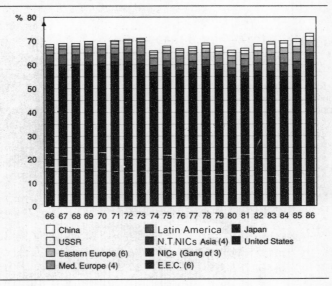

☐ China	▨ Latin America	■ Japan
☐ USSR	■ N.T NICs Asia (4)	■ United States
▨ Eastern Europe (6)	▨ NICs (Gang of 3)	
▨ Med. Europe (4)	■ E.E.C. (6)	

Chart 4:

IMPORT SHARES: Industrial Countries and LDCs (1966-1986)
(Percentages of Total World Imports)

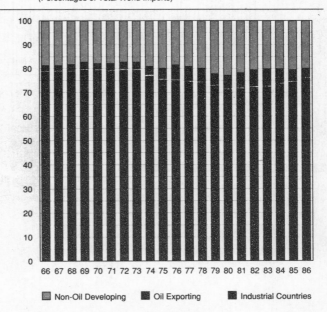

▨ Non-Oil Developing	■ Oil Exporting	■ Industrial Countries

Chart 5:   **TOTAL WORLD TRADE – 1985**

(Exports: Selected Countries)

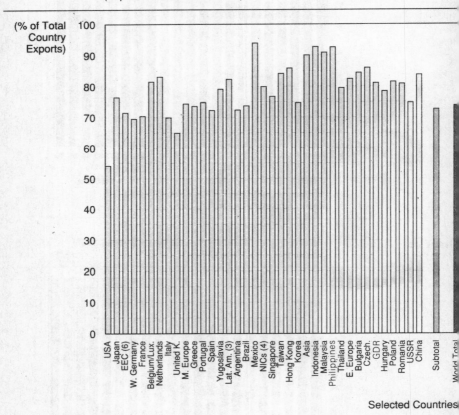

(% of Total Country Exports)

Selected Countries

Chart 6: **TOTAL WORLD TRADE – 1985**
(Imports: Selected Countries)

of Total
Country
Imports)

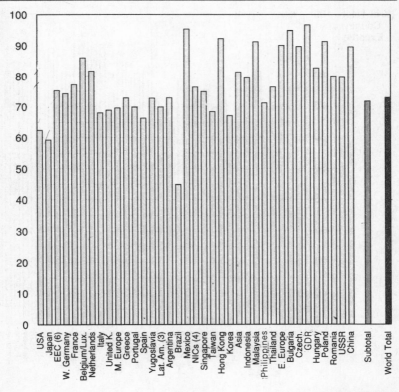

Selected Countries

Chart 7:   **WORLD TRADE OF MANUFACTURES– 1985**
(Exports: Selected Countries)

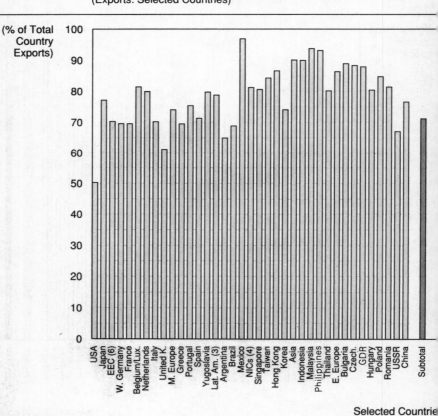

(% of Total Country Exports)

Selected Countries

hart 8:

WORLD TRADE OF MANUFACTURES – 1985
(Imports: Selected Countries)

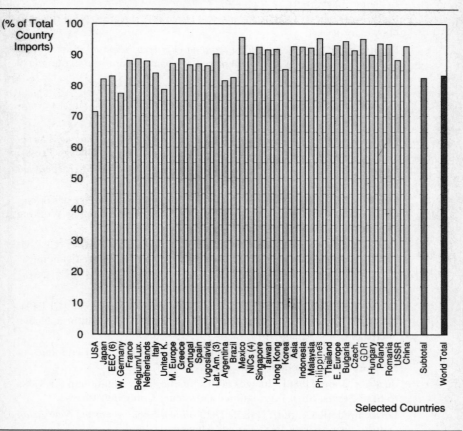

(% of Total Country Imports)

Selected Countries

References

Assetto, Valerie J. [1988], *The Soviet Bloc in the IMF and the IBRD* (Boulder, Colo.: Westview Press).

Balassa, Bela. [1981], *The Newly Industrializing Countries in the World Economy* (New York: Pergamon).

Baldwin, David A. [1985], *Economic Statecraft* (Princeton, NJ: Princeton University Press).

Bitar, Sergio. [1987], *America Latina en el Nuevo Mapa de la Economia Mundial* Santiago de Chile: Centro Latinoameri cano de Economia y Politica Internacional (CLEPI).

Bradford, Colin I. [1987], 'Trade and Structural Change: NICs and Next Tier NICs as Transitional Economies' *World Development*, Vol. 15, No. 3, pp. 299–316.

Bradford, Colin I., and William H. Branson (eds.) [1987], *Trade and Structural Change in Pacific Asia* (Chicago: The University of Chicago Press).

Bryant, Ralph, C. [1980], *Money and Monetary Policy in Interdependent Nations* (Washington, DC: The Brookings Institution).

Buhler, Warren B. [1988], 'Financing Development in the Age of Globalized Financial Markets.' Washington, DC: Strategic Planning Working Paper, World Bank.

Centre d' Études Prospectives et d'Informations Internacionales (CEPII). [1983(a)], *Economic Mondiale 1980–1990: la Fracture?* Paris: Economica.

———. [1983(b)], *Economic Mondiale: la Montée des Tensions*. Paris: Economica.

Centro Latinoamericano de Economia y Politico Internacional (CLEPI). [1988], *El desaio de la incertidumbre*. (Santiago de Chile: Editorial Nueva Sociedad).

Commission of the European Communities. [1988], 'The Economics of 1992' *European Economy*, No. 35.

de Vries, Joop. [1988], 'Images of the Nineties', presentation in the Talks to Staff Series, Shell International Petroleum Company, Ithaca.

Deyo, Frederic C., (ed.) [1987], *The Political Economy of the New Asian Industrialism* (Ithaca, NY: Cornell University Press).

Gilpin, Robert. [1987], *The Political Economy of International Relations* (Princeton, NY: Princeton University Press).

Guerrieri, Paolo, and Pier Carlo Padoan (eds.) [1988], *The Political Economy of International Co-operation* (London: Croom Helm).

Harding, Harry. [1987], *China's Second Revolution: Reform After Mao* (Washington, DC: The Brookings Institution).

Herzka, Claudio J. [1988], 'Economic Integration Efforts Among

Developing Countries and the Future World Bank Role.' Washington, DC: Strategic Planning Working Paper, World Bank.

Hewett, Ed A. [1988], *Reforming the Soviet Economy: Equality Versus Efficiency* (Washington, DC: The Brookings Institution).

Hough, Jerry F. [1988], *Opening Up the Soviet Economy* (Washington, DC: The Brookings Institution).

Kennedy, Paul. [1987], *The Rise and Fall of the Great Powers: Economic Change and Military Conflict from 1500 to 2000* (New York: Random House).

Köves, András. [1985], *The CMEA Countries in the World Economy: Turning Inwards or Turning Outwards*. Trans. G. Hajdu (Budapest: Akadémiai Kiadó).

Krugman, Paul R., (ed.) [1986], *Strategic Trade Policy and the New International Economics* (Cambridge: MIT Press).

Lincoln, Edward J. [1988], *Japan: Facing Economic Maturity* (Washington, DC: The Brookings Institution).

Lodge, George C., and Ezra F. Vogel (eds.) [1987], *Ideology and National Competitiveness: An Analysis of Nine Countries* (Boston: Harvard Business School Press).

Organization for Economic Cooperation and Development [1988], 'The Major Developing Economies and the OECD' (Report by The Secretary-General), Paris.

————. 1987. 'The Newly Industrializing Countries: Implications for OECD Industries and Industrial Policies.' Paris.

Padoa-Schioppa, Tommaso, *et al.* [1987], *Efficiency, Stability, and Equality: A Strategy for the Evolution of the Economic System of the European Community* (Oxford: Oxford University Press).

Park, Eul. [1988], 'Japanese Foreign Direct Investment in the 1980s' Washington, DC: Strategic Planning Working Paper, World Bank.

Rosecrance, Richard. [1986], *The Rise of the Trading State: Commerce and Conquest in the Modern World* (New York: Basic Books Inc.).

Sagasti, Francisco R. [1988], 'National Development Planning in Turbulent Times: New Approaches and Criteria for Institutional Design' *World Development*, Vol. 16, No. 4, pp. 431–48.

Schrenk, Martin. [1988], 'The CMEA System of Trade and Payments; Today and Tomorrow' Washington, DC: Strategic Planning Working Paper, World Bank.

————. [1988], 'Contours of the Future of CMEA' Washington, DC: Strategic Planning Working Paper, World Bank.

Scott, Bruce R., and George C. Lodge (eds.) [1985], *US Competitiveness in the World Economy* (Boston: Harvard Business School Press).

Sheaham, John B. [1986], 'Alternative International Economic Strategies and Their Relevance for China', World Bank Staff Working Papers, No. 759. Washington, DC: The World Bank.

Stremlau, John. [1988], 'Security for Development in a Post-Bipolar World' Washington, DC: Strategic Planning Working Paper, World Bank.

Suzuki, Yoshio. [1986], *Money, Finance and Macroeconomic Performance in Japan* (New Haven, Conn: Yale University Press).

Swiatkowski, Lucia. [1988], 'Perestroika of the Council of Mutual Economic Assistance: The New Science and Technology Policy' Washington, DC: Strategic Planning Working Paper, World Bank.

The World Bank. [1985], *China: Long-Term Development Issues and Options* (Baltimore: The John Hopkins University Press).

Turner, Louis, Neil McMullen *et al.* [1982], *The Newly Industrializing Countries: Trade and Adjustment* (London: George Allen & Unwin).

Watkins, Alfred J. [1988], 'US Fiscal & Financial Imbalances' Washington, DC: Strategic Planning Working Paper, World Bank.

Wozencraft, George. [1987], 'Classifying the Rise of the New Industrializing Countries in the Context of Differentiated Development Patterns in the Third World' Senior Essay, Yale University.

Yamamura, Kozo, and Yosukichi Yasuba (eds.). [1987], *The Political Economy of Japan*. Volume 1: The Domestic Transformation (Stanford, California: Stanford University Press).

5   Some Reflections on the 'Outward-Oriented' Development Strategy of the Far Eastern Newly Industrializing Countries

LUDO CUYVERS AND
DANIEL VAN DEN BULCKE

5.1. Introduction

Although there is a growing amount of literature on the so-called 'Newly Industrializing Countries' (NICs), general agreement as to the definition of this special group of countries or economies is still missing. For example Bradford [1988] reports on a clustering of NICs, the results of which clearly conflict with some of his former results (Bradford [1987]), and which surprisingly rank Hong Kong in a cluster separate from Singapore, Korea and Taiwan.[1]

On the other hand, certain studies (e.g. Terweduwe [1987]) have shown that these classifications lack a clear basis: countries that were taken into account do not all correspond to the criteria by which they were presumably selected, while some countries which were not included do. To avoid this issue, our reflections will mainly be directed towards the four Far Eastern Newly Industrializing Countries (FENICs), Hong Kong, Singapore, South Korea and Taiwan, which are taken up in practically all classifications of NICs or semi-industrialized countries (SICs).

The 'little dragons' or 'baby tigers' or 'gang of four', as these economies are often labelled by economic journalists, not only achieved spectacular results, they also adopted rather straight-forward economic policies which have made them into 'examples to follow' for other developing countries. As a matter of fact the adherents of the so-called 'new orthodoxy' in economic development

---

[1] Moreover, Bradford's clustering exercise neglects the growing importance of trade in services for some of these countries (see below).

theory present the remarkable performance of the FENICs as evidence of the superiority of outward-looking and 'laissez-faire' development strategies. There are indications, however, that the economic policy that was followed by the FENICs was much more interventionist than is generally believed and that their economic success may be due not so much to a 'hands off' policy during favourable circumstances but to the specific actions by the government in choosing and switching to the right policies at the appropriate time.

Outward-looking policies in this paper are not only limited to export promotion strategies but also include the liberalization of capital flows, in particular direct foreign investment (both inwards and outwards). The terms direct foreign investment (DFI) and Multinational Enterprises (MNEs) or Transnational Enterprises (TNEs) will be used interchangeably.

The four FENICs, i.e. Hong Kong, Singapore, South Korea and Taiwan, certainly have a number of similarities, the most important ones being that they are: densely populated, poorly endowed with natural resources, and yet have achieved during the last 20 years continuous self-sustained growth. Other characteristics include the small size of their domestic markets, their adherence to a market oriented economic system, their active participation in the international division of labour, their favourable attitude towards DFI and MNEs and the active participation of the government. Of course there are striking differences between, on the one hand, the city-state economies of Hong Kong and Singapore where the domestic markets are very small indeed and certain policy measures are much more pronounced, and on the other hand the somewhat larger economies of South Korea and Taiwan.

In the following section we will give some evidence of the importance of trade in manufactures and services, and of direct foreign investment in the FENICs. The economic policies which are held responsible for the spectacular export and growth performance of these countries, are reviewed in the third section. The final section of the paper is devoted to the question whether the 'outward-oriented' strategy of the FENICs can be successfully copied by the less developed countries.

5.2. Importance of foreign trade and direct foreign investment for Far Eastern NICs

5.2.1. *Foreign trade*

In 1973, the FENICS accounted for 2.9 per cent of world exports. In 1985 this share had more than doubled and reached 7.3 per cent (GATT [1988:34]). In 1980 (see Table 5.1) the Far Eastern NICs represented 17 per cent of the total exports of all developing countries (expressed in prices of 1975) as compared with 11 per cent for the Latin American NICs (Argentina, Brazil, Chile, Mexico and Uruguay). Although the FENICs had already a high export share of 32.2 per cent in manufactured products in 1963, they increased this proportion to 55.8 per cent in 1980. The Latin American NICs also gained a larger share in manufactured export markets of developing countries, but their expansion only went from 8.6 per cent in 1963 to 12 per cent in 1980.

TABLE 5.1:   *Exports of Far Eastern NICs as percentage of total of developing countries (1963, 1973, 1980)*
(in prices of 1975)

Group of products	1963		1973		1980	
	$ billion	%	$ billion	%	$ billion	%
Fuels	1.30	2.1	2.53	1.8	1.78	1.5
Non-fuel primary products	1.91	4.8	2.90	6.0	4.85	7.8
Manufactured goods	2.38	32.2	14.61	50.5	35.44	55.8
Non-fuel products	4.29	9.1	17.51	22.9	40.59	32.3
Total	5.59	5.1	20.04	9.2	42.37	17.3

Source: Balassa [1987:445]

The Far Eastern Newly *Exporting* Countries (NECs), i.e. Indonesia, Malaysia, the Philippines and Thailand, went from 2.8 per cent in 1963 to 5.8 per cent in 1980 in total manufactures exported from developing countries. Since the 1970s the rate of growth of industrial products by the Asian NECs has surpassed the expansion of the FENICs. In view of the high absolute size of their exports, the higher wage levels and the protectionist reactions of some industrialized countries towards the FENICs, this should not come as too much of a surprise. Yet, the average annual increases in export volume are still very impressive. During 1986–7 the growth rates of export volume were as high as 23 per cent for Hong Kong, 20 per cent for Taiwan, 18 per cent for South Korea and 16 per cent for Singapore. In 1987 the combined exports of the FENICs came close to surpassing the aggregate exports of the non-OPEC developing countries. (GATT, [1988:24]).

5.2.2. Trade in services

The performance of the FENICs' exports of manufactured products is sufficiently documented. During the past decade, however, a marked increase in international trade in services also occurred, in which the FENICs and Asian NECs took an active part. When development strategies in general, and the 'outward-oriented' strategy of the FENICs in particular are discussed, services should be taken into account.

As is clearly shown in Table 5.2, Asia's exports of non-factor services have increased more than five-fold between 1976 and 1986. The development of service industries in the FENICs as well

TABLE 5.2:   *World trade of non-factor services (1977–86)*

	in billion SDRs			per cent			growth rates	
	1977	1983	1986	1977	1983	1986	1976–81	1982–6
World	190.0	373.2	405.1	100.0	100.0	100.0	14.7	3.4
Industrial countries	152.8	276.5	309.5	80.4	74.1	76.4	13.7	3.2
Developing countries	36.1	95.1	94.9	19.0	25.5	23.4	18.7	0.9
– non oil LDCs	32.6	85.1	86.2	17.2	22.8	21.3	18.9	1.3
– oil-exporting LDCs	3.5	10.1	8.5	1.8	2.7	2.1	19.2	−3.5
– Asia	8.6	37.0	36.8	4.5	9.9	9.1	21.8	4.3
of which Korea	2.5	6.2	6.1	1.3	1.7	1.5	43.5	4.7
Singapore	2.6	8.7	5.4	1.4	2.3	1.3	21.2	−5.0
Hong Kong	2.3	4.5	—	1.2	1.2	—	16.4[a]	4.7[b]

Source: IMF, Balance of Payments Statistics, Part 2, Yearbook 1981 and 1987.
      Hong Kong calculations based on Lin and Chou [1984:19]
[a] 1978–81
[b] 1982–3

as in the rest of the region (the NECs) is quite impressive. However, the most spectacular results were achieved during the period 1976–81, although after 1981 the Asian countries (with exceptions such as Singapore) kept the growth rate of their service exports well above those of the industrial world. Hence, it becomes increasingly arbitrary to make a taxonomy of the NICs resting exclusively on merchandise trade, as is the case with Bradford's clustering exercises (see Bradford [1987 and 1988]).

At least two reasons for these developments can be given. Firstly, large MNEs have transferred not only industrial production to the Asian NICs, but also service activities such as transport, regional banking and off-shore financial services, insurance, etc., for reasons related to taxation, government incentives and regulations, labour cost, as well as to the increasing weight of the Pacific rim in world trade.

Secondly, the FENICs have developed service exports of their own. As their industrial activities are to a large extent organized within industrial groupings, encompassing steel works, shipyards, shipping companies, banks, trading companies, etc. the development of services in these groupings is a logical consequence of the need to diversify activities and to maximize turnover and cashflow. Foreign direct investment of the FENICs themselves (see below) evidently entails exports of non-factor services (project development, consulting, engineering, etc.).

Famous are examples of industrial grouping in the FENICs, such as the Korean 'chaebol', which work closely together with the government. The 10 largest of these groupings account for a quarter of Korean GNP. The Samsuy group, for instance, is engaged in shipbuilding, electronics, car construction, department stores, etc. The Korean Huyndai group is involved in heavy industries, metal works, shipbuilding, construction and trading. In Hong Kong, the Chueng Kong group participates in electricity generation, hotels, dock terminals, etc. Singapore's conglomerate United Industrial Corporation has branches in the USA, Australia, Hong Kong, the UK and Thailand, and is controlling various companies engaged in industry, shipping, consulting, trading, property, hotels, etc.

5.2.3. *Inward foreign investment*

DFI was not a very important component of total gross domestic capital formation in any of the four FENICs, except Singapore. In

Taiwan it averaged only 3.3 per cent of the total gross capital formation from 1951 to 1980, as compared with only 2 per cent for Korea during 1972–7 (Tsiang and Wu [1985:328]). Other foreign capital inflows and transfers (e.g. US aid to Taiwan and Korea) constituted important sources of funds until the beginning of the 1960s.

Yet DFI played a more significant role in the industrialization process of the FENICS than is shown by the total amount of funds invested.

It is extremely difficult to get accurate figures on the impact of DFI in Hong Kong, since it has no official balance-of-payments accounts. In the middle of the 1980s, overseas investment accounted for 10 per cent of manufacturing employment and output, and about 17 per cent of total domestic exports (Lin [1984:106]). Hong Kong has always followed an open door policy towards DFI.

When Singapore broke away from Malaysia in 1965 it followed the example set by Hong Kong and adopted a rather liberal attitude towards DFI and MNEs. Especially the growth of the export-oriented manufacturing sector has relied upon the attraction of foreign capital. Between 1972 and 1982 DFI in Singapore on average represented almost 80 per cent of total investment commitments. By 1982 majority-owned foreign companies contributed 64 per cent of manufactured value added and produced 84 per cent of manufactured exports (Kirkpatrick [1986:43]). In 1984 all foreign companies in Singapore employed 184,050 people, as compared with 128,625 in 1975. Indirect employment creation is probably limited because the small domestic market provides fewer opportunities for local sourcing than large market economies. In 1984 63 per cent of total output resulted from the activities of foreign subsidiaries, while these same companies took care of 74 per cent of total exports (Fong [1987:95]).

According to Ranis and Schive [1985:132–3] DFI provided important assistance to Taiwan's success story that has evolved over the past three decades, although it does not deserve 'star billing' from either friends or foes of DFI. In 1979 foreign subsidiaries employed 357,000 people, i.e. 5.5 per cent of total employment in Taiwan. Practically all of these jobs were situated in the manufacturing sector (346,000) where they reached 16.5 per cent of total manufacturing employment. While DFI does not occupy a really dominant position in total manufacturing investment, it is quantitatively important in certain specific sectors and contributes a lot in a qualitative way, by providing contact and access to international technology and markets. 'As the economy moves into the more sophisticated output mixes characteristic of secondary import and export substitution, the product choice, specialized information, and access contributions of DFI gain in importance' (Ranis and Schive [1985:135]).

In Korea employment in foreign firms attained 315,000 in 1978 as compared with only 159,000 in 1974. Ninety per cent of these jobs (288 thousand) were created in the manufacturing sector. The shares of foreign owned subsidiaries in total employment and manufacturing employment were respectively 2.3 and 9.5 per cent in 1978 as compared with 1.4 and 7.6 per cent in 1974. (Koo [1985:196]). Also the indirect employment effects are thought to be important in Korea.

The structure of DFI in the manufacturing sector of the FENICs (see Table 5.3) is not completely comparable. In Taiwan and Hong Kong electrical and electronic products dominate with respectively 44 and 32 per cent out of total manufacturing. In Singapore and Korea the chemical and petroleum sectors rank first with respectively 46 and 37 per cent. The fact that textiles and clothing have become much less important over the years is also shown in Table 5.3. Textiles and clothing represent 16 per cent of total manufacturing

TABLE 5.3: *Structure of direct foreign investment in the manufacturing sector of the Far Eastern NICs*
(in %)

Major Industries	Taiwan (1952–79)	Korea (1962–80)	Hong Kong (at end of 1980)	Singapore (1965–80)
Electrical & electronics	43.8	17.5	2.2	16.1
Chemical & petroleum	14.9	37.5	12.0	45.9
Metal & machinery	17.5	21.3	13.5	20.5
Textile & clothing	6.9	16.1	16.3	4.9
Others	16.9	7.6	26.0	12.6
Total	100.0	100.0	100.0	100.0

Source: Tsiang and Wu [1985:329]

in both Hong Kong and Korea and get an even lower share in Taiwan (7 per cent) and Singapore (5 per cent).

DFI in the FENICs is thus not limited to labour-intensive electronics and textiles but extends to the capital-intensive chemical industry as well. DFI-firms with a heavy domestic market orientation, such as the once important food processing, pulp and paper, and non-metallic minerals, by now generally represent only trivial proportions of the total DFI-presence in Taiwan (Ranis and Schive [1985:11]) and the other Far Eastern NICs.

5.2.4. *Outward foreign investment*

Dunning [1986:23] has estimated the total stock of DFI emanating from developing countries in 1982 between 29 and 34.6 billion US dollars. Table 5.4 lists these figures for the four FENICs and the Latin American NICs. The FENICs represent about one-third of all DFI by developing countries, at least when the oil investments (mainly from the Middle East, Indonesia, Nigeria and Venezuela) and the tax haven and shipping investments are excluded. With the inclusion of the latter two special categories, DFI originating in one of the four FENICs still takes up 16 per cent of the total. Hong Kong alone takes up almost half of the DFI that comes from the 12 most important developing home countries.

The outward DFI of the FENICs is geographically concentrated in the neighbouring countries, although there are already a number of ventures of Korean and Hong Kong firms in North America and Europe. For 'second tier' countries such as Indonesia and Thailand, DFI out of other Asian countries (mainly FENICs) is as high as 15.9 and 13.7 per cent of all foreign investment on their territory (Agarwal [1985:237]). Since 1967 Indonesia has received more DFI from Asian countries than Europe or North America (Kahn [1986:2]).

As for the motives for DFI from developing countries, in particular for the Far Eastern NICs, the main reason is to maintain existing markets and/or gain new ones. 'This investment motive, also found in developed country multinationals, is perhaps more important for the new multinationals since, in general, their products are almost standardized with low-technology inputs, and their marketing methods simple' (Kahn [1986:3]). MNEs from the FENICs have been very much aware of the deteriorating opportunities to export to certain markets because of increased protectionism in

TABLE 5.4: *Estimates of direct foreign investment of Far Eastern NICs and Latin American NICs and per cent of total of developing countries (1982)*

Countries	$ million	Per cent of subtotal	Per cent of total
Hong Kong	2,500 – 3,000	21.1 – 19.1	8.6 – 8.4
Singapore	1,500 – 1,750	11.9 – 11.2	5.2 – 4.9
Taiwan	300 – 325	2.4 – 1.9	1.0 – 0.9
South Korea	250 – 300	2.0 – 1.9	0.9 – 0.9
Argentina	750 – 1,000	6.0 – 6.4	2.6 – 2.8
Brazil	1,250 – 1,500	9.9 – 9.0	4.3 – 4.2
Chile	75 – 100	0.6 – 0.6	0.3 – 0.3
Colombia	250 – 300	2.0 – 1.9	0.9 – 0.8
Mexico	350 – 400	2.8 – 2.5	1.2 – 1.1
Uruguay	50 – 75	0.4 – 0.5	0.2 – 0.2
Other LDC Countries	5,318 – 6,940	40.9 – 44.4	18.3 – 19.4
Subtotal	12,593 – 15,690	100 – 100	43.3 – 44.0
Oil investments	4,000 – 5,000	— —	13.7 – 14.0
Tax haven and shipping investments	12,500 – 15,000	— —	43.0 – 42.4
Total	29,093 – 35,690		100 – 100

Source: Dunning [1986:23]

their export markets or higher costs in the country of origin. These factors were extremely important for Singapore firms (Fong and Komaran [1987:37]). The search for lower costs (Wells [1983]) in countries like Thailand and the Philippines, where wages were 5 to 6 times lower is very much related to this.

Another motive for DFI from the FENICs consists of gaining access to third markets via host countries that have a preferential trade agreement with industrial countries. An example of this strategy is provided by Hong Kong textile firms that have established joint ventures, e.g. in Mauritius to supply the European Community. The desire to reduce risk through diversification is also quite relevant to Singapore MNEs, especially for the cash-rich ones in mature industries which have invested in high technology areas like computers and micro-electronics (Fong and Komaran [1987:37]). MNEs from Hong Kong and Taiwan to some extent engage in diversifying strategies to avoid the political uncertainties (with respect to the People's Republic of China) that are linked with their home base. Investment undertaken to secure raw materials does not seem to occur very often.

Most authors seem to accept that DFI from other developing countries is more relevant to the development needs of the host countries (e.g. Wells [1983], Lall [1983], Agarwal [1985] and Kahn [1986]). The ownership advantages of MNEs from developing countries mainly stem from scaling down technologies from industrial countries and making them more suitable for the smaller markets of the poorer countries. Because of this their products are more adapted to local climatic and social circumstances, their technology is more appropriate and their production process will be more labour-intensive.

Subsidiaries which belong to Third World MNEs are not as integrated in the global rationalized network of MNEs from industrial countries and are therefore not to be confronted with less centralized sourcing and selling strategies (Agarwal [1985:246]) and likely to absorb a larger proportion of raw materials and semi-finished products from local producers in the host country. The larger autonomy of Third World MNEs, in comparison with MNEs from developed countries, will also cause less reluctance because the danger of loss of sovereignty will be smaller. However, the fact that much DFI from the FENICs is tied to ethnic and cultural groups in the host countries (mainly Chinese) may cause special tensions.

Another element which makes the FENICs' outward investment more acceptable to their neighbouring host countries, is the high degree to which they opt for joint ventures and more particularly accept or prefer minority positions. (Wells [1983], Agarwal [1985]). Although the limitations that exist in some host countries may have an effect, the choice of a limited form of ownership results mainly from the companies themselves and is an illustration of their risk-averse approach rather than a storage of funds. Over half of the Singapore- and Hong Kong-owned firms with foreign operations are involved in minority joint ventures (Fong and

Komaran [1985:38 and 41]). These proportions are much lower for MNEs from developed countries.

5.3. Understanding the economies of the outward-looking strategy

5.3.1. *Export-oriented approach*

The successful development strategy and the subsequent upsurge in exports of the FENICs can be explained by mainstream international economic theory. Balassa [1975] has, for instance, developed the concept of 'domestic resource cost' (DRC) to investigate the impact of export promotion policies versus that of import substitution. The DRC of exporting one dollar worth abroad is equal to the value of the domestic production factors divided by the net earnings of foreign exchange, i.e. taking into account the foreign exchange used to pay for imported raw materials, etc.

It is not always clear whether export expansion favourably affects economic growth in developing countries or whether the high export performance is a result of the unusual increase in the Gross Domestic Product. Only in the case of Korea could a clear causality between exports and growth be found, which means that the export-led hypothesis for the three other countries could not be confirmed (Darrat [1987]). Yet Balassa [1987:455] concludes from his study that an outward-looking strategy has a positive impact because of

gains from resource allocation according to comparative advantage; the exploitation of economies of scale and increased capacity utilization; improvements in technology; and increases in domestic savings and foreign direct investment.

Others have pointed to the impact of the outward-oriented strategies on accompanying macro-economic policies:

At the early stages of development the key seems to be the macro-economic policies made necessary by openness and the productive efficiency (at least in exports) resulting from competing in world markets, rather than openness or non-intervention per se (Campbell [1988:306]).

According to the advocates of the 'outward-looking' strategy, import substitution might be a useful development policy during a first phase (primary import substitution), i.e. until the limits for non-durable products for the domestic market have been reached. After having gone through a period of primary export substitution, i.e. the export of non-traditional export products, the DRC will decline as compared to the DRC of further producing import substitutes.

This will happen because:

1. In export promotion the abundant factors of production (unskilled labour) are used, hence production will be in line with the comparative advantage of the country. Import substitution will increasingly put the scarce factors of production (capital, skilled labour) into operation.
2. Economies of scale can be exploited because of specialization on larger markets (domestic and export markets), while import substitution often results in underutilized capacity and higher costs of production as a result of the limited size of the national markets.
3. Exposure to international competition will oblige the export sector to adapt continuously, e.g. by reducing costs, introducing the newest technology and management methods, etc.
4. Export promotion forces the country to abandon import restrictions, which will also eliminate bureaucratic measures, bribery, etc. and will have a beneficial effect on efficiency.
5. An outward-looking economy leaves more room for combining expenditure-reducing with expenditure-switching policies in case of external shocks which have effects on the balance of payments.

From the early 1950s onwards, Hong Kong pursued an export-oriented policy, whereas Taiwan and South Korea were at that time still inward-looking and following import substitution policies. The policy orientation of Hong Kong was very much linked to its role of commercial entrepôt in the Far East and, hence, the importance of re-exports. However, Hong Kong also benefited from the advantages of the Commonwealth Preference System during this period (Kam Hon [1982]).

While the other three Far Eastern NICs adopted restrictive measures to protect their own industry they also introduced export incentives such as: the remittance of indirect taxes on imported inputs for export production; income tax exemptions on part of the export earnings; tax concessions on interest on foreign loans; and the establishment of export-processing zones, etc. In Taiwan direct export subsidies were also granted by manufacturers' associations in some industries, such as cotton spinning and rubber products. In Korea an official trade organization was established to provide assistance in export promotion while former President Park is known to have personally exerted pressure on business leaders to meet their export targets.

Balassa [1978] has given much weight to the non-discrimination stance of commercial policies in Taiwan and Korea with respect to exporters. As exporters were exempted from indirect taxes on their inputs and outputs, and paid no duty on imported inputs, they were free to choose between domestic and imported inputs. Therefore, the commercial policies of the FENICs come close to what he calls 'ideal trade policies for developing countries', which means a system of equal incentives to exports and to import substitution, which provides stability and certainty to exporters, and minimizes the chances of retaliation from the importing countries. Nevertheless, a number of additional incentives were also applied to non-traditional exports, which have undoubtedly contributed to the diversification of their manufactured exports.

Later on, the Far Eastern NICs were hit by protectionist measures taken by the developed countries. The 1962 Long-Term Arrangement Regarding International Trade in Cotton Textiles and, since 1974, the Multi-Fibre Arrangement, are known to be protectionist anti-NIC policies of the rich countries. The bilaterally agreed ('voluntary') export restrictions of the NICs, or unilateral import quotas by the developed importing countries have similar restrictive effects.

There can be no doubt that the FENICs have been seriously affected by such policies, which as economic theory suggests, in the short period (not taking long-run dynamic interactions into account) give rise to global inefficiencies. From a longer run perspective, however, some disadvantages have had positive effects: for instance the Multi-Fibre Arrangement created pressures to diversify both industrially and geographically. Industrial diversification consisted of moves into the production of other products which were subject to less restrictions. FENICs also engaged in geographical diversification and set up production units in other low-wage countries, such as Thailand, Malaysia, the Philippines, Sri Lanka, etc. in order to escape quota limitations (Keesing and Wolf [1980:123–5]).

5.3.2. *Macro-economic policies in the FENICs*

5.3.2.1. *Investment and savings policy*

In order to gather sufficient capital, the FENICs pursued macro-economic policies that stimulated domestic savings and attracted foreign capital. In 1965, South Korea doubled its nominal interest rate on deposits. This increased savings to such an extent that more than half of all investment could be financed by domestic savings (Bunge [1982:112]). During the 1960s, when US aid to South Korea was cut back, the role of foreign borrowing and investment gradually increased. The Korean 'Foreign Capital Promotion Act' of 1966 contributed to an expansion of DFI.

Similar policies were adopted in Singapore and Taiwan. The relatively high interest rates in these countries provided sufficient incentives to domestic savings, but at the same time avoided these savings being used to finance low-return investment projects. In countries like Korea and Taiwan exchange controls discouraged capital outflows. The phenomenon of using domestic savings for investment in the rest of the world (through an export surplus), rather than for investment at home, is relatively recent. Balassa and Williamson [1987:6–7, 15–16] have argued that this is a doubtful policy.

In the 1970s the FENICs increasingly financed imports of capital goods by external borrowing, thereby contributing to a large extent to the recycling of the OPEC surplus (Bradford [1982:174]). The importance of government policies of reducing capital cost in order to bring about sufficient capital formation has recently been documented by Bradford [1987].

5.3.2.2. *Exchange rate policy*

Unlike countries following a policy of self-reliance based on import substitution, the FENICs made the exchange rate into one of the pillars of their export-oriented policies. When they switched to a more export-oriented policy they subsequently abandoned their multiple exchange rate systems, devalued their overvalued exchange rates and maintained a low but realistic rate.

Taiwan replaced its system of multiple exchange rates by a dual rate in 1958, and in 1959 by a single exchange rate of 40 Taiwanese dollars per US $, which remained in effect until the demise of the Bretton Woods system in 1971. Although Korea unified its dual exchange rate system in 1961, it later introduced multiple exchange rates to limit domestic inflation and the foreign exchange crisis. However, the exchange rate system was unified again in 1964.

In the period 1970–4, real effective exchange rates (i.e. the trade-weighted exchange rates adjusted for domestic inflation and inflation in the trading partner countries) of the FENICs fluctuated widely. Between 1975 and 1985 they not only varied very little but also much less than in most other developing countries (Edwards [1987]).

Apart from Taiwan, the real effective exchange rate of Hong Kong, South Korea and Singapore showed a tendency to increase (i.e. to depreciate), thus favouring their export sectors. It can also be argued that the relative stability of the real effective exchange rate in the four FENICs reduced the uncertainty in economic decision making, and encouraged exports as well as investment.

Since 1985, the real effective exchange rate of the four FENICs depreciated together with the US dollar, which means that their currencies are now undervalued. This undervaluation contributed significantly to the current account surpluses of Taiwan, Korea and Singapore, which have already led to retaliation by the developed countries (especially the US) and endanger the economic prospects of the FENICs both at home and on the world market (Balassa and Williamson [1987]).

5.3.3. *Industrial policy and policies with respect to DFI*

It is often believed that the success of the FENICs stems from their absolute devotion to economic liberalism and their support of private enterprise. In reality the governments of the FENICs are quite active participants in the economy and have intervened continuously. According to Macomber [1987:474] the difference between the Latin American and Far Eastern NICs 'lies in the nature of the policies and the way in which they are implemented. The East Asians know how to harness market forces in their economic policies and achieve impressive rates of growth. Latin Americans, on the other hand, seem to make almost conscious effort to move against market forces.' And Hamilton [1987:1254] adds to this that

It is not the quantity of government intervention that matters but its quality. In the successful NICs the quality has been consistently high while the quantity has varied considerably.

The nature and the implementation are thus extremely important.

Unlike Hong Kong, the three other Far Eastern NICs only switched to an outward-looking policy in the early 1960s: Taiwan in 1958–60, South Korea in 1962–6, Singapore in 1965. South Korea especially provides a good example of direct government intervention and a successful industrial policy. Because at the end of the Korean War steel production was largely concentrated in North Korea, South Korea built up its steel industry—against the advice of the World Bank—with substantial government funds. The government's decision was on the one hand influenced by its nationalistic goal to become a leading world producer of steel and on the other hand by the high priority of import substitution for the development of the shipbuilding and automobile industry.

South Korea launched its first Five-Year Plan in 1962. Like the following Five-Year Plans it focused on both export-oriented industrialization and on import substitution. Korea's development strategy was not just outward-looking. The Five-Year Shipbuilding Plan and the Shipbuilding Encouragement Law, which were adopted in 1962, provided the legal basis for substantial tax and financial incentives to this sector. Since 1974 when measures were taken to increase production capacity and to substitute for imported parts, the automobile industry has become Korea's newest strategic sector. In 1969 the 'Electronics Industry Promotion Law' gave rise to financial aid and tax benefits for the production of electronics.

Even Hong Kong, the champion of economic liberalism, adopted coordinating and stimulating policies, although without using distorting measures or subsidies. In order to acquire new technologies, foreign industrial investment was actively solicited. However, the main attractions of Hong Kong for foreign investors were not financial incentives, but low wages, low taxes, freedom to transfer profits abroad, infrastructure, etc.

Table 5.5 presents the major changes in the policies of the FENICs towards DFI. Hong Kong has been so liberal that no measures were even imposed.

Of the four FENICs Korea undoubtedly has started out as the most restrictive towards DFI. The Korean policy was to a certain extent inspired by the Japanese example of 20 years ago and basically only allowed the entry of foreign firms when their role was considered compatible with the government's development

TABLE 5.5   *Major dates of changes in the policies of the Far Eastern NICs
             with respect to direct foreign investment*

Country	Restriction on foreign ownership		Tax incentives		Export covenants required		Special import protection	
	Imposed	Relaxed	Granted	Withdrawn	Imposed	Relaxed	Granted	Eased
Hong Kong	--[a]	--	--	--	--	--	--	--
Korea	1960	1984[c]	1960		1973	1984	1960	[b]
Singapore	--	--	1967	--	1967	--	1963	1967
Taiwan	1954		1954	--	1954	--	1954	--

Source: Hughes and Dorrance [1987:50]. Major dates of changes in the policies of the Far
         Eastern NICs with respect to Direct Foreign Investment
Notes: [a] __: Indicates no adoption of a particular programme or no important changes
          [b] __: Indicates that it is almost impossible to identify a date of change
          [c] There are, for example, environmental and health controls on investment

strategies. Its policy was shaped gradually and often adapted to the
changed circumstances.

The first attempt by the Korean Government to draw the attention of foreign capital was made in 1960 (Foreign Capital Inducement Promotion Act) at a time when the country did not yet have
any foreign companies established on its territory (Kahn [1986:35]).
However, it took quite a while before MNE ventured into Korea.
The normalization of diplomatic relations with Japan (1965), the
revision of the Foreign Capital Inducement Promotion Act (1966),
the improvement of administrative procedures by the 'Measure to
Promote the Inflow of Direct Foreign Investment and to Foster the
Activities of Foreign Subsidiaries' (1969) and the establishment of
the Export Free Zone in Masan (1970) directed considerable DFI
into Korea.

When the government feared that unlimited approval of DFI
might create some adverse effects on the Korean economy, a major
revision of its attitude was carried out in 1973 (Koo [1985:178–9]).
Although joint ventures were already informally receiving preference the new measures explicitly gave priority to co-ownership
projects with Korean nationals. The foreign participation ratio was
basically limited to 50 per cent, although a number of exceptions
were provided, e.g. for entirely export-oriented projects that did
not compete with domestic firms in overseas markets; projects in
export-free zones; technology-intensive projects that produced or

induced the production of important export- or import-substituting products, etc.

Until 1979 foreign ownership limitations were very stringent. In line with the general changes in attitudes towards DFI by developing countries in general (Van den Bulcke [1988]), Korea reversed its policy again, not only for reasons of balance-of-payments problems but mainly to allow for increased competition for its domestic firms and to enhance their efficiency and productivity. The new open-door policy is another revision of the Foreign Capital Inducement Act that came into effect in 1984 (Kim and Song [1987]). The major plank of the new law was its replacement of a negative list by a positive list which specified those areas open to foreign investment. Of the 1084 sectors in the Korean economy only 49 are completely closed to foreign investors, mainly on grounds of public policy. New projects above a level of US $ 1 million will be automatically approved. Although the joint venture preference is still present for particular sectors it is applied less rigorously than before and even in these special categories wholly owned subsidiaries are allowed if they meet specific criteria.

Taiwan's experience with DFI goes back to the pre-World War II period, when it was occupied by Japan and Japanese capital established natural resource linked companies (modern sugar mills). After the Pacific War the numerous Japanese private companies were consolidated into 22 large government-controlled corporations. After going through its import-substituting policy during the 1950s, the reforms of 1960 were not only intended to strengthen export promotion efforts but also to improve the investment climate. Although, as early as in 1954 Taiwan had promulgated a Statute for Investment by Foreign Nationals and had taken special measures in 1955 to repatriate investment from overseas Chinese, the inflow of foreign capital had been very limited. The 'Statute for the Encouragement of Investment' (1960) with a number of tax advantages, the 'Statute for the Establishment and Management of Export Processing Zones' (1985) and the first zone in Kaohsiung (1960), have resulted in an important expansion of off-shore production by foreign MNEs. The major purpose of Taiwanese policy towards DFI was to attract new technology or to provide employment (Hsieh and Chen [1987:433–44 and 464–73]).

Singapore adopted an open strategy towards inwards DFI from its very beginning as a nation-state in 1965. Contrary to some West

European countries the role of the government was not altogether absent and Singapore authorities used transnational companies to restructure their manufacturing sector from a low wage- and low productivity-economy towards a relatively high wage- and higher added-value-economy. Singapore's development policy emphasizes economic efficiency and growth, rather than national ownership of the industrial sector. As Singapore does not insist on joint ventures, MNEs establish wholly owned subsidiaries, particularly in the technology and export-oriented sectors.

In trying to create a favourable investment climate, the Singapore government has applied not only traditional measures such as tax holidays and export incentives, but has also taken more controversial measures such as curbing trade unions, extensive labour interventions and the suppression of domestic political opposition (Fong [1987:97–8]).

The state of Singapore has played a critical role in determining the economic conditions on which its comparative advantage is based.

The fundamental objective of this intervention has been to establish the preconditions for the attraction and retention of foreign capital, upon which Singapore's export-oriented industrialization strategy is founded. (Kirkpatrick [1986:45]).

The most important of these interventions has been the labour market. Until the end of the 1970s the main thrust of the policy was to continue the surplus labour situation which was necessary for export-oriented liberalization of labour-intensive products. After 1979 its 'New Economic Policy' strategy of economic restructuring raised the price of unskilled labour while at the same time increasing its supply. Although the system of across the board wage increases has been abandoned because the increased costs resulted in a certain decline of Singapore's cost competitiveness, it is likely to remain a major attractive base for DFI on the basis of its many vocational advantages such as its political stability.

DFI is not a prerequisite for development, but the experiences of the FENICs suggest that for countries seeking to compress industrialization and the accompanying transformation of poor and predominantly agricultural economies into wealthy modern states in a mere generation, DFI can complement and stimulate domestic investment (Hughes and Dorrance [1987:64]).

5.4. The Far Eastern NICs: an example to follow?

With regard to their value as standards for other developing countries the success of the FENICs is a matter of fierce debate. Ten years ago Joan Robinson [1979:109–10] stated, 'If development means overcoming poverty and building up self-reliance, these miracles can hardly be regarded as examples of success.' Other critics have argued that the experience of the 'Gang of Four' cannot be generalized as these countries are quite unique and the external circumstances have been exceptionally favourable (Streeten [1982]).

5.4.1. *External limitations*

Instead of making a list of the so-called 'Potential NICs' (or 'Near-NICs' or 'Second Tier NICs') some general comments will be made about the chances of other countries to emulate the growth experience of the FENICs. First of all, it would be wrong to assume that the starting position of other countries is comparable to that of the four countries of the Far East in the 1950s and 1960s. The growth of the world economy has slowed down, while competition among the developing countries themselves has increased markedly.

According to an influential paper by Cline [1982] (on the basis of an assumed import penetration limit of 15 per cent) the generalization of the NICs model to the rest of the developing world would multiply the manufactured exports of the LDCs seven-fold. The market share of the developing countries in the industrial economies would probably lead to oversaturation and result in protectionist reactions which would greatly limit the possibilities of this generalized strategy. This implies that the model may work well if pursued by a limited number of countries, but is likely to break down if taken up by a great number of developing countries. Cline advises against too many countries imitating the export-biased policies of the Asian NICs, since a great part of their success is to be explained by the fact that they were first to switch policies in the 1950s and 1960s. Bradford [1982:173]) concludes that

Newly developing countries will surely appear, some achieving new status as exporters on a world scale. But the number will be limited and the occurrences will be unusual.

His later findings (Bradford [1987:309–10]) tentatively show that—apart from Malaysia—the other 'next tier NICs' (Colombia, Thailand and the Philippines) and India are more on a general development path and have more in common with the 'non-transitional' LDCs than with the NICs.

A much more positive view is embraced by Balassa [1987:462–6] who concludes from a time series analysis that supply-side rather than demand-side variables dominated export growth in the developing countries during the post-war period. Even the protectionist policies of industrial countries may not be sufficient to stem the export growth of the NICs. In textiles and clothing the exports of developing countries increased again in 1984 as

developing country exporters increasingly shifted to the exportation of products that do not encounter barriers, in particular engineering products, which came to account for nearly two-fifths of the manufactured exports of the developing countries.

Notwithstanding their rapid growth in the last 20 years, in 1983 the developing countries supplied only 2.3 per cent of the manufactured goods consumed by the developed countries.

It should not be forgotten that a growing part of the trade between developed and developing countries consists of intra-industry specialization so that changes occur in the product composition of the firm rather than in the industrial structure of the economy. Moreover the growing importance of intra-firm trade within multinational groups undoubtedly limits the protectionist pressures in the industrial home countries of MNEs. (Helleiner [1981], Van den Bulcke [1985] and Little [1986]). Also the fact that Far Eastern NICs have developed their own MNEs is to a large extent due to their attempts to establish subsidiaries abroad to avoid existing and potential trade restrictions in their export markets.

5.4.2. *Other limitations*

Other exceptional circumstances that reinforced the momentum of the policy switch from import-substitution to export-promotion for the FENICs were:

1. The resurgence of national pride and solidarity after the fall of the Japanese colonial empire and the Communist threat.

2. The wish to imitate the Japanese post-war industrial miracle (Linder [1985]).
3. The changes in the economic structure that could be realized because of US aid in countries like South Korea and Taiwan. After the Korean war, South Korea received an annual flow of US public aid of an average of $270 million between 1953 and 1958 (Bunge [1982:31]). The gradual reduction of this aid forced the Korean and Taiwanese authorities to try out the outward-looking strategy. In Hong Kong, the loss of the Chinese market (on which the largest part of its transit trade was based), as a result of the UN embargo of 1951, had pushed Hong Kong towards open policies much earlier than the other FENICs.
4. The inflow of cheap labour as a result of the massive emigration to Taiwan, South Korea and Hong Kong from North Korea, Japan and China. Hong Kong's textile industry was to a large extent developed by Chinese entrepreneurs coming from Canton and Shanghai.
5. The absence of raw materials and domestic sources of energy, which resulted in an important impetus for export-oriented growth strategy in order to acquire the necessary foreign exchange to finance their development. Countries with intensive natural resource exports are much less constrained in terms of foreign exchange and more eager to develop an inward-oriented strategy for the development of their manufacturing industry.

If one takes together the above-mentioned factors it is evident that the FENICs have been operating in a somewhat special situation. The great merit of the policy makers has been that a number of disadvantages have actually been turned into advantages. It is far from certain that other countries will be able to face such tremendous challenges, and, like the FENICs, rise out of the ashes of underdevelopment.

References

Agarwal, J. P. [1985], 'Intra LDCs Foreign Direct Investment: A Comparative Analysis of Third World Multinationals', *The Developing Economies*, September, pp. 236–53.

Balassa, B. [1975], 'Reforming the System of Incentives in Developing Countries', *World Development*, June, pp. 365–82.

Balassa, B. [1978], 'Export Incentives and Export Performance in Developing Countries: A Comparative Analysis', *Weltwirtschaftliches Archiv*, Band 114, Heft 1, pp. 24–61.

Balassa, B. [1987], 'The Importance of Trade for Developing Countries', *Banca Nazionale del Lavoro, Quarterly Review*, December, pp. 437–69.

Balassa, B., G. Bueno, P. Kuczynski and M. Simonsen [1986], *Toward Renewed Economic Growth in Latin America* (Washington Institute of International Economics).

Balassa, B. and J. Williamson (1987). 'Adjusting to Success: Balance of Payments Policy in the East Asian NICs', Institute for International Economics, p. 156.

Bradford, C. [1982], 'Newly Industrializing Countries', *The World Economy*, September, no. 2, pp. 171–86.

Bradford, C. [1987], 'Trade and Structural Change: NICs and Next Tier NICs as Transitional Economies', *World Development*, no. 3, pp. 299–316.

Bradford, C. I. [1988], 'The NICs in the World Economy' (this volume).

Bunge, F. [1982], *South Korea: A Country Study* (Washington: The American University).

Campbell, B. [1988], 'The Little Dragons have Different Tables', *The World Economy*, June, pp. 305–10.

Cline, W. [1982], 'Can the East Asian Model of Development be generalized?', *World Development*, vol. 10, no. 2, pp. 81–90.

Darrat, A. [1987], 'Are Exports an Engine of Growth? Another Look at the Evidence', *Applied Economics*, February, no. 2, pp. 277–83.

Dunning, J. [1986], 'The Investment Development Cycle and Third World Multinationals', in K. Kahn (ed.), *Multinationals of the South: New Actors in the International Economy* (London: F. Pinter, pp. 15–47).

Edwards, S. [1987], 'Real Exchange Rate Variability: An Empirical Analysis of the Developing Countries Case', *International Economic Journal*, vol. 1, no. 1, Spring, pp. 91–106.

Euh, Y-D. and S. Min [1986], 'Foreign Direct Investment from Developing Countries: The Case of Korean Firms', *The Developing Economies*, June, no. 2, pp. 149–68.

Fong, P. E. [1987], 'Foreign Investment and the State in Singapore', in

V. Cable and B. Peraud (eds), *Developing with Foreign Investment* (London: Croom Helm, pp. 84–100).

Fong, P. E. and R. Komaran [1985], 'Singapore Multinationals', *Columbia Journal of World Business*, Summer, pp. 35–43.

GATT [1988], *International Trade 1987/1988* (Geneva) (Advance copy).

Hamilton, C. [1987], 'Can the rest of Asia emulate the NICs?' *Third World Quarterly*, October, pp. 1225–56.

Helleiner, G. [1981], *Intra-Firm Trade and the Developing Countries* (London: Macmillan).

Hsieh, A. and T. -J. Chen. [1987], 'The Role of Foreign Capital in the Economic Development of Taiwan', in Chung Hua Institution for Economic Research, Conference on *Economic Development in the Republic of China on Taiwan* (Taipeh Conference Series, no. 7, pp. 433–81).

Hughes, H. and Dorrance, G. [1987], 'Foreign Investment in East Asia', in V. Cable and B. Persaud (eds.), *Developing with Foreign Investment* (London: Croom Helm).

Juul, M. and L. Welch [1981], 'Structural Adjustment and Growth in East Asia: Threat and Prospect', Paper, Joint AIB-EIBA-Conference (Barcelona, 26 pp).

Kam-Hon, L. [1982], 'Development of Hong Kong's Place in International Trade', *The World Economy*, September, no. 2, pp. 187–200.

Keesing, B. and M. Wolf [1980], *Textile Quotas against Developing Countries*, (London: Trade Policy Centre).

Kahn, K. [1986]. *Multinationals of the South, New Actors in the International Economy*, London, F. Pinter, p. 250.

Kim, S. H. and Y. K. Song [1987], 'US Private Investment in Korea', *Columbia Journal of World Business*, Winter, pp. 61–6.

Kirkpatrick, C. [1986], 'Singapore at the Crossroads: The Economic Challenges Ahead', *National Westminster Bank Review*, May, pp. 43–51.

Koo, B. Y. [1985], 'The Role of Direct Investment in Korea's Recent Economic Growth', in W. Galenson (ed.), *Foreign Trade and Investment: Economic Growth in the Newly Industrializing Asian Countries* (Madison: University of Wisconsin).

Lall, S. [1983], *The New Multinationals: The Spread of Third World Enterprises* (Chichester: John Wiley).

Lin, T. B. [1984], 'Foreign Investment in the Economy of Hong Kong', *Economic Bulletin for Asia and the Pacific*, United Nations, vol. XXXV, no. 2, December pp. 96–106.

Lin, T. B. and W. L. Chou [1984], 'Recent Economic and Social Developments in Hong Kong', *Economic Bulletin for Asia and the Pacific*, United Nations, vol. XXXV, no. 1. June.

Linder, S. B. [1985], 'Pacific Protagonist—Implications of the Rising Role of the Pacific', *American Economic Review*, May, no. 2, pp. 279–84.

Little, J. S. [1986], 'Intra-Firm Trade and US Protectionism: Thoughts Based on a Small Survey', *New England Economic Review*, pp. 42–51.

Macomber, J. [1987], 'East Asia's Lessons for Latin American Resurgence', *The World Economy*, December, no. 4, pp. 469–82.

Marton, K. [1986], 'Technology Transfer to Developing Countries via Multinationals', *The World Economy*, December, pp. 409–26.

Ranis, G. and C. Schive [1985], 'Direct Foreign Investment in Taiwan's Development', in W. Galenson (ed.), *Foreign Trade and Investment: Economic Growth in the Newly Industrializing Asian Countries* (Madison: University of Wisconsin, pp. 85–137).

Robinson, J. [1979], *Aspects of Development and Underdevelopment* (Cambridge: Cambridge University Press).

Streeten, P. [1982], 'A Cool Look at "Outward-Looking" Strategies', *The World Economy*, September, no. 2, pp. 159–69.

Terweduwe, D. [1987], 'The Newly and Semi-industrialized Countries: A Critical Appraisal of the Country Classifications', *Tijdschrift voor Economie en Management*, no. 1, pp. 55–71.

Tsiang, S. and Wu Ring-I [1985], 'Foreign Trade and Investment as Boosters for Take-off: The Experience of the Four Asian Newly Industrializing Countries', in W. Galenson (ed.), *Foreign Trade and Investment: Economic Growth in the Newly Industrializing Asian Countries* (Madison: University of Wisconsin).

Van den Bulcke, D. [1985], 'Intra-Firm Trade of Multinational Enterprises: Characteristics and Implications for Developing Countries', *EADI-Bulletin*, no. 1, pp. 95–121.

Van den Bulcke, D. [1988], 'Deregulation of Foreign Direct Investment in Developing Countries', in D. van den Bulcke (ed.), *Recent Trends in International Development, Direct Investment Services, Aid and Human Rights* (Antwerp: RUCA, pp. 29–64).

Wells, L. [1983], *Third World Multinationals: The Rise of Foreign Investment from Developing Countries* (Cambridge: MIT-Press).

Wells, L. [1987], 'Evaluating Foreign Investment: With Special Reference to Southeast Asia', in R. Robinson (ed.), *Direct Foreign Investment: Costs and Benefits* (New York: Praeger, pp. 17–39).

6   Labour Intensive Manufactured Exports: A Direct Attack on Poverty

HARMEN VERBRUGGEN

6.1. The causes of success

Quite a number of studies have been published on the all-important question: how the NICs—and South Korea, Taiwan, Hong Kong and Singapore in particular—have managed to achieve such a boom in their manufactured exports and to keep up, almost uninterrupted, such high GDP growth rates. Evidently, the important companion question that arises concerns the lessons that can be learned from the experiences of the NICs and to what extent their strategies can be adopted by other countries. Numerous explanations have been put forward. For simplicity reasons these explanations can be grouped into four categories, which of course, are not strictly exclusive.

The prevailing explanation of the *first* category is that of the avowed superiority of the export-oriented trade and industrialization strategy, meaning a strategy that does not bias industrial production toward the domestic market, but instead integrates industrial production into the international economy through trade. This does not necessarily involve completely free trade; it has at least to be ensured that there is no bias against exports in the incentive system. South Korea, Taiwan and Singapore have been so successful because they were the first to implement export-promotion policies. Moreover, these countries have typically followed the most comprehensive export-promotion policies, amounting to free-trade conditions for exporters in these countries. Hong Kong has always been a free-trade area. The World Bank World Development Report 1987, and the numerous underlying background and other supporting studies, can be seen as the principal proponent of this view (World Bank, [1987]).

In the *second* group of explanations the NICs are simply designated as atypical. Both Singapore and Hong Kong are city-states, which should mean that their economies are not burdened with a backward agricultural sector. Moreover, city-economies should be more easily manageable. South Korea and Taiwan are special cases because both countries have gratefully enjoyed the political interest of and protection from the Western countries. The basis for their successful economic development was laid down in the 50s and 60s. They started with an efficient agricultural sector, a relatively well-developed infrastructure and sizeable foreign economic assistance, mainly from the United States.

The *third* group of explanations points to the stability and strong political control of the governments and institutions of the NICs, and hence their ability to promote change. Apart from Hong Kong, the economies of the NICs operate under a highly centralized guidance, characterized by an unusual degree of harmony between the individual objectives of the entrepreneurial class and national economic aspirations. A feature common to the NICs is a public policy commitment to export-oriented industrialization.

The *fourth* category of explanations attributes the success of the NICs to conducive industrial relations, the social environment and cultural factors. Thus, the labour force in the NICs is well-educated, industrious, mobile and non-militant, and the state, employers and employees are all united in and driven forward by Confucianism.

The dispute that still has to be settled concerns, of course, the assessment of both the relative importance and the policy relevance of the various explanations. At least two features stand out. First, economists feel most at home with the first category of explanations. It is not by accident that this school of thought is most adequately typified by the slogan 'getting the prices right'. Thus, policies should be directed at establishing a neutral incentive system between import substitution and export activities, and avoiding price distortions, improving the operation of product and factor markets by attacking market failures nearest to their sources, setting an appropriate exchange rate, and by affording protection—if deemed necessary—only selectively and for a limited and preannounced time period. Second, it becomes increasingly clear that the success of the NICs is at least partly due to deliberate government intervention and guidance. It has not only been simply a matter of reducing the discrimination against exports. On the contrary, elements of a command economy can clearly be recognized, such as: jointly (government and private sector) formulated export strategies and targets, import protection of specific industrial sectors or production processes, policies to establish industrial conglomerates, concessional credits, public investments and government measures to stimulate the transfer and absorption of (imported) technology. This line of thought corresponds to the third group of explanations mentioned above.

6.2. Strategic trade model

Bradford's studies into the phenomenon of NICs also point to the impact of guided government intervention. From his research, it appears that structural change and rapid export growth in the NICs is primarily brought about by sectoral strategies and deliberate underpricing of investment goods (Bradford, [1987]). Also in his contribution here, 'The NICs in the World Economy', Bradford expresses the view that the success of the NICs is first of all to be explained by a deliberate strategy of export push, investment drives and structural change, brought about by a close public sector–private sector collaboration, rather than by simply reducing discrimination against exports and eliminating various other market distortions. That is what he calls 'the NIC model of managed openness', in which the government plays an important role in promoting trade.

The element of a national strategy, carried into effect by a close collaboration of firms and government agents in establishing a limited number of large strategically export-oriented conglomerates is also given predominant weight in the recent new theories of international trade. This so-called strategic trade theory emphasizes strategic behaviour of firms and governments and takes due account of real-life facts in the world economy, such as technological advantage, learning curves, scale economies and imperfect competition (Krugman, [1986] Chapter 1).

My criticism concerns Bradford's opinion that this model 'provides us with a window to the future'. In other words, this model is an example for and will be followed by other major countries and trade blocs in the future. I have serious doubts about the transferability of this model, mainly because it very much rests upon specific characteristics of the Asian NICs, namely the strong political control and the public policy commitment to export-oriented industrialization. It should be emphasized that many factors affect the ability of a country to adopt a more outward-oriented strategy and generate manufactured exports. Among these factors are a country's political configuration and the strength of vested interests in continued protection. Factors that should also be reckoned with are a country's domestic market size, its natural resource endowment, the quality of the labour force, and its density of population. It will take a country-by-country assessment to attribute due importance to these factors. There is, therefore, no generally applicable policy prescription, with the exception, perhaps, of the export-processing free zone (EPFZ) as an instant device to generate manufactured exports.

Moreover, it still remains to be seen whether it is desirable that other countries should copy the political climate of the NICs with such a high degree of political influence and government intervention. The present economic ideology in the Western countries especially is rather one of less government and less guidance.

Admittedly, the strategic trade theory might provide a new rationale for both government support and a more active trade policy. And indeed, a few examples of strategic protectionism in Western countries, mainly in the fields of aircraft industry and electronics, can be given as illustrations. But the point remains that these new theoretical insights do not yet provide straightforward guidelines for policy, and that the identification of strategic sectors is surrounded by uncertainty and substantial financial risks.

6.3. Basic question

The foregoing discussion suggests that, although in certain fields of economic policy lessons can indeed be learned from the experience of the NICs, simple and general recommendations in order to achieve rapid growth of manufactured exports cannot be provided. There is still too little insight into the basic question as to the economic mechanisms through which these export successes are actually brought about. Put differently, which mechanisms are at work in the interaction between the expansion of manufactured exports on the one hand, and growth and structural change of the domestic economy on the other? Bradford's research highlights the role of the production factor capital. His findings seem to suggest that forced capital formation is an important means of accelerating structural change in manufacturing production for both the domestic and the export markets, and a key instrument in the strategy for becoming a NIC (Bradford, [1987]). This contribution focuses on another causal relationship, namely how the production stimuli emanating from an expanding export sector can best be passed on to the other sectors of the economy. The angle of incidence in analysing this relationship is the role of the production factor labour in the export-oriented industrialization strategy (Verbruggen, [1987]). In discussing this role, it is also hoped that the relationship between export-oriented industrialization and the reduction of poverty can be illuminated. Before doing so, it should be made clear that in this contribution the reduction of poverty is primarily interpreted as the generation of productive employment opportunities. This view implies that here we assume a developing economy with excess capacity expressed in unemployment and underemployment at a given wage rate.

6.4. Employment effects and production linkages

The important question can now be asked what the employment effects are of an export-oriented industrialization strategy compared to domestic-market-oriented manufacturing production. Three different types of employment effects can be distinguished, namely:

1. direct employment effects;
2. indirect employment effects;
3. secondary employment effects.

The extent of indirect employment effects is related to the extent of *domestically* supplied intermediate inputs and the labour intensity of these inputs. The secondary employment effects comprise the employment creation throughout the economy after spending the wage incomes earned in export and input supplying industries on *domestically* produced goods. By envisaging three successive stages of employment creation, insight is at the same time gained into the degree of interrelatedness between the export sector and the rest of the economy. This addresses the above basic question most directly. Apart from the realization of indirect and secondary employment effects, there are two other effects that are closely related to the degree of integration of the export sector in the domestic economy. The first effect is the net inflow of foreign exchange from exports, which equals export value less imported inputs that are directly and indirectly required in the production of exports. The second effect has to do with the elusive, but highly important category of externalities which might accrue to domestic industry. It is frequently assumed that the foreign-trade sector is the channel through which embodied and disembodied technologies are introduced and diffused throughout the economy. These externalities may also refer to the increased availability of trained labour and management, and the use by domestic industry of special facilities in infrastructure, banking and other services that were initially created in support of the export sector. It is thought that there is a strong positive relationship between the backward integration of the export sector with the domestic economy and the realization of these externalities.

The empirical evidence presented in this contribution is drawn from in-depth studies of seven East and South-East Asian countries, i.e. Indonesia, Malaysia, the Philippines, Singapore, Thailand, together with the founders of ASEAN, South Korea and Taiwan. Analyses of input-output tables of these countries, covering the 1970s, have been made to grasp the impact of the export sector on overall employment, foreign-exchange creation and the integration of the economy. The selection of precisely these seven countries is interesting as they show marked differences in *per capita* income level and structural national characteristics, such as domestic market size, population density and availability of natural resources. One can also observe differences among these countries in manufactured export performances and in industrialization and trade strategies pursued.

At the one end we find Indonesia which meets all the salient features of an import-substitution regime. At the other end are the generally known NICs, South Korea, Taiwan and Singapore. Their export-promotion policy is accompanied by a fairly open and liberal trade regime, although South Korea and Taiwan still use the instrument of protectionism to encourage some branches of industry. EPFZs contribute relatively little to the export performance of these two countries. By contrast, the EPFZ-type of export production plays a crucial role in Singapore's export drive. In between these extremes, we find the Philippines, Thailand and Malaysia. These countries pursue a combined or dualistic strategy: domestic production is protected, whilst the discrimination against exports is reduced via subsidies or EPFZs. The intercountry differences within this group, however, may not be disregarded. Protection given to domestic industry in Thailand is moderate and no EPFZs were in operation during the 1970s. As in Thailand, domestic industry in Malaysia is protected moderately, but export manufacturing, on the contrary, has from the outset taken place in EPFZs. The Philippines, in turn, combines a heavily protected manufacturing sector with a policy of export promotion based on both subsidies and EPFZs. Thus, three fairly distinct groups can be identified. Indonesia alone belongs in the first group and represents the pure strategy of import substitution. The second group consists of the Philippines, Thailand and Malaysia which have achieved a remarkable upsurge in manufactured exports by pursuing a dualistic trade strategy. The third group, comprising South Korea, Taiwan and Singapore, stands out as the prime example of a genuine, comprehensive export-oriented industrialization strategy.

6.5. Main research findings

6.5.1. *Direct employment effects*

The main research findings that are presented here only refer to the exports of non-natural-resource-based manufactures.[1] Considering firstly the direct factor intensity of manufactured exports, the specialization pattern of manufactured exports in the case-study countries is clearly labour-intensive, except in Indonesia. Apparently, the inward-looking policies in Indonesia are biased against labour-intensive exportables. Export-promotion policies in the other countries do produce the desired effect. This holds especially for the countries that pursue a comprehensive export promotion strategy. It can be established that manufacturing industries in South Korea, Taiwan and Singapore with a higher export-output ratio show a higher labour intensity of production, generate less value added per employee and pay lower wages. In these industries, the labour force is predominantly unskilled. Another striking feature of export industries is the predominance of female workers in the labour force. The rationale for active policies to increase female labour force participation in these countries is—

---

[1] Thus, the term manufactured exports does not include food products, beverages, tobacco, wood and cork products (except furniture), petroleum products, iron and steel, and non-ferrous metals.

apart from specific abilities and skills—the reduction of wage costs in export industries, as (young) female workers earn substantially less than their male colleagues in comparable functions.

The specialization pattern in the other case-study countries is less distinct. Indeed, manufactured exports are on average relatively labour-intensive, except for Indonesia, but in these countries exports are not consistently concentrated in the most labour-intensive products. Exports also include a substantial share of relatively capital-intensive products produced in relatively high-wage industries. Consequently, for these countries no significant correspondence can be found between a sector's export orientation, factor intensity and average wage level.

6.5.2. *Production linkages and foreign exchange effects*

The level of domestic production linkages emanating from manufactured export production is influenced by technical product characteristics, the degree of sectoral interrelatedness of the economy in which production takes place and the trade and industrialization strategy pursued. In turn, the degree of sectoral interrelatedness is strongly influenced by structural country characteristics. The impact of differences in country characteristics may briefly be summarized as follows.

As an economy develops and becomes more specialized, inter-industry relations become more pronounced. In general, the ratio between the demand for intermediate and final products increases. At higher levels of economic development, technologically advanced sectors producing intermediate and capital goods have the strongest inter-industry linkages. Apart from the level of economic development, domestic market size and natural resource endowment have a sigificant impact on the structure and interrelatedness of production. Given the level of *per capita* income, large economies tend to be more industrialized and tend to have a higher level of sectoral integration than small economies. Small economies have a more specialized structure of production, resulting in a higher trade dependence. This is reflected in a higher export orientation of production and a larger import leakage. Finally, if countries amply endowed with natural resources achieve the processing of these resources domestically, this results in the creation of strong linkages between manufacturing and primary sectors.

In general, the empirical analysis shows a relatively high import dependency for non-natural-resource-based manufacturing production in the case-study countries. But contrary to what is often suggested, the empirical evidence indicates that an export-oriented industrialization strategy does not as such result in an increasing import dependence. This is explained by the finding that in developing countries the level of production linkages is generally higher for labour-intensive low-wage industries than for capital-intensive industries, except if production takes place under EPFZ conditions. This finding contradicts the general impression that inter-sectoral linkages are stronger for technologically more advanced and relatively capital-intensive sectors. This appears only to be true at higher levels of economic development. Apparently, at a lower stage of development it is easier to supply labour-intensive production processes with domestically produced intermediates than capital-intensive processes. Thus, a comprehensive export promotion of labour-intensive manufactures reduces rather than increases the import dependence of production. This finding is easily accounted for considering that, during the mid-1970s, intermediate- and capital-goods-producing industries were largely undeveloped in all seven countries. South Korea, Taiwan, Singapore, and to a lesser extent also Malaysia, are representatives of a group of forerunners that embarked on an export-oriented industrialization strategy following the completion of a first stage of import substitution of mainly non-durable consumer goods. These countries did not move into a secondary or backward-linkage type of import substitution, but extended the first stage to export markets. The larger countries, Indonesia, the Philippines and Thailand, reached the limits of the domestic market roughly ten years later than the forerunners; they were then confronted with the choice between turning to exportation of manufactures or moving to second-stage import substitution. In other words, all the countries in our study were still in a first-stage industrialization process during the mid-1970s. At this stage of industrialization, production of non-durable consumer goods is highly import-dependent, whatever its market orientation.

6.5.3. *Indirect and secondary employment effects*

The higher level of production linkages generated by labour-intensive manufactures does not fail in its effect on the extent of indirect and secondary employment creation. With respect to the indirect employment effects of exports, it appears that the relative extent of this effect is larger in those cases where the composition of exports is more labour-intensive than that of production in general. Thus, if the direct employment effect is higher per unit of exports than per unit of total production, this is equally true for the indirect employment effects. This does not hold for Malaysia and Singapore. These two exceptions may be taken to reflect the small extent of production spread effects associated with export production in EPFZs. In both countries, the direct employment effect per unit of manufactured exports exceeds that of the average for total manufacturing production, whereas the indirect employment impact of these exports falls behind the average for manufacturing.

The same pattern emerges if the secondary employment implication of manufactured exports is considered, with only one modification. The direct employment effect of manufactured exports in Malaysia is sufficiently large to compensate for the low indirect effect, resulting in a secondary employment effect just exceeding the average for manufacturing production. This compensation does not occur in Singapore.

6.6. Employment and income distribution

It can now be asked how export-oriented industrialization influences an economy's income distribution. The foregoing analysis as well as the experiences of the four Asian NICs suggest the following conclusions. First, the labour absorption capacity of this strategy is relatively high, particularly for low-skilled labour. Second, the rapid employment growth that accompanied this strategy in the four Asian NICs led to tight labour markets and concomitant wage increases from the early 1970s onwards. Whether a country embarking on an export-oriented industrialization strategy will indeed observe a significant equalizing influence on the income distribution also depends, of course, on the developments in other sectors of the economy, notably in agriculture. In this respect, the four Asian NICs have a good record. Agriculture is virtually absent in Singapore and Hong Kong, whereas South Korea and Taiwan went through radical land reforms in the late 1940s and early 1950s. This is most likely the decisive factor that contributed to the relatively equal income distribution of these countries. This equality in income distribution has certainly not been reduced by the industrialization policy of stimulating labour-intensive exports (Van Liempt [1988] Chapter 5; Fei, Ranis and Kuo [1979] Chapters 2–3).

6.7. Two lessons

At least two lessons can be learned from the experiences of the seven countries under consideration. The first lesson offered is the proven effectiveness of a comprehensive as compared to a dualistic export-promotion strategy in generating labour-intensive manufactured exports, and, consequently, its superiority in both production and employment spread effects. It is true that one unit of foreign exchange earned in exporting is equivalent to one unit of foreign exchange saved through import substitution. But, for one thing, the net foreign-exchange earnings per unit of output from labour-intensive exports are generally higher than, or at least equal to, the net foreign-exchange savings from capital-intensive production oriented towards the domestic market. A second point is that direct, indirect and secondary employment effects associated with one unit of foreign exchange in exporting labour-intensive exports are each clearly more extensive than corresponding employment effects which are associated with one unit of foreign exchange saved through capital-intensive domestic-market-oriented production. We may therefore safely conclude that developing countries' exports of labour-intensive manufactures tend to have an equalizing effect on an economy's distribution of income. In terms of its low-skilled labour absorption capacity, this strategy constitutes a direct effect on poverty.

The second lesson to be learnt refers to the poor record of spread effects associated with the EPFZ-type of export promotion. This fact emerges quite clearly from the experiences in Singapore and Malaysia, and from the EPFZ production especially of electronics in South Korea and Taiwan. The direct employment effects are the only substantial gain to be reaped from this specific export-promotion device. This strategy can therefore only be advocated for those countries which have no policy alternative, most notably small countries that are poorly endowed with natural resources and, in absolute terms, a small labour force. In all other cases, EPFZs are less favourable, especially where these zones are grafted on to a protected import-substitution sector.

In one respect the latter conclusion has to be modified. The

EPFZ described here is typical of the first or 'easy' phase of export-oriented industrialization based on specialization in a rather narrow range of labour-intensive exportables. Recent experiences in the NICs, but also in India and China, however, indicate that the EPFZ-type of export production can be upgraded and diversified in the course of time, and moreover, that a backward integration with the domestic economy can be developed (Basile and Germidis [1984]; Spinanger [1984]; Oborne [1986]). Here we are dealing with the second generation of EPFZs. Employment generation is not the prime objective anymore; instead, the aims are acquisition and diffusion of technology and generation of foreign exchange. The closed characteristics of the EPFZ will then have to change, for instance, through the establishment of joint ventures between domestic and foreign firms, the establishment of research and training institutes within the zone, and the development of a system of sub-contracting in order to involve domestic input-supplying firms in EPFZ production. In fact, the second generation of EPFZs shares some characteristics with a so-called science park.

The ongoing upgrading and diversification of the EPFZ-type of export production also provides an argument against those who fear that a generalization of the NIC model of export-oriented development across all developing countries is not feasible because of a threatening saturation of export markets (Cline [1982]; Ranis [1985]). There is a limit to the absorption capacity of the international market and this limit is already believed to have been reached by the present-day NICs. Reality shows, however, that in the course of time the first NICs make room for the second-tier NICs, and there is no reason to believe that this process of continued changes in economies' comparative advantages will end. One caveat should indeed be added. Developing countries that now embark on export-oriented growth may not expect to yield such spectacular results as were achieved by the first NICs. Since the mid-1970s, the world economy has been less buoyant, and protectionism in Western countries is still on the rise.

References

Basile, A. and D. Germidis [1984], *Investing in free export processing zones* (Paris: OECD).

Bradford, C. I., Jr. [1987], 'Trade and Structural Change: NICs and Next Tier NICs as Transitional Economies', *World Development*, vol. 15, no. 3.

Cline, W. R. [1982], 'Can the East Asian Model of Development Be Generalized?', *World Development*, vol. 10, no. 2.

Fei, J. C. H., G. Ranis and S. W. Y. Kuo [1979], *Growth with Equity—The Taiwan Case* (New York: Oxford University Press).

Krugman, P. R. (ed.) [1986], *Stategic Trade Policy and the New International Economics* (Cambridge/London: The MIT Press).

Liempt, G. van [1988], *Bridging the gap: Four newly industrializing countries and the changing international division of labour* (Geneva, ILO).

Oborne, M. [1986], *China's special economic zones* (Paris: OECD).

Ranis, G. [1985], 'Can the East Asian Model of Development Be Generalized?—A Comment', *World Development*, vol. 13, no. 4.

Spinanger, D. [1984], 'Objectives and impact of economic activity zones— some evidence from Asia', *Weltwirtschaftliches Archiv*, vol. 120.

Verbruggen, H. [1987], 'Gains from Export-Oriented Industrialization— With Special Reference to South-East Asia', Part II in: H. Linnemann (ed.), P. van Dijck and H. Verbruggen, *Export-Oriented Industrialization in Developing Countries* (Singapore: Singapore University Press).

World Bank [1987], *World Development Report 1987* (New York: Oxford University Press).

PART 3

The Least Developed Countries

7   The Development Experience of Post-Colonial Sub-Saharan Africa

NELSON P. MOYO
N. AMIN[1]

7.1. Introduction

Starting from a position of reasonably good growth following independence (in the 1960s), Africa's position in the Third World development league has been deteriorating sharply through the seventies and eighties. The 1980s have been an especially serious period for SSA. The continent has become characterized in the 'development' and popular press as the 'poorest of the poor' or the 'Fourth World'. Following this characterization SSA has increasingly been seen as needing special treatment or as requiring special concessions of one kind or another from the international community. Secondly, as growth and development failed and as SSA became more and more debt ridden, the international organizations, notably the IMF and the World Bank, began to give greater attention to Africa, imposing their stabilization and structural adjustment programmes and generally trying to supervise these economies, largely in the interests of international finance capital. The underlying pre-supposition of IMF and World Bank policy recommendations has been the belief that it is the domestic policies of SSA countries and not the external influences caused by changes in the world economy which have been primarily responsible for the economic difficulties of these countries.

We will argue that far from laying the foundations for future development, Fund and Bank stabilization and structural adjustment policies have led to a reversal of development, indeed, to the de-industrialization of some SSA countries. Ironically, the adoption

[1] The authors would like to thank the Conference participants for comments received during discussion and in particular, Dr P. Terhal and Dr L. Berlage for their written contributions.

of these policies has led to more unemployment and increased poverty in the most vulnerable population groups.

While the IMF and World Bank also speak of the African 'crisis' we must be sure that for us the meaning of the term crisis and the corrective action that this implies differs substantially from that of the IMF, the World Bank and its African and Africanist acolytes. For us, the crisis is not only economic, but social and political and is underlined primarily by imperialism which, we contend, has a strong social basis in Africa (namely, the compradorial ruling classes, which have for some time now been reaping the fringe benefits associated with an alliance with imperialism). When the IMF and World Bank talk of the African crisis and proceed to produce policy documents and impose conditions to force 'liberalization' they essentially mean to open the door further to imperialist penetration and to ensconce the African masses deeper into their 'places' within the presently structured international division of labour, first shaped for Africa during the colonial period.

If the international aid-donor agencies do not escape the part they have played in fostering the crisis, what of the African ruling classes and their states? As implied earlier, the latter have been at the forefront of the Bank's criticism. It has to be acknowledged that in the tremendous social upheaval unleashed on the continent over the past few decades, the ruling classes operating the state machinery have not been innocent bystanders. Far from it, their part in aiding and abetting the 'crisis' has been significant, but not in our view for their failure to realign the African economies towards conditions more suitable for international capitalist expansion. Precisely the opposite is the case: African states and the ruling classes have been singularly unable to effect capitalist development which can be truly termed 'national' and have instead been active in nurturing neocolonial links rather than severing them. It is an undeniable fact that most African states, including those espousing socialist paths of development, have not seriously managed to break their neocolonial connections even though some states have attempted to do so in certain periods.

In Africa today the majority of the population is still based in the rural areas and the mass of them are peasants producing commodities for own consumption and for sale. Despite market relations linking independent peasant producers to state and international capital, differentiation of these producers has not developed beyond a certain point. Rich and poor peasants exist but rarely in

Africa are agrarian capitalists and a sizeable rural proletariat to be found. In recent times in Africa, especially since the seventies, it is agricultural production which has been declining. Peasant incomes have consequently dropped and markets for food and other goods have not expanded. In the cities, as old industries close and others remain under-utilized, the expansion of productive wage-employment has come to a halt or even been reversed. But, the service sectors have continued to grow (although less so recently as the IMF/World Bank austerity measures have begun to bite into this sector).

We attempt to develop some of the arguments presented above in the rest of the paper. Section 7.2 provides a very brief outline of colonial rule in sub-Saharan Africa (SSA), the struggle for independence and the character of the state that emerged after decolonization. Section 7.3 describes the pattern and pace of economic growth in SSA during the sixties and seventies. It is suggested that a significant economic decline set in during the seventies in most parts of SSA. This economic decline or 'crisis' has continued into the eighties as we indicate in section 7.4. In section 7.4 our focus turns to a critical examination of the interventionist role of the IMF and the World Bank. We suggest that the take-over of control of economic management from African states by these institutions, while intended to cure the crisis has actually made conditions worse. Section 7.4. also discusses the less well-known Lagos Plan of Action put out by the Organization of African Unity (OAU) again in response to what the latter perceived to be a mounting crisis in Africa. The LPA is discussed for it contrasts in its recommendations with the World Bank's 'Berg' report.[2] Finally in section 7.5, by way of a conclusion, we make an attempt to point a way forward or at least to indicate what form of social change could under the present circumstances herald a way out of the crisis. While no easy solutions or concrete policies are recommended by us, we suggest that both politically and economically, any way out must deal with the primary contradiction facing Africa today, i.e. imperialism.

7.2. Colonialism, the struggle for independence and the post-colonial state

All the countries of SSA were, prior to independence, objects of imperialist exploitation and plunder. Much has been written about

[2] World Bank [1981].

the nature and motives of imperialism. At the beginning the imperialist powers wanted raw materials to feed their home industries and food for their expanding cities. But, as industry and finance grew, capitalists sought new and profitable areas in which to invest their capital. They also wanted markets for their industrial goods. What distinguished the empire-builders of the pre-capitalist era and those of capitalist times is that while the former more or less left the economic basis of their victims intact, the capitalist conquerors were determined to impose great changes on the economic and traditional social systems and cultures of their subject peoples. Thus private property in land was introduced and so was wage labour which was extracted by direct and indirect means. By various devices the colonies were gradually integrated in the capitalist division of labour as producers of raw materials and food for the imperialist centres and as centres for profitable investments.

Before 1880 colonial possessions in Africa were relatively few and limited to some coastal areas. Subsequently, however, the conquerors penetrated further inland and subordinated huge populations. By 1900, almost the entire African continent had been split up into separate territories owned by European nations. Of course, the specific experiences of the colonies differed. Suffice it to say that the colonial experience in Africa had profound effects on Africa's later development. At independence most African states inherited distorted economies characterized by external orientation and sectoral disarticulation. Some critics of the dependence school,[3] have argued that colonial imperialism had some positive effects: it established the conditions of capitalist development whose pace of development, however, was unfortunately held back by the short-comings of the colonial state. According to Warren and his disciples political independence created conditions for the state to play a more decisive and beneficial role in the economy and to advance the development of the forces of production. Has SSA really seen a period of undiluted capitalist expansion and growth as has been claimed by some recent academics? In later sections of this paper we consider the extent to which Warren's thesis holds true for sub-Saharan Africa.

The struggle for independence in Africa was in many ways an outcome of contradictions emerging from late colonial rule itself.

---

[3] For example, Warren [1980] and Sender and Smith [1986].

For while suppression and exploitation of the indigenous peoples had been effectively brought under the control of the colonial state, the imperatives of local-level government increasingly generated the authorities' need for a faithful, supportive class of people from the ranks of the colonized 'natives'.[4] This social stratum, later to gain a political cohesion and an ideology of rebellion, was composed of petty traders, small shopkeepers, religious converts or servile pastors, landowners and most notably, obliging chiefs or chiefly clans. The new middle class increasingly came to mediate between state and people, the rulers and the ruled.

Africanist academics and intellectuals in Africa and in the USA sought to challenge the hitherto colonially dominated science about the 'African Man', his 'Culture', or the lack of it, his 'History', his 'Kingdoms' and so on. While there was a general celebration that Africans indeed possessed a history which was not only that of colonialism, there emerged some consensus that the future lay in 'Nation-building'. However, as commentators of this notion have recently pointed out,

. . . by nation-building . . . they (the Africanists) meant no more than state-building, and at that really the building of strong bourgeoisies on the continent . . . [and] . . . in practice . . . understood as a project to be realized in partnership with the erstwhile imperial powers![5]

The adoption of 'modernization' as a programme and an ideology to be pursued by the nationalists when they came to power after independence provided the ideal point of contact between them and the 'Africanists'. The modernization perspective gave the nationalists then (i.e. after independence) and to this very day, albeit in a much changed form, the philosophical basis for establishing a strong state which was to oversee the transition (take-off) from a traditional (backward) society to a modern (capitalist) one. In effecting this transition, the precepts of modernization theory held, the state had to contain popular uprisings which called for more democracy and for a reduction in inequalities. The latter type of politics were a luxury which backward countries could ill-afford to entertain.[6]

---

[4] For further details refer to Freund [1984] and Sandbrook [1985] among others.

[5] Mamdani et al. [1988:2].

[6] For a detailed elaboration on the ideology of 'developmentalism' see Shivji [1988a].

As Mamdani *et al.* have recently pointed out, the ideology of modernization which,

. . had begun as an attempt to explain change in the Third World turned into a recipe for how to contain change [and] through its confrontation with reality and through its internal changes, the modernization theory had produced a 'pedagogy of the oppressed'.[7]

More recently of course modernization theory has undergone a transformation. For whereas in the sixties 'strong states' and 'modernizing elites' were seen in Africa to be the social agents of transformation in cahoots with international finance capital, the African political, social and economic crisis materializing over the last three decades has produced a crisis of confidence in the ability of the state and the ruling classes to effect the desired transformation.

The brunt of the blame for three decades of development failure, it is argued, must now be borne by the state and the ruling classes which have been far too preoccupied with fighting factional wars, mostly of a tribal nature. If peace and order had not been established by the African ruling elite in the sphere of politics—for coups continued—neither had the conditions for successful capitalist growth been laid. By the latter, namely the absence of conditions amenable for the expansion of capitalism, what is generally meant is the government crowding out of private entrepreneurship, the endemic administrative inefficiency of African governments and the mismanagement of domestic and external economic policies.[8] African states have therefore 'failed to deliver the goods' and in the present era the imperialist powers (through the so-called multi-lateral organizations—IMF, IBRD, OECD, EEC) are desperately in search of new alliances (outside the state) in Africa. But first African state power has to be undermined and this is precisely the mission being accomplished under the guise of 'structural adjustment'.[9]

The dismal economic record of the post-independence period cannot in our view be fully grasped in abstraction of the following:

1. the colonial legacy and the historical shaping of Africans and African social formations in the world division of labour;
2. that de-colonization left colonial administrative structures and the state relatively untouched;

---

[7] Mamdani *et al.*[1988].   [8] World Bank [1981].
[9] See World Bank [1981]; and for a critical review of World Bank policies with regard to Africa see IDS Bulletins [1983, 1985, 1986].

3. that unlike other neocolonies, in most of SSA an indigenous bourgeoisie was at independence weak and undeveloped;
4. that modernization theory formulated and re-formulated in the halcyon days of the fifties and early sixties provided theoretical space and ideological justification. for a state-led, foreign-backed, economic take-off;
5. that in most of Africa the post-colonial state has been an instrument used to consecrate power, be it exercised by a military authority group, party, nationality, or person. A swelling state has without exception been used to pave the way for the ruling classes and monopoly capital to accumulate such that an important aspect of the national question—the right to economic self determination—and the social question—democracy—remain to this day unsolved;
6. that while independence brought an end to direct imperial rule, it did not usher in an epoch which changed in substance the fundamental connections between the ex-colonies and their erstwhile rulers. The form had changed, the content had not. As Sandbrook remarks:

The weak legitimacy of African governments is further undermined by the manifest and abject dependence of various strongmen upon foreign patrons who play the tune to which the leaders dance. Neither reform nor popular change of a regime is attainable if foreign powers manipulate events to suit corrupt and despotic leaders. Clandestine campaigns to replace rulers who incur the displeasure of the imperialists ignite factional and violent conflict, exacerbate political instability and corrupt new layers of aspirant politicians. Capitalism thus assumes a particularly repressive and unstable cast in Africa and the masses sink deeper into cynicism and despair.[10]

If this passage describes the situation of many Third World countries it is even more true of Africa. We turn now to examine the economic record.

7.3. From political downturn to economic downturn: the sixties and seventies

This section of the paper traces the economic record of development in SSA through the independence period to the late seventies. Both the extensive coverage of the economic experience of SSA

[10] Sandbrook [1985:111].

countries and the time period, namely two decades, impose a strict constraint on the type of analysis that can be offered in this paper. The exercise is therefore a limited one, to trace in very broad and general terms the economic trends and tendencies. Moreover, our assessment of this period is based on selective economic criteria owing to the limitations of space. Additionally, it should be noted that we have chosen to treat SSA as if it were an economic unity and some data presented relate to the entire group of countries south of the Sahara (excluding South Africa). It must be stressed, lest we are misinterpreted, that this procedure has been adopted in order to bring out the dominant features and tendencies of SSA economies and not to thereby deny the real differences which exist between them.

While the seventies and eighties have been highlighted to be the period of Africa's crisis, the sixties, for several SSA countries appear to have been a period of relative stability and some growth.[11] Figures for per capita GNP growth for low income and middle income SSA countries are provided in Table 7.1 which shows quite clearly that growth in the sixties, although well below 2 per cent per annum, was considerably better than that achieved during the seventies when annual rates, particularly in the group of low income countries, declined drastically. Annual growth rates in GDP for SSA were similarly much higher in the sixties than during the seventies when rates had dropped to 1.6 per cent from being 3.9 per cent in the previous decade.[12] Further aspects of the worsening economic situation during the seventies are examined below.

Given the importance of agriculture in the economies of most SSA countries it is important to examine the performance of that sector in the period being considered. Table 7.2 shows that in the sixties, by comparison with other Third World regions, Africa as a whole recorded moderately better rates of growth in per capita food production and that while total food production increased from the rate witnessed over the previous decade (i.e. the 1950s), the gain was tempered by rising population growth rates in the sixties.

[11] Although, in comparison to other areas of the world, per capita GNP growth for SSA was lower in the 1960s. Average per capita incomes in SSA exceeded only those in South Asia between 1960 and 1980 but remained consistently below levels in East Asia, Middle East, North Africa and Latin America.

[12] In the eighties, we note that economic decline had worsened, for between 1980 and 1985, GDP growth for SSA was −0.7 per cent per annum.

TABLE 7.1: *GNP per capita and GDP-average annual growth rates in sub-Saharan Africa*
(per cent)

	Annual Average GNP per Capita		Annual GDP Growth	
	1960–70	1970–80	1960–70	1970–79
SSA[a]	1.3	0.8[b]	3.9	1.6[c]
of which:				
low-income	1.6	0.2[d]	--	--
middle-income	1.7	2.1[e]	--	--

Source: Adapted from World Bank Reports [1980, 1981 and 1987]
Notes: [a] Sub-Saharan Africa excluding South Africa
    [b] Pertains to period 1970–79
    [c] Excluding Nigeria
    [d] The Berg report stated an average growth rate of -0.3% for this period, 1970–79; this difference in estimate may be due to a weighting difference or due to differences in country classification
    [e] Excluding Nigeria, the growth rate for this group would be 1.5%; Nigeria's growth rate for the period 1970–79 was 4.2%

TABLE 7.2: *Annual growth rate of food production, total and per capita*
(per cent)

	1952–62		1961–70		1970–78	
	total	per capita	total	per capita	total	per capita
World	3.1	1.1	2.9	0.9	2.5	0.8
Developed market economies	2.5	1.3	2.6	1.5	2.2	1.3
Western Europe & USSR	4.5	3.0	3.8	2.7	2.6	1.8
Developing market economies	3.1	0.7	2.8	0.2	2.7	0.4
Latin America	3.2	0.4	3.1	0.2	3.0	0.2
Asia	3.1	0.8	2.6	0.1	2.7	0.1
Africa	2.2	0.0	2.9	0.4	1.4	-1.3

Source: Adapted from Gakou [1987:4]

However, in the seventies, we notice a severe deterioration in Africa's food production capacity. Not only did the rate of output decline in that period, but more seriously, per capita production rates fell between the sixties and seventies from 0.4 per cent per annum to −1.3 per cent per annum. Africa was the only region to have experienced a dramatic decline in annual growth rates in per capita food production. During the seventies out of 39 SSA countries for which data are available, 27 experienced negative annual rates of growth in per capita food production,[13] of which 20 countries showed declines of 1 per cent per annum or more. Further corroboration of the decline of agriculture in SSA during the seventies is obtained from an examination of absolute and relative indices of yields for major food and non food crops (see Table 7.3).

The severity of this decline for the African countries and more so for the majority of its inhabitants can only be grasped by an appreciation of the place occupied by agriculture in these economies. In most SSA countries more than 70 per cent of the population derive (or attempt to derive) a livelihood from agriculture. The share of agriculture in GDP has declined over the seventies due to the rising importance of the so called 'industrial and service sectors'. However, the contribution of agriculture to GDP for all SSA countries is still significant: thus while in 1960 agriculture accounted for 49 per cent of GDP, in 1979 its share was down to 32 per cent, and 34 per cent in 1985. The dominance of agriculture in many economies of Third World countries, but especially in SSA, has meant that the aggregate performance of that sector determines to a large extent the overall success of the economy. During the seventies the growth of per capita agricultural production actually declined.[14] Thus in such a situation a crisis in agriculture would very quickly translate into a national economic crisis.

That indeed has been the hallmark of economic development in Africa over the past few decades, but especially since the 1970s. The malaise in agriculture has spread into other spheres.

Retrogression in agriculture and declining per capita growth rates for food and non-food commodities has of course led to a

[13] World Bank [1981:167].

[14] For SSA, the World Bank estimate for the period 1969/71 to 1977/79 for the average annual per capita growth rate of total agricultural production was −1.4 per cent, thus also indicating that the poor performance in agriculture applied to both food and non-food sectors (World Bank [1981]).

TABLE 7.3: *Yields of principal crops in sub-Saharan Africa*
(per cent)

| | index of yields (1961–63 = 100) | | index of relative yields (world = 100) | | |
	1969–71	1977–79	1961–63	1969–71	1977–79
cocoa					
world	121	121	100	100	100
d'ing c	121	120	100	100	100
SSA	124	108	94	97	84
coffee					
world	108	112	100	100	100
d'ing c	108	113	100	100	100
SSA	112	97	83	86	71
tea					
world	96	102	100	100	100
d'ing c	116	142	101	122	140
SSA	148	159	90	139	141
maize					
world	120	144	100	100	100
d'ing c	115	126	56	54	49
SSA	114	109	42	40	32
millet					
world	110	113	100	100	100
d'ing c	109	108	94	93	89
SSA	98	94	107	95	88
sorghum					
world	121	145	100	100	100
d'ing c	115	151	70	67	73
SSA	92	93	82	63	53
wheat					
world	129	151	100	100	100
d'ing c	120	145	85	78	81
SSA	160	138	67	82	61
groundnuts					
world	106	112	100	100	100
d'ing c	102	107	94	91	90
SSA	93	96	95	84	81
seed cotton					
world	116	132	100	100	100
d'ing c	119	127	72	74	69
SSA	133	124	46	53	43

Source: Adapted from World Bank [1981:169]
Note: d'ing c = developing countries

rising volume of agricultural imports. For example for SSA, cereal imports in the sixties and seventies rose to 9.0–9.5 per cent per annum. This trend in SSA, of a rising dependence on imported staple food, whether achieved through commercial means or through aid measures, does not appear to be slowing down. Indeed, between 1976/77 and 1986/87 the FAO have estimated that Africa's (North and SSA) total cereal imports rose from 13.7 million tons to 27.2 million tons.[15]

Yet another indication of the dependence of Africa on imported food can be seen from Table 7.4 which shows that low income countries of Africa received the highest amount of food aid in cereals during the period 1979/81 and 1985/87. Thus, currently Africa appears to be absorbing between 45 and 50 per cent of the world shipments of food aid with no obvious signs that this dependency is likely to decrease in the near future. Rather, most expectations are that it will increase given the continued balance of payments problems faced by many African countries and the willingness of the USA and the EEC to conduct their cereal trade through non-open market channels, which has the additional advantage in that their economic and political leverage on African countries is increased.

TABLE 7.4:   *Distribution of food aid in cereals*

Receiving regions	1979–81	1982–4	1985–7
	(Million tons grain equivalent)		
1. Low-income food deficit countries[a]	7.2	8.7	9.7
of which:			
Africa	4.2	5.5	5.6
Asia	2.6	2.7	3.2
2. Other developing countries	1.4	1.4	1.6
3. Other countries	0.3	0.06	0.01
4. World[b]	9.0	10.5	11.4

Source: Adopted from FAO,'Food Outlook' [1987]

Notes: [a] Includes all food deficit countries with per capita income below the level used by the World Bank to determine eligibility for IDA assistance (i.e.US $835 in 1986), which in accordance with the guidelines and criteria agreed by the CFA should be given priority in the allocation of food aid

[b] Totals do not add due to rounding

[15] FAO [1987].

A further aspect of the African economies which deserves mentioning, however briefly, for it is common knowledge nowadays, is their acute dependency on the export of primary commodities—agricultural and/or mineral. In most African countries export trade has been heavily reliant on the exports of two or three commodities and in fact, over the past few decades the three commodity concentration in total exports for all SSA countries actually increased.[16]

Further features of the export trade structures and their developments for most SSA countries over the sixties and seventies are described below.

1. The trade patterns determined in the colonial period remained to a large extent unchanged in the post-colonial period, i.e. the economies remained reliant on exporting primary commodities.

2. As already seen above, the share of three principal exports in total exports for the majority of SSA countries increased during the seventies implying therefore an increased dependence on the sale of commodities to the world market in which prices are not only highly volatile but prone to secular decline relative to the price of manufactured goods.

3. The destination of exports revealed no marked shift away from markets established during the colonial period.

4. The barter and income terms of trade while having improved in the sixties deteriorated sharply during the seventies for many SSA countries (see Table 7.5). Indeed for several of them annual growth rates in the net barter terms of trade during the seventies were negative particularly for the low income countries. For 12 out of 20 SSA countries, the annual growth in terms of trade during the seventies was actually negative.[17] This downward trend was most marked for the mineral exporters (−7.1 per cent per annum between 1970 and 1979). However, it should be mentioned that a number of SSA countries exporting fuel and other primary commodities did experience some improvement

[16] See World Bank [1981:156]. It should be noted that this aggregate shift in the export concentration for SSA as a whole conceals a number of changes in the pattern of exports for a range of countries: thus, between 1961 and 1976/78, in 16 out of 39 SSA countries the three commodity share of the total exports declined, indicating therefore some diversification. However, for the other 23 countries the shares actually increased over the same period suggesting more dependence on the export earnings of the three principal commodities—most of which are agricultural or mineral in nature (ibid.).

[17] See World Bank [1981].

TABLE 7.5:   *Terms of trade—average annual growth rate*

| | Average annual growth rate of: | | | |
| | Net Barter Terms of Trade (%) | | Income Terms of Trade (%) | |
	1961–70	1970–79	1961–70	1970–79
Low-income countries	**0.9**	**0.8**	**5.1**	**−0.8**
low-income semi-arid	**−0.1**	**−1.3**	**4.8**	**3.0**
1. Chad	−1.0	1.6	2.9	−1.7
2. Somalia	−1.6	−2.7	0.5	2.2
3. Mali	7.0	−0.6	4.5	5.7
4. Upper Volta	3.5	−1.3	15.6	6.2
5. Gambia	−0.1	−1.3	5.4	3.0
6. Niger	0.5	−2.2	4.8	9.0
7. Mauritania	−2.1	−5.2	38.5	−6.1
low-income other	**0.8**	**0.7**	**5.5**	**−1.3**
8. Ethiopia	0.5	2.4	3.3	−0.7
9. Guinea-Bissau	--	--	--	--
10. Burundi	−0.2	−0.9	4.7	−19.0
11. Malawi	−3.0	−0.5	7.9	3.5
12. Rwanda	0.8	6.3	15.1	7.2
13. Benin	1.2	−2.8	8.7	−14.5
14. Mozambique	--	--	--	--
15. Sierra Leone	1.5	−1.6	2.4	−6.6
16. Tanzania	0.2	0.7	3.8	−4.4
17. Zaire	7.7	−7.8	7.2	−8.7
18. Guinea	--	--	--	--
19. Central African Rep.	0.9	1.3	8.0	1.1
20. Madagascar	−0.3	−0.9	4.1	−1.3
21. Uganda	1.3	3.1	5.5	−0.8
22. Lesotho	--	--	--	--
23. Togo	2.2	9.0	11.3	6.0
24. Sudan	0.8	1.4	2.1	−2.8
Middle-income oil importers	**1.6**	**2.6**	**6.4**	**0.6**
25. Kenya	−1.6	2.2	4.8	0.9
26. Ghana	2.3	6.9	1.5	−0.8
27. Senegal	1.3	1.4	1.3	0.2
28. Zimbabwe	--	--	--	--
29. Liberia	−4.7	−4.1	12.6	−2.2
30. Zambia	10.0	−9.0	12.3	−9.7
31. Cameroon	1.9	6.1	8.0	6.7
32. Swaziland	--	--	--	--
33. Botswana	--	--	--	--
34. Mauritius	−3.3	3.7	−1.6	8.6
35. Ivory Coast	2.0	3.0	9.2	8.2
Middle-income oil exporters	**1.0**	**12.9**	**17.0**	**12.8**
36. Angola	1.7	8.5	10.2	0.3
37. Congo	0.1	1.0	2.5	8.6
38. Nigeria	1.0	17.2	7.0	16.9
39. Gabon	1.0	17.2	7.0	17.0
Sub-Saharan Africa	**0.9**	**1.2**	**5.5**	**0.6**

Source: Adapted from World Bank [1981:155]

in terms of trade.[18] In part these gains were due to the 1976–78 commodity price boom. But in general as is well known, world market prices for the main export commodities of SSA declined fairly substantially reducing the purchasing power of many countries.

5. The annual growth in export volume of the whole of SSA fell quite dramatically in the seventies.[19]

6. The continent's share of non-fuel world trade, not surprisingly then, fell from 3.1 per cent in 1960 to 1.2 per cent in 1978. Moreover, Africa's share of developing countries non-fuel exports between 1960 and 1978 declined from 18 to 9.2 per cent respectively.

7. Finally, all of the above, i.e. 1 to 6 occurred under conditions of increased trade protection in advanced capitalist countries. Falling export volumes, declining commodity prices and adverse terms of trade accompanied by rising food imports, mounting external debts and a huge balance of payments deficit are all characteristics which together come to constitute 'Africa's macro-economic crisis' which we argue culminated to an acute point in the seventies. As we have already implied, the balance of payment deficits of SSA countries were primarily due, on the one hand, to falling export volumes and declining commodity prices in world markets as the demand for primary commodities in the advanced capitalist countries fell during the recessionary years, and on the other hand, to rising oil prices which in the seventies affected Third World oil-importing countries the most.

Table 7.6 shows how significant the deficit in the current account had become by 1980 in the oil-importing African countries. Furthermore, Table 7.7 shows that the deficit was heavily financed by official external aid flows. The rising burden of external debt on the economies of sub-Saharan African countries between 1970 and the mid-eighties is amply demonstrated in Table 7.7 which shows that the external public (official) debt burden of SSA countries expressed in terms of GNP and exports had by 1985 come to approximate the burden experienced by the group of the so-called

[18] Of the non-fuel exporters, positive shifts were experienced by Cameroon, Ghana, Kenya, Uganda, Rwanda, Ethiopia, and Chad (see Table 7.5).

[19] In fact, compared to the sixties for 19 out of 29 SSA countries (i.e. 65 per cent) the growth rate of the volume of exports was negative during the seventies (see World Bank [1981:157]).

TABLE 7.6: *Oil-importing African countries: current account deficit and its financing*
(billions of dollars, 1978)

Item	1970	1973	1975	1978	1980
Current account deficit[a]	1.5	1.9	6.4	6.6	8.0
Financed by:					
1. net capital flows:					
Official Development					
Assistance (ODA)	1.6	2.1	3.2	3.2	4.3
commercial loans	0.8	1.1	1.9	1.9	2.1
2. change in reserves &					
short-term borrowing[b]	−1.4	−1.7	1.0	1.1	1.3
Current account deficit					
as % of GDP	2.4	3.6	9.5	8.8	9.2
ODA as % of GDP	2.7	3.9	4.7	4.4	5.0

Source: World Bank [1981:17]
Notes: [a] Excluding from current accounts net official transfers (grants), which are included in capital flows
[b] A minus sign indicates an increase in reserves

TABLE 7.7: *Debt service ratios of developing countries*

	Debt service as percentage of:			
	GNP		exports of goods and services	
	1970	1985	1970	1985
Developing economies	1.5	4.3	11.2	19.7
Oil exporters	1.7	5.9	12.6	25.6
Exporters of manufactures	1.2	2.7	11.8	13.6
Highly indebted countries	1.6	5.1	12.4	27.8
Sub-Saharan Africa	1.2	4.8	5.3	21.5

Source: Adapted from World Bank [1987:239]

'highly indebted countries' (mainly from Latin America). The significance of the debt crisis in SSA becomes more apparent when one bears in mind that many of the SSA countries are by most international standards the poorest of the group of Third World countries and moreover, that their capacity to finance these huge debts has since 1970 been progressively deteriorating.

The above review of broad economic trends in SSA indicates two phases of growth: an upward trend during the sixties when both agricultural and manufacturing sector output was increasing, and a downward trend in the seventies when several indicators point towards economic stagnation and, in many instances, to a general economic decline. Of course it must be acknowledged that experiences in individual countries differed in degree and complexity within this broad characterization. Thus, in some countries the downturn came earlier or in some later, but regardless of the precise timing, or the actual severity of the economic downturn, in our view the universal characterization we present above for SSA as a whole still holds.

Further to the above account on the economic record of SSA we must add that in Africa too, since the sixties, following the Latin American experiences of the fifties and sixties, Import-Substituting Industrialization (ISI) also acquired considerable significance. In Africa state-assisted ISI over the past two decades could be argued to have brought considerable benefits when judged in terms of conventional economic indicators, as Sender and Smith[20] have recently attempted to show. On the issue of state intervention it has been argued by the same authors that in post-colonial SSA, a favourable climate for investment and accumulation was created. The forms of intervention included the

expanded provision of credit; legislation to reverse colonial discrimination and provide privileged access for Africans to certain avenues of accumulation; nationalization and direct state production; measures to control and influence the pattern of both foreign and domestic private investment—fiscal incentives, tariffs, foreign-exchange licensing and preferential allocation systems; and the provision of transport, energy and irrigation infrastructure, frequently financed by means of expanded access to concessional capital inflows from abroad.[21]

While we have no disagreement with Sender and Smith's 'list of interventions' by which states attempted to promote industrialization in SSA, we do not share their conclusion that these measures actually did lead to a period of rapid capitalist growth[22] during

[20] Sender J. and S. Smith [1986].
[21] Ibid.
[22] Two excellent reviews of Sender and Smith's book are by Bernstein [1987] and Mkandawire [1987]. Both come to a similar conclusion that Sender and Smith wildly exaggerate the positive impact of imperialism in Africa.

which it could be suggested that a firm industrial base was laid in Africa.

An examination of the record of industrialization in SSA indeed reveals a pattern of performance which is not too dissimilar to that already charted above with respect to agriculture, GDP growth, trade, etc. The 1978 World Bank report stated that in spite of 'widespread attempts to force the pace of industrialization . . . the results . . . have generally been unsatisfactory'.[23]

In the early sixties despite the difficulties faced by Latin American countries with large-scale Import-Substituting Industrialization (ISI) several African countries (e.g. Zambia, Kenya, Ghana, Nigeria) proceeded on similar lines of development. Among many such countries ISI became highly popular and even though constraints of a severe lack of trained manpower, of undeveloped indigenous technological capacities and of small domestic markets would have made it plain enough that large-scale industrialization would later only lead to a creation of a large number of 'white elephants', the programme of industrial development went ahead usually in partnership with foreign based multinationals. For Africa as a whole, the proportion of manufactured value added in GDP has remained relatively insignificant even though much policy effort has been directed towards its promotion. In 1976, the proportion of GDP accounted for by manufactured value added for the whole of Africa was less than 8 per cent in 19 countries, 8–12 per cent in 10 countries, 12–15 per cent in 8 countries and more than 15 per cent in 6 countries (Egypt, Ivory Coast, Kenya, Mauritius, Zimbabwe and Swaziland).[24] Moreover, Africa's share in world manufacturing value added (MVA), rose from 0.7 per cent in 1960 to 0.8 per cent in 1975 and to 1 per cent in 1982.[25] As one might expect, equally unimpressive was Africa's contribution to the world exports of manufactures, for the share between 1970/71 and 1975/76 declined from 1.12 to 0.6 per cent. Although these growth figures indicate that levels of industrialization in Africa remain low in comparison to other areas, it is necessary to focus on the character of industrial development in order to obtain a fuller appreciation of this aspect.

The most notable feature of African industrialization achieved over the past few decades is that its structure is relatively undiversified. The manufacture of consumer goods dominates over the

---

[23] Quoted in Fransman [1982:1].
[24] See Fransman [1982] chapter 20 by UNIDO.   [25] UNIDO [1983].

production of intermediate goods and capital goods. Over the past 25 years even with respect to the consumer goods sector, it is food processing, beverages, tobacco products and textiles which account for a large part of industrial production.[26] Furthermore as a United Nations report indicated, a large proportion of the food processing and beverage industries are dominated in Africa as in other Third World countries by foreign multinationals.[27] Thus, though the desire to industrialize has been particularly high in the planning agendas of many African countries, performances over the last two decades have been poor. But it needs stating that some countries between 1970 and 1976 did succeed in having fairly high growth rates in manufactured valued added; 8 SSA countries had achieved rates of growth of between 5 and 10 per cent in this period and some others (7 countries) had more than 10 per cent (Botswana, Congo, Gabon, Mauritius, Nigeria and Swaziland). However, as mentioned above, growth rates alone provide insufficient information either about the type of industrial development or about the pattern of wage employment.

Reviews of industrialization in Africa and other Third World countries indicate that high prices of domestically produced goods and the existence of low wages throughout the economy combine to limit the size of the market and lead to the under-utilization of capacity. Secondly, a high import dependence coupled with multinational control over industry and trade serve to further limit the size of the market (i.e. high import prices leading to high product prices) as well as contribute to the foreign exchange drain since, in addition, foreign companies export profits out of the countries by means of transfer pricing. In a recent comprehensive survey of ISI, Nixson summarized his conclusions as follows:

ISI has not, in practice, significantly alleviated the balance-of-payments constraint; it has led to a growing dependence on a largely imported, capital-intensive technology and has thus not created extensive employment opportunities or indigenous technological development; the process has been heavily dependent on foreign capital and has emphasized the establishment of consumer goods industries at the expense of investment and capital goods industries; it has led to what many would regard as an undesirable redistribution of income and in general it has failed to generate a sustained process of economic growth.[28]

[26] For further details see Fransman [1982] and Barker *et al.* [1986].
[27] UNCTAD [1979].   [28] Nixson [1982:49].

We would add that the same could be said of the export-oriented phase of industrialization which occurred mainly in the seventies in Africa, except of course this phase has in individual countries (e.g. Ivory Coast) made some contribution to alleviating balance-of-payments difficulties. Problems besieging African industrialization essentially boil down to the following points:

1. that development patterns begun during the colonial period have not been decisively broken, so consumer goods production (but not for mass consumption) dominates;
2. that the capital required for industry has been provided mainly by foreign investors; and
3. that 'industrial growth in the Third World has often been characterized by the absence of a bourgeoisie and the absence of a proletariat'.[29]

Our review of the economic record in SSA since the period of independence up to the eighties shows that for many countries an economic deterioration of a substantial nature set in during the seventies. Various kinds of internal and external factors have been mentioned as contributing to this situation, although so far not in any great detail. We will discuss this at some length in the next section. Here we need to stress that though the economic situation in SSA has been observed to worsen during the post-independence period we should take note of the fact that the economies inherited from the colonials were themselves structurally very weak. Put into this context the crisis assumes a different significance for post-colonial governments introduced very few radical structural changes. In fact the later governments built upon and expanded the colonially inherited structures, practices and relationships (notably the external ones). The origins of the contemporary crisis, which as we have noted has manifested itself primarily as an agrarian crisis, are rooted in the colonial period itself. It is only now that the contradictions are coming to acquire such a severe expression. One example relating to agriculture can be cited to illustrate this point.

Agricultural marketing boards have recently been the subject of much criticism for their role in oppressing the peasantry and more generally in contributing to the poor agricultural performance in SSA.[30] State monopoly control of agricultural output marketing in

---

[29] R. B. Sutcliffe quoted in Barker *et al.* [1986:6].
[30] See especially Bates [1981] and World Bank [1981].

the form of 'marketing boards' was, however, a colonial creation. The colonial state intervened particularly in the depression years of the 1930s to control competition and to guarantee to even the least efficient producers a cost plus pricing system.[31] Later, during and after the Second World War, this monopoly intervention came to be institutionalized in the form of state marketing boards which acquired the right to set prices for both growers and intermediaries. In the forties, state power was used to ensure high profits for foreign-controlled marketing sectors and to extract huge surpluses from the producers. Monopoly rents earned by foreign traders and the state marketing boards thus led to a tremendous squeezing of the peasantry which simultaneously inhibited the development of the productive forces in agriculture and blocked the emergence of an indigenous merchant class.

The state, in the marketing board mechanism, now had additional means to extract surplus from the direct producer, thus further reinforcing the fact that the most certain source of personal enrichment must be through the capture of state power and the monopoly rents that went with it rather than through the actual expansion of the forces of production.[32]

In coming to power the nationalist governments in Africa nationalized the state marketing corporations and continued to operate them on much the same lines as their predecessors had done, albeit under a new ideology of 'development', 'planning' and/or 'socialism'. But the effect on the peasantry was the same. The new ideologies could not change the logic or content of the state apparatus which had been undemocratically constituted. As Brett says,

Having begun as an agency captured from the colonialists on behalf of the nation, it (the state marketing board) had come to be seen as a mechanism for the extraction of surpluses from many for allocation to an increasingly favoured few.[33]

7.4 Growing indebtedness, recession and the increasing role of international organizations in SSA during the 1980s

This period in Africa's development history has been marked by an unprecedented rise in external indebtedness. But secondly, as the major creditors became increasingly worried about whether they would get their money back, leading international organizations—

---

[31] Mamdani [1976].   [32] Brett [1986:24].   [33] Ibid.

the IMF and the World Bank—stepped up their activities in Africa with their stabilization and structural adjustment programmes. What has been the impact of these programmes? Have they helped African economies? These and other questions are examined in this section.

During the 1980s Africa's social and economic crisis has intensified. It is shown by the great suffering of the working classes and the peasantry, by the generally poor state of Africa's economies and by the falling living standards of most Africans. Poverty, unemployment and social and economic inequality have been on the increase. To date no effective world policies have been devised to improve, let alone reverse, the situation. The signs are that the social and economic conditions of Africa will worsen in the years to come.

While developing countries as a whole experienced growth in their gross domestic product, averaging about 3.3 per cent between 1980 and 1985, SSA experienced a fall in GDP over the same period. When Africa's rapidly growing population is taken into account, living standards for most people have fallen sharply. GDP per capita is estimated to have fallen by an average of 3.4 per cent per annum between 1980 and 1986.[34] The average figures of GDP growth and GDP per capita of course mask the highly unequal income distributions in most SSA countries. The little evidence that is available suggests that in some countries as much as 60 per cent of income goes to the richest 20 per cent of households while the poorest 20 per cent receive only 3 per cent of income. Chronic unemployment contributes to this maldistribution of income: about half of SSA's working age population is either unemployed or underemployed.[35]

The collapse in the growth rate of most African countries has been accompanied by a sharp rise in their external indebtedness. The external debt position of the 44 SSA countries which are members of the IMF deteriorated sharply relative to other developing country groups experiencing debt-servicing problems. The rise in the region's debt-service ratio was also substantially higher. IMF estimates of SSA's external debt for the period 1976–87 (Table 7.8) show that the absolute value of debt in 1987[36] was more

---

[34] Harris [1987].   [35] Davies and Moyo [1988:63].

[36] The estimate of Fund credit was $7 billion while external payments arrears amounted to roughly $11 billion. About 24 countries had to seek rescheduling of their debt between 1980 and 1987—four of them repeated schedulings 5 or more times (IMF [1988]).

TABLE 7.8: *Sub-Saharan Africa: external debt outstanding*

	1976	1980	1981	1982	1983	1984	1985	1986	1987
Sub-Saharan Africa[b]									
Total debt[a]	**21.1**	**57.5**	**68.1**	**80.2**	**90.6**	**93.4**	**106.6**	**122.4**	**137.8**
Medium-and long-term[a]	18.4	45.6	53.2	59.0	65.3	69.1	79.5	97.2	111.8
Publicly guaranteed[a]	16.9	41.9	48.3	53.6	60.0	64.0	74.1	91.7	106.0
of which (% share)									
multilateral[c]	20	21	21	22	23	24	23	23	24
bilateral[d]	48	43	44	46	46	48	49	51	51
institutions[e]	20	28	29	25	24	21	19	19	18
other[f]	12	8	6	6	8	8	8	7	7
Nonpublicly guaranteed[a]	1.5	3.7	4.9	5.4	5.3	5.1	5.4	5.5	5.8
Short-term[a]	1.7	6.1	7.0	9.5	10.8	9.6	9.9	7.2	8.0
Outstanding use of fund credit[a]	1.0	2.0	3.4	4.0	5.1	5.3	6.0	6.4	7.1
Arrears[a]	--	3.8	4.5	7.7	9.5	9.4	11.2	11.6	10.9
Number of countries	--	19	24	25	27	26	26	27	23

Contd.

Table 7.8 (*Contd.*)

	1976	1980	1981	1982	1983	1984	1985	1986	1987
Total debt of market borrowers[a]	4.2	16.3	20.5	26.4	34.1	34.2	37.6	43.8	48.1
Total debt of official borrowers[a]	13.7	31.2	36.2	40.9	41.6	43.5	51.0	58.8	68.4
Total debt of other borrowers[a]	3.2	10.0	11.4	13.0	14.9	15.7	18.0	19.9	21.3

Source: Adapted from IMF Survey [June 1988:183]

Notes: [a] billion US dollars
      [b] Including Nigeria
      [c] Loans and credits from the World Bank, regional development banks, and other multilateral and intergovernmental agencies
      [d] Loans from governments and their agencies (including central banks) and loans from autonomous public bodies
      [e] Loans from private banks and other private financial institutions and publicly issued and privately placed bonds
      [f] Suppliers' credits, external liabilities on account of nationalized properties and unclassified debt to private creditors

TABLE 7.9: *Developing countries: debt and debt service ratios, 1980–86*
(in percentage of exports of goods and services)

	1980	1981	1982	1983	1984	1985	1986
Total debt	**634**	**478**	**849**	**900**	**949**	**1012**	**1100**
(in billions of US $)							
Debt ratio	82	95	120	134	134	148	169
By region							
Africa	92	119	154	170	170	185	231
Asia	72	75	88	94	89	101	100
Europe	127	137	147	150	145	162	172
Middle East	27	33	46	60	70	82	123
Western hemisphere	183	210	273	292	277	293	349
Debt service ratio	13	16	20	19	20	22	25
By region							
Africa	15	18	22	25	27	28	35
Asia	9	10	12	12	12	13	14
Europe	21	25	26	24	25	28	30
Middle East	4	5	7	8	10	11	16
Western hemisphere	34	42	51	46	41	43	50

Source: IMF Annual Report [1987]

than six and a half times its 1976 level. For those countries that have had to borrow from the open market, the comparable figure was eleven and a half times. Africa's external debt has undergone major changes in structure: the concessionary component has fallen substantially and the use of Fund credit has risen considerably despite the very onerous conditions attached to such loans.[37]

Table 7.9 shows the total value of external debt of developing countries since 1980. For the African region, the ratio of debt to exports of goods and services was 231 per cent in 1986 compared to 92 per cent in 1980. The debt-service ratio jumped from 15 per cent in 1980 to 35 per cent in 1986. These average figures, however, hide the seriousness of debt burdens in some individual countries.[38]

In a recent statement the South Commission identified the following causal factors in the debt crisis of developing countries:

[37] With effect from May 1988 five SSA countries—Liberia, Sierra-Leone, Somalia, Sudan and Zambia—were declared ineligible to use the general resources of the IMF owing to their failure to meet their obligations to the Fund.

[38] South Commission [1988].

1. over-lending by banks until 1981 and sudden withdrawal of bank credit thereafter;
2. an extremely hostile international environment characterized by sluggishness of world trade;
3. an unprecedented fall in commodity prices and abnormally high rates of interest in the international capital markets; and
4. defective economic policies in some debtor countries.

7.4.1. *External versus domestic causes*

An issue which has come up in the recent debate is the relative contribution of external factors (such as the two oil price shocks and the world recession) and that of domestic policies to Africa's economic malaise. For example the World Bank in its 1981 report—the 'Berg Report'—was firm in its judgement that domestic policies were at the heart of the crisis. It focused on over-valued exchange rates, price distortions, costly industrialization and the 'over-extension' of government as being the root cause of Africa's problems. Although the 1983 and 1984 Bank reports put greater emphasis on external factors than their predecessor had done, this did not lead to 'the shift in diagnosis to affect the policy prescriptions'.[39] A point that needs to be emphasized is that since SSA's economies are small and open, domestic policy must, of necessity, be conditioned by external factors. These external factors became particularly unfavourable for SSA in the early 1980s. Firstly, primary commodity prices collapsed due to the weakness of world demand. As these falling commodity prices were not accompanied by similar reductions in import prices the terms of trade declined[40] and gave rise to immense balance-of-payments pressures. Three other features compounded the situation.

Firstly, largely as a consequence of the domestic policies of the United States, interest rates and other terms of borrowing rose sharply at a time when SSA was in need of greater credit. There is little prospect for increased Official Development Assistance. Secondly, the rise in the cost of international borrowing and external debt-servicing was accompanied by the instability of the exchange rates of the major international currencies which not

---

[39] Stoneman [1985:6].

[40] The World Bank has estimated that the national income of SSA as a whole would have been 1.2 per cent higher in 1982 if the terms of trade had remained at their 1980 level.

only contributed to fluctuations in foreign exchange earnings but also made any form of forward planning immensely difficult. Finally, protectionist practices among the leading capitalist countries increased. Such protectionism has been directed not only at traditional exports, notably against agricultural products, but also at the non-traditional exports of manufactured goods, especially those in which developing countries have recently been acquiring a growing comparative advantage, for example, textiles and clothing.

The combination of these external factors and natural disasters, principally drought and floods, have wreaked havoc in many SSA countries. Stoneman emphasizes the primacy of external factors when he says,

far from arising through inappropriate internal state-oriented policies (some manifesting themselves simultaneously in all developing countries), the problems of the 1980s are primarily caused by the world market. Indeed, the supposed need for new market-oriented policies is being used indiscriminately not only as pressure to change the policies of, say, Tanzania (which has suffered severely and is therefore identified as having had particularly bad policies), but also those of quite successful countries pursuing self-reliant policies (like India and Zimbabwe), and on the other hand to confirm the market-oriented policies of countries like Kenya and Ivory Coast, which have also suffered severely. Many countries certainly have been pursuing ill-conceived policies, (and in many cases corruption and lack of political will has meant that actual policies have borne little resemblance to the rhetoric), but this fact should be located in the structural constraints provided by the world market conditions, and not regarded as determining.[41]

7.4.2 *The role of the IMF and the World Bank*

The abysmal economic performance of most SSA countries under the weight of a hostile external economic environment has brought them under the increasing scrutiny, indeed supervision, of the IMF and the World Bank. The World Bank has, for example, established a temporary special facility for SSA, and it has pledged that half of the new concessionary credit to be disbursed by the IDA in 1988–90 will be committed to SSA. Since 1979, the IMF has devoted a large proportion of financing facilities, including conditional credit, to SSA. Furthermore, the new IMF credit facility—structural adjustment facility—which was initiated in March 1986 to provide

[41] Stoneman [1985:2].

concessional long-term credit to low-income countries with protracted balance-of-payments problems, has been directed mainly to SSA countries.[42] Given their main concerns, it is doubtful whether the involvement of SSA countries with the IMF and the World Bank will be to the former's long-term advantage. Harris has recently argued that many critics of these international organizations assume, wrongly, that the main concern of the two institutions is in helping the individual national economies. The critics' suggested reforms such as,

some greater emphasis on growth and less on balance-of-payments equilibrium; some greater social protection for the poor to give a stronger humanitarian and political underpinning to structural adjustment programmes; or some greater and more flexible emphasis on relative prices with less emphasis on macro-economic policies,[43]

have in recent years, proved to be largely acceptable to the two institutions.

The main role of the IMF and World Bank, [Harris suggests] is the construction, regulation and support of a world system where multinational corporations trade and move capital without restrictions from national states.[44]

A main feature of 'stabilization' and structural adjustment programmes is that the obligation to 'adjust' is put almost exclusively on the deficit countries not the surplus ones. And, with respect to the deficit countries, the pressure is put largely on the developing countries not on the strong ones like the United States, which is the biggest deficit country in the world.

What exactly are the contents of 'stabilization' and structural adjustment programmes? It has to be remembered that IMF and World Bank programmes and policy prescriptions are being recommended (by the institutions, and the powerful donors and international banks) as the only hope for many developing countries of Africa. Firstly, let us examine IMF stabilization programmes.

---

[42] Harris [1987]. In December 1987 the IMF established an enhanced structural adjustment faculty (ESAF) 'to assist eligible member countries to undertake strong three-year macro-economic and structural adjustment programmes to improve their balance of payments positions and foster growth' (IMF, 1988). Malawi which received SDR 55.8 million recently is the first Fund member to use resources under the ESAF.

[43] Harris [1987].   [44] Harris [1987].

Basically, the IMF argues that balance-of-payments deficits and inflation will result if the country consumes more goods and services than it is able to produce.

The possible remedies, according to Fund conventional wisdom, are (1) to cut down overall demand to the level of the available supply or (2) to try and boost production. The former has dominated Fund stabilization or 'economic recovery' programmes. The main instruments of policy are: devaluation of the currency, reduction of the government's budget deficit, restrictions on domestic credit and cuts in subsidies for public goods and services. It is thought that devaluation will improve the balance-of-payments by making exports more competitive on international markets while imports are made more expensive. It is never made clear, however, who would buy the exports if all developing countries devalue. Devaluation is usually combined with the elimination or gradual reduction of import and foreign exchange controls both of which are thought to hinder trade. Simultaneously, Fund programmes in line with the interests of creditors, call for the elimination of restrictions on international payments, for example, profit and dividend transfers and debt-service.

The next set of measures—reduction of the government budget deficit, restrictions on domestic credit and cuts in subsidies—are all designed to cut down the level of aggregate demand, but perhaps more importantly, to hone down the size and role of government in the economy. The main focus is to shift resources from the state sector to the private sector which is believed to use resources more efficiently. Thus, it is argued that the government budget deficit must be cut down. Fund programmes also usually include freezes in government employment and in wages and salaries generally. Apparently, wages and salaries are exempt from the demand to give free rein to market forces in price determination. The Fund however, favours reductions in taxes. The belief is that the government is 'over-extended' yet it does not have the capacity for such 'over-extension'. In the area of monetary policy the volume of domestic credit must be restricted, interest rates must be raised and money supply must be controlled. Another focus is on 'price distortions'. Here Fund programmes always insist on the elimination of subsidies on basic foodstuffs and economic and social services like transport, electricity and water, health, education, etc. The result has been sharp rises in prices which the Fund insists must be de-controlled.

The social and political consequences are of little concern to the Fund. The main preoccupation appears to be the creation of 'free market' economies in which multinational corporations (MNCs) can invest profitably.

The diagnosis and remedies of the IMF have been found to be faulty. They tend to deal with symptoms, not with the real causes of the diseases. As Korner *et al.* put it:

The causes of inflation and balance of payments deficits in developing countries are frequently high import bills. Price rises for oil and capital goods imports, in particular, as well as high interest levels on money markets, have imposed severe strains on the balance of payments of Third World countries. If this cost inflation is treated with demand-reducing therapies, the result is inevitably worse than the disease. Economic activity is throttled, the incentives for private investors frequently have no effect and the economy drifts into recession. Inadequate use of production capacities and high unemployment are, however, precisely the reasons for the subsidies and transfer payments in national budgets which the IMF condemns as inflationary.[45]

The reaction of the IMF to such criticisms has been to point out that it is concerned only with short-term balance-of-payments aid and not with development aid but that monetary stability is a pre-condition for development. But experience with IMF 'recovery programmes' in a number of African countries suggests that the preoccupation with monetary and financial stability has not produced the 'pre-conditions' for sustainable growth. Surely the introduction of the World Bank's 'structural adjustment loans' (SALs) must have originated from such a realization. As is well known the two institutions work very closely. The IMF 'seal of approval' has become almost (though not formally) the pre-condition for further loans from international donors and the reschedulings of debt with public and private creditors. The international banks increasingly rely on the IMF for assurance that a country is a good credit risk.

A growing amount of research shows some association between the Fund's adjustment programmes and human rights violations in many developing countries where a number of what have come to be called 'IMF riots' have been ruthlessly crushed and the so-called 'ring leaders' rounded up. Such riots have followed sharp rises in not only food prices and cuts in social services, but real shifts in

[45] Korner *et al.* [1986:57].

income from workers to property owners, a drop in real wages and mounting unemployment which the austerity measures trigger. Central to Fund policies is the reduction of the autonomy of the state especially with respect to the dominant classes in society. This has served to intensify class conflicts. Mittleman and Will writing about the IMF and human rights say:

The Fund deprives the state of critical tools of a non-coercive kind. In terms of economic and social rights, both of an individual and collective nature, conditionality depresses real wage rates, contributes to high levels of unemployment, and facilitates resource extraction . . . Violations of human rights stemming from the contradiction between the rights of property and the rights of persons are fostered by IMF policies that advance the internationalization of capital and entrench the international division of labour.[46]

The World Bank's SALs were introduced in 1980 to finance structural adjustment programmes in developing countries. The SALs usually last for 3–5 years. As in the case of IMF loans the recipient government must sign a letter of intent in which it undertakes to comply with certain conditions. While (unlike the IMF) the World Bank does not insist on exactly quantifiable macro-economic variables, it too demands reductions in trade restriction, abolition of price controls combined with increases in the prices of public goods and services, promotion of exports through tax incentives and devaluation. In addition, however, World Bank programmes call for specific institutional reforms and government measures to assist specific economic sectors which may be in industry, agriculture, mining, etc. Because they are often linked to IMF stabilization programmes, there are no shining examples in Africa where structural adjustment programmes could be said to have successfully laid the foundation for future growth. In fact, the policies of the IMF and the World Bank have in many developing countries proved to be counter-productive to achieving sustainable development. There is overwhelming evidence that the most disadvantaged people, those most dependent on subsidized basic goods and services, have borne the brunt of these programmes.[47] The policies of the IMF and World Bank have had, as their main aim, the creation in developing countries of a climate favourable

---

[46] Mittleman and Will [1987:68].
[47] See, among others, Cornia *et al.* [1988].

to foreign investors particularly the MNCs. They have been pre-occupied above all with ensuring that developing countries repay their loans.[48] Now with several years of 'experimentation' with the IMF's and World Bank's policy doses, higher rates of economic growth in SSA are still illusory.

7.4.3 *The Lagos Plan of Action*

The IMF and World Bank have put forward one clear alternative—the 'free market' approach through SALs—as a way out of the crisis. There is hardly any African country in the 1980s that has not implemented an IMF or World Bank programme. Yet the crisis has continued relentlessly. We have argued that IMF/World Bank schemes and programmes will merely serve to further integrate SSA into the international division of labour which is precisely the very factor which has been the main source of independent Africa's economic problems over the previous three decades.

An alternative approach has been put forward in the Lagos Plan of Action and the Final Act of Lagos (LPA) which was adopted at the Special Economic Summit of the OAU in 1980.[49] Its basic thrust was the long-term economic restructuring of African economies—the achievement of a more self-reliant, more economically integrated Africa by the year 2000. The broad outlines of the LPA were articulated in the basic guidelines and stated in its preamble in the following manner.

1. Africa's huge resources must be applied principally to meet the needs and purposes of its people.
2. Africa's almost total reliance on the export of raw materials must change. Rather, Africa's development and growth must be based on a combination of Africa's considerable natural resources, her entrepreneurial, managerial and technical resources and her markets (restructured and expanded) to serve her people. Africa, therefore, must map out its own strategy for development and must vigorously pursue its implementation.
3. Africa must cultivate the virtue of self-reliance. It is not to say that the continent should totally cut itself off from outside contributions. However, these outside contributions should only supplement our own effort; they should not be the mainstay of our development.
4. As a consequence of the need for increased self-reliance, Africa must mobilize her entire human and material resources for her development.

[48] See IMF Annual Report [1987].
[49] Organization of African Unity [1981].

5. Each of our States must pursue all-embracing economic, social and cultural activities which will mobilize the strength of the country as a whole and ensure that both the efforts put into and the benefits derived from development are equitably shared.
6. Efforts toward African economic integration must be pursued with renewed determination in order to create a continent-wide framework for the much needed economic co-operation for development based on collective self-reliance.[50]

Does the LPA really constitute an alternative to the IMF/World Bank approach? The LPA is clearly 'Pan-Africanist' in tenor, with its appeal to African unity and economic integration. It is also in rhetoric clearly anti-imperialist. But it is doubtful whether the founding fathers were really thinking of a radical form of development which is people-centred and involving a complete de-linking from Western imperialism. But it did nevertheless contain a number of useful ideas: for example, the emphasis on strategies for expanding food production for domestic markets as opposed to a concentration on cash crop production. This is important, especially in view of the fact that SSA has been plagued by recurrent famines over the past few decades. Furthermore, the LPA clearly recognized the importance of concerted action by African States for effecting a restructuring of African economies through increased trade and other forms of economic cooperation. It also recognized that Africa as a developing region must make its contribution towards promoting economic cooperation with other developing regions within the framework of the non-aligned movement and the group of 77. It is only through the development of collective self-reliance through cooperation that developing countries could possibly increase their strength in global deliberations on social, economic and political issues.

But the LPA is little known outside of Africa. It has been completely overshadowed by the IMF/World Bank SALs. The main problem is that the LPA does not provide an outline of the concrete steps or measures which would be necessary for the realization of its objectives. It merely identifies the areas in which action is needed and suggests, in very general terms, the type of action that would be required. There is one further weakness of the LPA, namely the weakness of its thrust. The point is that what gives force and appeal to IMF/World Bank programmes is that they are not only tough (calling for real sacrifices now) but they have promises of money for the implementation of these programmes. The LPA provides only a framework (without any conditions or promises attached to it) within which more concrete measures could be formulated and implemented by nation states. In July 1985, the OAU heads of state and government met to thrash out short-, medium-, and long-term sectoral measures (for Africa's economic recovery in the period (1986–90) in order to accelerate the attainment of the objectives of the LPA. It is doubtful whether African states are actually taking any notice of the LPA.

7.5. Conclusion

What is the way forward for sub-Saharan Africa?

In a paper such as this, it would be presumptuous for us to offer a simplistic blueprint for a way out of the crisis. No easy solutions or remedies are available and, in our opinion, nor can they be. A mere alignment of exchange rates here and a shift in fiscal policies there or a drawing of the curtains on the state everywhere is not going to make the crisis disappear—as the World Bank or IMF would wish us to believe.

It is clear that whatever the weight of external causes to the social and economic crisis in Africa, domestic restructuring is imperative. That is, national strategies and policies must be formulated and implemented to achieve sustained and balanced development. To achieve real economic transformation such strategies must be based on a realistic identification and better utilization of indigenous resources and capabilities.

To begin with, a country which seriously wants to get out of the crisis and to eliminate the recurrence of such crises, will require a coherent and clearly articulated development strategy. Such a development strategy must identify necessary linkages—both horizontal and vertical—between economic sectors (in particular between industry and agriculture and within each of these) and it must clearly spell out the roles of the public and private sectors and that of domestic and foreign capital. The organizing theme must be 'self-reliance'. SSA has for too long placed too much reliance on foreign capital sources. These have in most cases failed to materialize; or when they have, their attached conditions have been so onerous that it has ended up imposing real burdens on the working people. The labour effort of large sections of the working people in SSA is currently committed, and is pledged to be in the medium-term, to produce commodities for the repayment of foreign loans. This is an aspect which is often overlooked in discussions of the 'debt crisis' but is highly relevant considering that many if not most peasants and workers receive wages (or their equivalent) which are well below that required for necessary consumption. Thus, both the existence of wages which for the most part are well below the value of labour-power and the commitment to produce certain types of commodities (mainly agricultural) for sale in the world market in order to meet debt-servicing requirements, generate a double-edged burden on the masses. On the one hand domination by foreign capital (and the debt burden) squeezes workers to the extent that even the necessary consumption for the majority fails to be met, and on the other hand export commodities have to be produced which under prevailing SSA production conditions imply a substitution of commodities against production for domestic markets hence exacerbating the shortages of commodities required for meeting the basic needs of labour (e.g. food).

A nationally oriented programme would broadly speaking include the following main priorities:

1. Eliminate hunger by increasing food self-sufficiency with effective distribution systems. In many African countries peasant farmers have stopped producing surpluses not because of shortages of foreign exchange or lack of skills and know-how but because of the failure of agricultural authorities and marketing boards to provide farmers with the required incentives such as consumer goods, transport, storage facilities, social services and appropriate inputs at sensible prices.
2. Maintain exports of traditional items while every effort is made to increase non-traditional exports through increased intra-African or South-South trade.
3. Reduce too heavy a reliance on foreign borrowing by redoubling efforts to mobilize domestic resources and savings; raise the effectiveness of utilization of foreign aid and domestic savings.
4. Eliminate excessive restrictions on the informal sector.
5. Cut down the excessive expenditure of the political and administrative elite.

6. Eliminate grandiose projects which eat up a lot of resources (foreign and local) and which are of no benefit to the masses.
7. Encourage, by means of incentives, production for domestic markets.
8. Facilitate the spread of collective and cooperative forms of production in all sectors of the economy.

Also we need to stop and think about the crisis a little more. For who is it that is crying 'Crisis! Crisis!' the loudest at the moment? The international organizations are for sure, the African ruling classes are, the international banks are and more generally international finance capital is. The masses in Africa however, while having been the greatest victims of the crisis have in the main remained silent, but let it be said that this is not because they have no axe to grind or because they have nothing to say or have no alternatives, potentially or otherwise, to offer.

It is now well known that the masses shared little of the spoils of independence. Economically the masses (here meant as the peasants, working classes and the lower rungs of the petty bourgeoisie) have not progressed. Politically theirs is a constituency not truly represented; indeed the post-independence experience shows clearly and consistently everywhere, that their independent organization outside the control of the state has been something which the African states have tolerated the least.[51]

The state has attempted to control and if necessary to co-opt autonomous representative organizations of the people—whether peasant associations, cooperatives, community-based bodies, trade-unions or working class organizations, or militant student associations. The absence of such democratic organs in Africa coupled with the increasing staticness of economic and political life has blocked the emergence of a popular coordinated resistance to the crisis from its currently subterranean expression to an open and challenging force. Hitherto, the people's response to the crisis has been to by-pass the state (which is itself in many ways more and more showing signs of decay) to evade covert and overt coercion through active engagement in the parallel economy. Such people's involvements outside of the state nexus are essentially survival strategies employed in order to cope with the declining living standards being faced by the masses. The hope for change lies in

[51] See Shivji [1988a] and Anyang' Nyong'o [1987].

the strengthening of mass popular organizations to open more space for democratic expression and class action. But as yet this democratic movement of the people is in its infancy and much effort will be required for the mere calls for democracy to be translated into an effective force in individual countries. Increasingly among African intellectual circles the state in Africa is being seen as an institution of repression, for the modernization ideology of 'developmentalism'[52] has not produced the desired economic change since independence nor has it succeeded in harnessing the creative energies of the African peoples towards broad-based development. As Anyang' Nyong'o has recently stated,

at the centre of the failure of African states to chart viable paths for domestic accumulation is the problem of accountability, the lack of democracy. The people's role in the affairs of government has diminished, the political arena has shrunk, political demobilization has become more the norm than the exception in regime behaviour, social engineering for political demobilization (i.e. repression) is the preoccupation of most governments; all this has come about to cement one notorious but common aspect of all African governments: the use of public resources as possibilities for viable indigenous processes of development is neglected or destroyed altogether. There is a definite correlation between the lack of democratic practices in African politics and the deteriorating socio-economic conditions.[53]

Discussing the crisis of the state in post-colonial Africa, another prominent African social scientist, Ntalaja, says the petit-bourgeois nationalist leadership has been interested more in

replacing Europeans in the leading positions of power and privilege than in effecting a radical transformation of the state and the society around it.[54]

In their preoccupation to enrich themselves, in alliance with imperialist capital 'they failed the crucial test for post-colonial development'.[55]

This introspection by some intellectuals in Africa marks the beginning of a new realization on the continent that neither the state as presently constituted nor increased international aid and donor meddling is likely to reverse the 'crisis'. The latter is not being seen merely as a balance-of-payments problem or a result of

[52] Shivji [1988a].   [53] Anyang' Nyong'c [1987:19].
[54] Ntalaja [1987:73].   [55] Ibid.

insufficient aid or its misuse. Rather, as a group of leading aca-
demicians (Africanist and African) collectively agreed at a seminar
in 1986: 'The present crisis in Africa is largely an institutional
crisis. In particular, it is a crisis of the state.'[56]

Reflections on the continent's problems cannot overlook the
fact that the crisis we speak of embodies a class character and that
resolutions, or attempted resolutions, will at some point underscore
particular class positions. We can be clear that the IMF/World
Bank crisis-resolving programmes give a fillip to further penetration
by international finance capital and to private merchant classes
within Africa. The Lagos Plan of Action contains some spirit of
anti-imperialism, but judging by its content and, in particular, its
programme of action, there seems little which is genuinely anti-
imperialist and people-centred. But it contains the germs of a plan
for what one may term 'national bourgeois democracy' by the fact
that it espouses greater inward orientation, use of available local
resources, self-reliance, regional trade and investment cooperation
and so on. Aside from these grand proclamations the social agents
which are to carry out these sweeping changes are not clearly spelt
out. By default, perhaps, the LPA visualizes the economic agent
to be the state itself. How different in social and ideological
content are the pronouncements of the LPA to what the African
states have been stating since independence anyway? Very little,
we think, in any real concrete sense.

Finally, given the foregoing discussion we would say that since no
ready national bourgeois force exists in contemporary Africa, given
the hold of finance capital of these social formations, the ultimate
and effective challenge to imperialism must come from the masses
(peasants, workers and progressive sections of the petty bourgeoisie).
It is the latter group (i.e. the masses) which conjecturally and
objectively have the most to gain by challenging imperialism in
Africa and paving the way to a real democratic transition to
socialism.[57] A national democratic revolution or what Mao called
'new democracy' is in our view the current stage of the struggle
towards the emancipation of the masses in Africa. For they are
potentially the only force, given the current situation, to usher in a
period of bourgeois democracy which the present African bourgeois

[56] Bgoya and Hyden [1988:6].
[57] See Shivji [1988b] for an interesting discussion of the 'new democratic revolution' in the context of Africa.

classes have failed to deliver. Under new democracy of course it is only the leadership of the working class which would ultimately ensure that this form of bourgeois democracy will be transitory to socialism. The intense class struggles which would be set free for expression under new democracy do not any way imply, let alone guarantee, the leadership of the working class or its ultimate victory.

While objectively the present stage of the struggle can be identified as new or national democratic, that is not to suggest that all throughout SSA we will witness in the next few years struggles taking this form. We are a long way from that and in any case in each separate social formation, concrete programmes to suit the particular social and economic configuration will have to be worked out in detail by the movements. Again no political blue-print exists, nor can it be provided, least of all for the whole sub-continent. But one central component to the struggle for new democracy throughout Africa will be the solution of the 'agrarian' question.[58] In some contexts the resolution of the agrarian question will entail dealing with the 'land question', in other situations with the 'state-marketing question', and in others some combination of both of these.[59]

References

Anyang' Nyong'o, P. (ed.) [1987], *Popular Struggles for Democracy in Africa* (London: UNU and Zed Books).

Barker, C. E. *et al.* [1986], *African Industrialization* (Aldershot, England: Gower).

Bates, R. [1981], *Markets and States in Tropical Africa: The Political Basis of Agricultural Policies*, (Berkeley: University of California).

Bernstein, H. [1987], Book Review of J. Sender and S. Smith, the Development of Capitalism in Africa 1986. *Capital and Class*, no. 33, Winter, 1987.

---

[58] We do not elaborate further on this in this paper for lack of space, but see Shivji [1987], Levin and Neocosmos [1987], Neocosmos [1987] and Mamdani [1986].

[59] See Mkandawire [1987] for a recent collection of essays on the agrarian question and the role of the state in several African countries. In particular note the introduction written by Mkandawire himself.

Bgoya, W. and G. Hyden [1988], 'The State and the Crisis of Africa: in Search of a Second Liberation', *Development Dialogue*, Uppsala, Sweden.

Brett, E. A. [1986], 'State Power and Economic Inefficiency: Explaining Political Failure in Africa', *IDS Bulletin*, vol. 17, no. 1, Sussex.

Cornia, G. A., R. Jolly and F. Stewart (eds.) [1988], *Adjustment With a Human Face* (Oxford: Clarendon Press).

Davies, R. and N. P. Moyo [1988], 'Dimensions of Africa's Economic Crisis', *Zibabwe Journal of Economics*, vol. 2, no. 1; January 1988.

FAO [1987], Food Outlook: Statistical Supplement, (Rome: FAO).

Fransman, M. [1982], *Industry and Accumulation in Africa* (New Hampshire, USA: Heinemann).

Freund, B. [1984], *The Making of Contemporary Africa* (London: Macmillan).

Gakou, M. L. [1987], *The Crisis in African Agriculture* (London: UNU University and Zed Books).

Harris, L. [1987], 'The Bretton Woods System and Africa', Paper presented at the IFAA Conference on The Impact of the IMF and World Bank Policies on the people of Africa, held at City University, London, 7–11 September, 1987.

IDS [1983], Accelerated Development in Sub-Saharan Africa: What Agenda for Action?, edited issue by C. Allison and R. Green, *IDS Bulletin*, vol. 14, no. 1, Sussex.

IDS [1985], Sub-Saharan Africa: Getting the Facts Right, edited issue by C. Allison and R. Green, *IDS Bulletin*, vol. 16, no. 3, Sussex.

IDS [1986], Developmental States and African Agriculture, edited issue by T. Mars and G. White, *IDS Bulletin*, vol. 17, no. 1, Sussex.

IMF [1987], *IMF Annual Report* (Washington: IMF).

IMF [1988], *IMF Survey*, vol. 17, Supplement, June 1988 (Washington: IMF).

Korner, P., G. Maass, T. Siebold and R. Tetzlaff [1986], *The IMF and the Debt Crisis*, (London: Zed Books).

Levin, R. and M. Neocosmos [1987], 'The Agrarian Question and Class Contradictions in South Africa: Some Theoretical Issues for Consideration', Paper presented at Workshop on The South African Agrarian Question: Past, Present and Future, University of the Witwatersrand, 22 to 24 May 1987.

Mamdani, M. [1976], *Politics and Class Formation in Uganda* (London: Heinemann).

Mamdani, M. [1986], 'Extreme but not Exceptional: Towards an Analysis of the Agrarian Question in Uganda', *DPP Working Paper*, no. 5, (Milton Keynes, England: The Open University).

Mamdani, M. *et al.* [1988], 'Social Movements, Social Transformation and the Struggle for Democracy in Africa', Working Paper 1/88 (Dakar, Senegal: Codesria).

Mittleman, J. and D. Will [1987], 'The International Monetary Fund, State Autonomy and Human Rights', *Africa Today*, 1st and 2nd Quarter, 1987.

Mkandawire, T. [1987], Book Review of J. Sender and S. Smith, the Development of Capitalism in Africa 1986, *Africa Development*, vol. 12, no. 2 (Dakar, Senegal: Codesria).

Mkandawire, T. (ed.) [1987], *State and Agriculture in Africa* (Senegal: Codesria).

Neocosmos, M. (ed.) [1987], *Social Relations in Rural Swaziland: Critical Analyses*, (Swaziland: Social Science Research Unit, University of Swaziland).

Nixson, F. [1982], 'Import-Substituting Industrialization' in M. Fransman [1982], *Industry and Accumulation in Africa*.

Ntalaja, N. [1987], *Revolution and Counter Revolution in Africa: Essays in Contemporary Politics* (London: Zed Press).

Organization of African Unity [1981], *Lagos Plan of Action for the Economic Development of Africa, 1980–2000* (Geneva: Institute for Labour Studies).

Sandbrook, R. [1985], *The Politics of Africa's Economic Stagnation* (Melbourne, Australia: Cambridge University Press).

Sender, J. and S. Smith [1986], *The Development of Capitalism in Africa*, (London: Methuen).

Shivji, I. [1987], 'The Roots of the Agrarian Crisis in Tanzania: A Theoretical Perspective', *East African Social Science Research Review*, vol. 3, no. 1, January 1987.

Shivji, I. [1988a], 'The Politics of the Left in Africa: Towards a Self-Criticism'. Text of a public lecture given in Harare, Zimbabwe, 21 January 1988 under the auspices of the Zimbabwe Chapter of the African Association of Political Science (Mimeo).

Shivji, I. [1988b], 'Fight, My Beloved Continent: New Democracy in Africa'. Revised text of the Farewell address to students of the University of Zimbabwe, 10 August 1988 (Mimeo).

South Commission [1988], 'Statement on External Debt', March 1988.

Stoneman, C. [1985], 'Strategy or Ideology? The World Bank and IMF approach to Development', Paper Presented to a Conference on Economic Policies and Planning Under Crisis Conditions in Developing Countries held at the University of Zimbabwe, Harare, 2–5 September, 1985.

UNCTAD [1979], *Transnational Corporations in Food Processing and Beverage Industries of Developing Countries*, (New York: Centre for Transnational Corporations).

UNIDO [1983], *Industry in a changing world* (Vienna: United Nations).

Warren B. [1980], *Imperialism: Pioneer of Capitalism* (London: New Left Books).

World Bank, [1980], *World Development Report*, Washington.

World Bank, [1981], *Accelerated Development in Sub-Saharan Africa; An Agenda for Action* (Washington: World Bank).

World Bank [1987], *World Development Report*, Washington.

Remarks on the Recent
Economic Performance of the
Low-Income Countries

LODEWIJK BERLAGE

In their paper Moyo and Amin discuss the economic performance
of sub-Saharan Africa. Their analysis includes both low- and middle-
income countries. They basically argue that the problems of sub-
Saharan Africa are due to the structural weakness of the economies
inherited from the colonial powers, to the integration of Africa in
the world economy, and to the collaboration of local elites with
imperialism. These explain both the low level of income and the
poor economic performance of the seventies and the eighties. They
suggest that without fundamental changes in the economic and
social system the downward economic trend will continue.

The question as to why some countries have a low standard of
living is intriguing, but difficult to answer. It is clear that a number
of low-income countries have a weak natural resource base, that they
are vulnerable to natural disasters and that their human resources
are underdeveloped. But these three characteristics do not apply
to all low-income countries.

It seems somewhat easier to explain the economic performance
of countries over a certain period of time. In this note I will
reconsider the recent economic performance of the low-income
countries, including the Asian ones. If economic imperialism is at
the root of the problems of the less developed countries, we should
observe more or less the same evolution in all parts of the world
which are presumed to be in a situation of dependency. As is well
known, this is not the case. During the seventies and especially the
eighties, there has been a growing differentiation between the
economic performances of Asian, Latin American and African
LDCs.[1] A number of Asian countries, although affected by shocks

---

[1] See e.g. section 2.5 of the text by Singer in this volume.

in the world economy like the oil price rises and the world recession of 1980–82, were able to stay on a growth course. The Latin American countries continued their growth during the seventies, though this entailed a debt burden which in the light of later events (the increase in the real interest rate and the world recession) turned out to be excessive. But economic growth in sub-Saharan Africa did slow down considerably even during the seventies (as illustrated by Table 7.1 in Moyo and Amin's text). Changes in the world economy by themselves apparently are not sufficient to explain these differences in economic performance.

When we consider the economic evolution of the low-income countries, a similar picture of diversity is obtained. The growth figures in Table 8.1 for low-income Africa conform to Moyo and Amin's vision. Per capita GDP showed hardly any change over the period 1965–80 and a marked decline during the eighties. However, the experience of the Asian low-income countries was different. India and the other low-income countries of Asia experienced a small increase of per capita GDP over the period 1965–80 and a marked increase during the eighties. (China of course is a special case). With some qualifications this was also true for the Asian least developed countries, for which statistics are available, i.e. Bangladesh and Nepal.

TABLE 8.1:   *Average annual growth rates of GDP per capita, low-income countries*[a]

Country group	1965–80	1980–86
African countries	0.2	−1.9
Asian countries (excluding India and China)	1.0	2.4
India	1.4	2.7
China	4.4	9.3
Haiti	0.9	−2.5
Average		
excluding India and China	0.6	0.3
including India and China	2.5	5.1
Of which least developed countries		
African countries	0.4	−1.8
Asian countries	−0.3	1.1
Average	0.1	−0.7

Source: Based on World Bank, World Development Report [1988]
Note: [a] Low-income countries listed in the World Development Report 1988; group averages are obtained by using 1986 populations as weights

Bangladesh's GDP declined slightly over the period 1965–80. Between 1980 and 1986 it grew at a yearly rate of 1.1 per cent, resulting in an overall growth rate close to zero over the 21 year period from 1965 to 1986. Of course stagnation at a low level of per capita income is not exactly spectacular. However, one should consider the fact that Bangladesh is an extremely resource poor country. Apart from some natural gas, it has hardly any natural resources except land and water. Of the latter there is too much during the summer and not enough during the winter season. It has an extremely unfavourable population-arable land ratio. And the literacy rate of its population (5 years and older) is less than 25 per cent. Moreover, during the period under consideration, the war of liberation and its concomitant destruction and dislocation and the institutional problems related to the take-over from the Pakistani business elite had a negative impact on economic performance. If one considers the initial conditions and the politico-military upheavals, stagnation rather than decline was quite a feat.

The difference in economic performance between African and Asian low-income countries may have several explanations:

1. extra-economic factors might have been more unfavourable in sub-Saharan Africa;
2. identical changes in the world economic environment might have had a differential impact in different countries; or
3. the quality of economic decision-making might have been fundamentally different in the two regions.

The purpose of this text is not to analyse in depth the merits of the three explanations.[2] The following comments are of a rather general nature and the result of casual observations.

Among the extra-economic events which did have an economic impact on the economies of low-income countries we might mention environmental problems and disasters and political instability. It is not an easy matter to state whether these have been more intense in low-income Africa than in Asia. Certainly the drought in the Sahel has had an unfavourable impact on the countries in this region. In some countries civil strife and war were prime determinants of

[2] For an attempt to unravel the impact of environmental factors and of national decision-making on the economic performance of sub-Saharan Africa see Wheeler [1984]. He comes to the conclusion that changes in the economic environment were more important than national decision-making.

the economic performance. Examples are Angola, Chad, Ethiopia, Mozambique, Sudan and Uganda. At the origin of these conflicts were such factors as the lack of a tradition of nationhood, of ethnical homogeneity and of political purpose of post-colonial states, and foreign, including South African, support for opposition movements. Such factors, while not limited to African countries, might have had a more adverse impact there.

Major unfavourable changes in the world economy included the rise in the price of oil in 1973 and again in 1979, the drop in commodity prices over the period 1978–86 and the rise of the real interest rate in the early eighties. Again, the issue is not whether these events were unfavourable, but rather whether their impact was heavier in sub-Saharan Africa than elsewhere. I will limit my comments to the drop in commodity prices and concentrate on three African countries and Bangladesh. The African countries are Ghana, Senegal and Zambia. All three of them were reclassified by the World Bank from the group of middle- to that of low-income countries. Table 8.2 gives data on terms of trade and on GDP growth for these countries.

TABLE 8.2: *Terms of trade (1980 = 100) and average annual growth rate of GDP (%)*

Country	Terms of trade			Growth of GDP	
	1966	1971	1986	1965–80	1980–86
Ghana	83	114	88	1.4	0.7
Senegal	136	114	87	2.1	3.2
Zambia	320	111	70	1.8	−0.1
Bangladesh		156[a]	109	2.4	3.7

Source: World Bank, World Tables [1987] and World Development Report [1988]
Note: [a] 1972

Of the four countries the experience of Zambia has been most dramatic. Over a twenty year period its terms of trade fell to less than 25 per cent of their initial value. This development was the result of the decline in the copper price and of the increase in the prices of oil and manufactures. It is evident that for any country it would be hard to adjust to such an unfavourable evolution of its terms of trade. Even a government fully conscious of the long-term nature of the evolution and of the necessity of policies to accommodate the implied loss of real income, would have found it hard to impose the necessary policy measures on its population. In reality the Zambian government, not different from any other, reacted slowly and hesitantly to the changing situation.[3] A similar story, though a less dramatic one, could be told for Senegal. Ghana on the other hand, a notoriously poor performer during the seventies and the early eighties, did not experience a similar long-term decline in its terms of trade. Of course there were ups and downs, with a high of 159 in 1977 and a low of 73 in 1982. But against the background of the twenty years from 1966 to 1986, these were short-term fluctuations. The implication would seem to be that the causes of the poor performance of Ghana are not to be found in the external environment, at least insofar as the terms of trade are a good indicator thereof. In this context we might quote R. H. Green [1988],

From 1973 through 1981 . . . there was no coherent policy but only a stream of inconsistent slogans, of temporary expedients and of increasingly frantic scrambling to salvage personal and narrow sub-class interests out of a steadily shrinking pot.

Of course one might ask why countries, which are faced with a sluggish demand for and an unfavourable development of the relative prices of their traditional exports, do not shift their resources to the production and export of other products. The argument that low income economies are by definition too inflexible to perform such a resource shift is appealing, but not entirely convincing. To show this, one might again refer to Bangladesh. This country is a traditional exporter of jute in raw and in manufactured form. In the seventies jute products generated more than 75 per cent of its total exports receipts. In the eighties its exports of jute and jute manufactures and of other traditional products stagnated. But between 1981 and 1987 Bangladesh's non-traditional exports, like frozen shrimps and garments, rose by almost 250 per cent. These two products provided 6 per cent of the export receipts in 1981, but 40 per cent by 1987. This does not mean that the country has solved once and for all its foreign exchange problem. Merchandise exports in 1987 covered less than half of merchandise imports. But

---

[3] For a discussion of adjustment policies in Zambia, see Colclough [1988].

without the upsurge in non-traditional exports the country would have had an even more difficult time to cover its import needs.

It is clear that the opportunities to shift to new export products vary from country to country. (It is difficult to breed shrimps in the desert!) But the only response to stagnating or declining revenues from traditional exports is not to undergo events passively.

A third set of explanations of the difference in economic performance has to do with the quality of economic decision making. We might consider this at a 'superficial' level, i.e. which were the specific policy measures that were or were not taken? Or at a 'fundamental' level, i.e. by discussing the deeper nature of policies and of the state itself.

As for the specific policy measures I suggest that rules of economic behaviour do exist which are applicable in a wide variety of circumstances and which, when neglected, sooner or later have negative consequences for the economy. The following are examples of such rules.

1. Production should be profitable. If the price of a product is kept artificially low by government regulations, output will suffer.
2. In an inflationary situation, prices should be adjusted. If in such a situation the price of some goods is kept constant, by forcing public firms to maintain fixed prices or by providing subsidies, the result will be growing financial problems for the public firms or the government treasury.
3. Real interest rates should be positive. If the real interest rate is negative, it becomes more likely that scarce financial resources are allocated to poor investment projects.
4. If domestic inflation is higher than world inflation, the nominal exchange rate should be adjusted. If this is not done, exports are discouraged.

It is difficult to say whether policies of Asian low-income countries have conformed better to such rules than those of sub-Saharan countries. I submit that at least in one respect Asian countries have done better. In the agricultural sector, they have as a rule pursued policies, be it in terms of prices, subsidies or expenditures on infrastructure, which were more favourable to production than was the case in many African countries.

The paper of Amin and Moyo considers the impact of the quality of economic decision-making at a more fundamental level. They discuss the specific nature of African states. They seem to advance at least two views, which are not necessarily contradictory. The first one is that 'decolonization left colonial administrative structures and the state relatively untouched' (para. 1); and that 'the petit-bourgeois nationalist leadership has been interested more in replacing Europeans in the leading positions of power and privilege than in effecting a radical transformation of the state'[4] (para. 5). The other view is that 'modernization theory . . . provided . . . ideological justification for a state-led, foreign-backed, economic take-off' (para. 1) but 'has not produced the desired economic change' (para. 5).[5]

I will not elaborate on the first view. The second one is partly corroborated by sketchy evidence on the origin of the debt of African low-income countries.

As is well known, the largest part of the debt of the low-income countries originated from soft loans. But in the seventies these countries also obtained on a limited scale loans at market conditions, and export credits which were guaranteed by export credit insurance agencies in the industrialized countries. Some of these loans and credits were granted for projects whose net social benefits were doubtful from the beginning (and also for the purchase of military equipment). Why were credits for such projects requested by governments of low-income countries and why were they granted by financial institutions in the industrial countries? On the part of the former there was an apparent urge to modernize in a big way whatever its cost. We might presume that a consequence of this was the failure to evaluate realistically the benefits and costs of a number of projects. In the lending countries exporters of equipment and technical know-how had sufficient political leverage to obtain the necessary credits and credit insurance.

In conclusion, the resource endowment of many low-income countries, be it for natural or for historical reasons, is poor. Their natural environment is chronically negative. The international economy has recently evolved in an unfavourable way for them. However this by itself does not explain why the performance of African low-income countries has been poorer than that of Asian

---

[4] The latter part is a quote in Amin and Moyo's paper from Ntalaja.

[5] For other references to the role of the African state see the review article by Smith [1988].

ones. The difference might have been caused by circumstances which were specific to Africa, but was probably also the result of the poor quality of decision-making there.

Foreign aid and debt alleviation could help to redress the situation. But the industrialized countries presently are unwilling to substantially increase their aid; the extent of the debt alleviation they are willing to concede remains unclear. The low income countries therefore cannot escape an adjustment to the drop in their real income. In principle it is better to do this by active policy measures than by letting the situation deteriorate. A realistic alternative to agreements with the IMF or the World Bank therefore is not to remain passive, but to develop elaborate national adjustment programmes, which, just like those agreements, will have some painful consequences.

Even if more aid and debt alleviation were forthcoming, this would not discharge African and other governments from improving their economic institutions and from formulating and implementing policies which are both realistic and conducive towards a resumption of growth. Given the constraints, there are no easy recipes to do this.

References

Colclough, C. [1988], 'Zambian Adjustment Strategy—With and Without the IMF', *IDS Bulletin*, vol. 19, no. 1, pp. 51–60.

Green, R. [1988], 'Ghana: Progress, Problematics and Limitations to the Success Story', *IDS Bulletin*, vol. 19, no. 1, pp. 7–16.

Smith, L. [1988], 'Africa's Crisis', *Journal of Development Studies*, vol. 24, pp. 250–7.

Wheeler, D. [1984], 'Sources of Stagnation in Sub-Saharan Africa', *World Development*, vol. 12, pp. 1–23.

9 The Fourth World: Concept, Reality and Prospects

> . . . We are not idiots to believe that there is possibility of life
> for us outside of where the origin of our life is. Respect our
> place of living, do not degrade our living condition, respect
> this life.
>
> We have no arms to cause pressure, the only thing we have
> is the right to cry for our dignity and the need to live in our
> land.[1]

9.1. Introduction

The paper by Moyo and Amin focuses on the group of countries
classified as sub-Saharan Africa. These countries are very severely
affected by a crisis in development, as Moyo and Amin document
extensively and convincingly. In their introduction the authors
loosely associate this group with the term 'the Fourth World'.

In this comment we will try to view the crisis in development in a
wider geographical perspective and from another viewpoint. For
this purpose we will use and elaborate the term 'the Fourth World'
according to a somewhat different meaning. We will expose this
meaning in the second section of this paper. The third section will
take us to parts of the Fourth World. In the concluding part of this
paper we will then discuss the future prospects of the Fourth World.
In this last section some of the fundamental notions will return which
Moyo and Amin propose at the end of their paper when facing the
question of how to find a way out of the crisis of sub-Saharan Africa.

9.2. An attempt at conceptualization

According to our understanding of it, the Fourth World consists
neither of countries, nor of regions within countries. It is people

---

[1] Ailton Krenak, Coordinator of Indian Nations' Union at WCED Public Hearing,
Sao Paulo, 28-9 October 1985, cited in: *Our Common Future* [1987: 115].

who ought to be considered. One may object that this creates confusion. The term 'Third World' clearly refers to countries. Why then should one similarly not use the term 'Fourth World'? The reason is that people and not nations have to be in focus, when we want to indicate—using the term 'Fourth World'—the hard core of the development problem. Ultimately this hard core consists of people's problems and not of the problems of nations.

People are dependent upon an 'environment' in order to be able to survive. Human life needs protection, in the basic sense of material sustenance, but also in terms of immaterial needs.[2] The environment in which people live has, therefore, to fulfil a number of protective functions. We use the concept of environment here in a multidimensional sense, a (human) life-sustaining 'niche'. The natural environment provides a number of basic facilities. In order to tap its potential people adapt their social behaviour, societal organization and culture. Individual human lives have to be embedded in these protective layers of ecology, social organization and culture, in order to be able to grow and develop. Culture moreover provides the 'environment' for the fulfilment of immaterial human needs, the development of creative capacities.

Changes can occur in this multidimensional environment which reduce or destroy its protective functions. People can lose their control over the environment, and it may become a threat to, instead of a guarantee for, survival and development as human beings. Beyond a certain level of vulnerability vicious circles increasingly start to play a role in making people more and more prisoners of their own situation: at the individual level the well known vicious circles of poverty, malnutrition and disease, lack of productivity leading again to the continuation of poverty; at the social level the isolation, discrimination and political repression, and finally the perverse interactions of poverty and environmental degradation.

Now we will define the Fourth World as consisting of those groups of people who are caught up in these vicious circles of vulnerability. While the Third World is considered to consist of countries, the Fourth World consists of people, struggling in vain to attain a minimum level of protection of their lives.[3]

[2] According to Dennis Goulet (1971) there are three sets of basic values which are common to all human cultures. These transcultural values are grouped by him under the titles of life-sustenance, esteem and freedom.

[3] The use of the term 'Fourth World' as we propose it is not new. The international solidarity movement ATD Quatrième-Monde—founded in 1957 in Paris by the

Often the causes of such a condition are sought in a *lack* of economic development. Our contention is that this is not necessarily the case. More particularly, the very factors which are supposed to promote economic development are often the cause of the emergence of a Fourth World. Throughout this paper we will concentrate on these cases, because they are really calling into question the quality of the development effort. Before we turn to reality we first will review the dimensions along which *in principle* development may cause greater vulnerability.

9.2.1. *Economic*

Irma Adelman [1979] has presented a theory of development in which enrichment and impoverishment are both a result of the application of productivity-increasing innovations. Development is described by her as follows:

The historical growth process of currently developed countries involved a set of transformations—from purely agrarian, to agrarian and commercial to primarily manufacturing and industrial economies. As part of this process the nature of the critical factor of production involved in the major economic activity changes over time, from land to financial capital, to physical and human capital. Whenever the critical factor of production changes, as part of that change, the productivity of the critical factor of production involved in the major economic activity was improved. With each change, a two-step sequence was initiated which entailed initial improvements in the productivity of the critical factor of production, followed, with a longish—one or two generation—delay, by an equalizing redistribution in the ownership of that factor.

With the concept of 'critical factor of production' Adelman wants to indicate, at every stage, that specific factor of production which, when its productivity is increased, will be mainly responsible for the dynamic behaviour of the economy. The crucial point which Adelman wishes to stress concerns the disequalizing effects of innovation.[4] Through technological innovation and/or through

---

priest Joseph Wresinski—was most probably the first to adopt this terminology, apparently after the idea of the Third World had become current. Alfred Sauvy used in 1952 for the first time the term 'Third World'.

[4] Applying this scheme of Adelman to the newly emerging critical factor of production which might be called 'information', one can easily see the disequalizing tendencies connected with recent innovations with respect to the capacity for gathering, processing and controlling 'information'.

institutional change the productivity of the critical factor of production is increased. However, the incidence of the innovation is not equally distributed among the population or even among all the owners of that critical factor of production, but rather follows the skewness of that particular distribution:

Unfortunately, in general it was the few who owned large amounts of the factor whose productivity was improved or large amounts of factors that could be transformed into it, who could adapt to the new technologies, while the many whose initial endowments of the factor were meagre could not (Adelman, op. cit. p. 6).

So, increasing returns were enjoyed by those who could take advantage of the increase in productivity of the critical factor of production in their hands, and by those who owned factors co-operating with the critical factor under the new technology. Decreasing returns were felt by those who—although owning a certain amount of the critical factor—could not take advantage of the innovation, and by those who owned factors which were displaced through the new technology. Marginalization and dispossession were reinforced by institutional changes. 'This combination of simultaneous enrichment and impoverishment is typical of the first step in the historical income effect of a productivity-increasing innovation in the medium run' (p. 6). After quite some time— possibly several decades—a kind of trickle-down process can be observed, leading to 'a certain amount of redistribution'. This, however, depends on 'political pressures in the form of demonstrations, strikes, revolts and revolutions' (p. 7). As in the next stage of the growth process the critical factor of production changes again, a new disequalizing increase in its productivity occurs 'followed by eventual redistributive revolt'.

This view implies that economic development continuously tends to create a Fourth World, consisting of those who are not simply left behind, but who face impoverishment due to the undermining of their traditional survival strategies.

Myrdal [1957] and Griffin [1969] have shown how the spatial dimension of economic development may reinforce these unequal development patterns. Whole regions can become economically worse-off through systematic patterns of unfavourable economic transactions with other developing regions. Cumulative backwash effects for the least-advanced region may occur through out-migration of the skilled people, adverse terms of trade and outflow of savings. This can even occur when the backward region is rich in natural resources under unequal conditions of ownership and control of technology. When the backward region is subject to environmental degradation, yet another aspect is added to its vulnerability.

9.2.2. *Ecological*

Environmental and economic vulnerability are closely related for those large groups of people living on the fragile soils of the Third World who are forced to over-exploit—in order to feed themselves— these soils because of increased population densities, but also because of the fact that the best and most productive lands are used for meeting the commercial demands of the rich. Considering the ecological dimension we are faced with a fundamental question, namely whether the Fourth World is to be defined in such a way as to include future generations. The answer to that question should be 'yes'. Those who, in the future, will face increased vulnerability due to some environmental crisis caused by present development surely are as much victims of that development as contemporary people who are marginalized now. However, while in the case of economic marginalization the victims—even if they revolt only after a considerable lag of time—may be able to reclaim their rights in the distribution of growth, future generations are by definition not able to intervene politically in present development trends if these *irreparably* reduce their chances of survival. As the World Commission on Environment and Development's report (Brundtland Commission) says (p. 8):

Many present efforts to guard and maintain human progress, to meet human needs, and to realize human ambitions are simply unsustainable— in both the rich and poor nations. They draw too heavily too quickly, on already overdrawn environmental resource accounts to be affordable far into the future without bankrupting those accounts. They may show profits on the balance sheets of our generation, but our children will inherit the losses. We borrow environmental capital from future generations with no intention or prospect of repaying. They may damn us for our spendthrift ways, but they can never collect on our debt to them. We act as we do because we can get away with it: future generations do not vote; they have no political or financial power; they cannot challenge our decisions.

But the results of the present profligacy are rapidly closing the options for future generations. Most of today's decision makers will be dead before the planet feels the heavier effects of acid precipitation, global warming, ozone depletion, or widespread desertification and species loss. Most of the young voters of today will still be alive. In the Commission's hearings it was the young, those who have the most to lose, who were the harshest critics of the planet's present management.

9.2.3. *Cultural*

We define culture as the whole of values (underlying human social behaviour) which are transmitted from one generation to the next through education and other forms of socialization. It is by now clear that the importance of the cultural dimension of development has been severely underestimated in the past. Kuznets in his Nobel Memorial lecture [1973] underlined the changes '*in the institutional and ideological spheres*' which were considered to be necessary for economic growth. According to Kuznets, without such changes the chain reaction which is the core of the process of economic transformation would be blocked by 'inappropriate' institutions and their underlying attitudes and values. Kuznets tends to view and value cultural change as a function of economic growth (see for a critique Terhal [1987]). Whatever may be the value of such a view, modern economic growth appears to be embedded in a broader process of change which in sociological literature bears the name of modernization. And modernization is transmitted through economic interaction on very unequal terms. The process through which modernized societies impose their values on traditional ones is not such a harmonious process as it is often depicted. In all (traditional) cultures the values underlying people's behaviour with respect to reproduction, environmental management, economic production and consumption form a whole which in its turn is rooted in a set of fundamental beliefs and attitudes. These relate to ultimate questions revolving around the meaning of the world, man's place within it, the balanced relation between individual and communal life, and the roles of social, moral and religious obligations.

What is at stake in modernization, therefore, is far more than functional adaptation. As Goulet [1971: 38–59] has rightly observed the 'values of modernity' are often as shocking and emotionally disturbing for the poor villagers of the Third World, as their deep poverty is for the Western observer. Modernity undermines and shakes the foundations of traditional social life and may deprive people of their sense of meaning and coherence of their world. It makes them more vulnerable psychologically as it destroys the mental security which traditional communal life provided them with.

9.2.4. *Political*

Development makes people more vulnerable politically. This is due to the fact that the emerging political systems in many developing countries are not capable of handling peacefully the manifold conflicts which are created by development processes themselves. Conflicts are often settled, then, through political violence, coups, civil war or military interventions, causing the uprooting of many millions of refugees. A. O. Hirschman [1981] has even attributed 'the decline of development economics' to the political chaos which has accompanied development. We quote (pp. 20–1):

But there was a more weighty reason for the failure of development economics to recover decisively from the attacks it has been subjected to by its critics. It lies in the series of political disasters that struck a number of Third World countries from the sixties on, disasters that were clearly somehow connected with the stresses and strains accompanying development and 'modernization'. These development disasters, ranging from civil wars to the establishment of murderous authoritarian regimes, could not but give pause to a group of social scientists, who, after all, had taken up the cultivation of development economics in the wake of World War II not as narrow specialists, but impelled by the vision of a better world. As liberals most of them presume that 'all good things go together' and took it for granted that if only a good job could be done in raising the national income of the country concerned, a number of beneficial effects would follow in the social, political, and cultural realms. When it turned out instead that the promotion of economic growth entailed not infrequently a sequence of events involving serious retrogression in those other areas, including the wholesale loss of civil and human rights, the easy self-confidence that our sub-discipline exuded in its early stages was impaired.

In the first part of their paper Moyo and Amin refer specifically to the problematic situation of the state in sub-Saharan Africa. They list a number of reasons why the African states 'failed to deliver the goods'. They blame the state and the ruling classes which have been far too preoccupied with fighting wars, mostly of a tribal nature. Political insecurity certainly is a major factor contributing to the vulnerability of oppressed minorities in Africa and elsewhere.

It may appear far-fetched to bring such different phenomena as economic impoverishment, environmental degradation, cultural alienation and political chaos under one heading, namely that of the Fourth World. One may acknowledge the pedagogical value of such an intellectual manipulation in that it brings together under one denominator all the dimensions in which development, as commonly understood, may fail. For development economists the message would then be indeed the same as is spelt out in the text of Hirschman quoted above: *not to take* it for granted that if only a good job could be done in raising the national income of the country concerned, a number of beneficial effects would follow in the social, political and cultural realms.

9.3. Reality

In this section we will consider three different classes of empirical phenomena. In two of them factors supposedly associated with development lead to the emergence and continuation of a Fourth World. These classes of phenomena are summarized under the headings of (9.3.1) rural impoverishment, (9.3.2) ecological degradation, and (9.3.3) international dependency. Thus we will leave out the political and cultural dimensions, although the latter will appear to be closely associated with aspects of ecological degradation.

In the subsections (9.3.1) and (9.3.2) we will restrict ourselves to examples from Asia. This, obviously, does not imply that rural impoverishment and ecological degradation do not occur on a much vaster scale in Latin America and Africa. It only indicates that even where macro-growth rates are comparatively favourable, such as in Asia, there exists a Fourth World, let alone under the (much) worse macro-economic conditions prevailing at present in the other continents. In particular the case of sub-Saharan Africa, as discussed in detail by N. P. Moyo and N. Amin, clearly illustrates the disastrous impact which the macro-economic environment (both international and national) can have on levels of living. In such a situation Fourth World conditions may acquire a virtually nationwide incidence.

In Table 9.1 we give the growth rates of GDP per capita for various continents. In subsection (9.3.3) we will briefly consider the effects on the poor of the international depression reflected in the negative growth rates in Table 9.1.

TABLE 9.1: *Developing market economies GDP per capita growth rates 1976–1986*
(annual percentage change at 1975 prices)

	1976–80	1981–85	1981	1982	1983	1984	1985[a]	1986[b]
All developing market economies	2.7	−1.1	−1.5	−1.7	−1.7	−0.5	−0.1	−0.3
Africa	2.4	−3.1	−5.1	−3.5	−2.5	−2.8	−1.5	−2.5
Latin America	2.9	−1.8	−1.2	−3.8	−4.9	0.8	0.1	−0.5
West Asia	−0.2	−4.4	−9.2	−0.2	−4.7	−4.1	−3.7	−2.9
South and East Asia	4.0	2.8	4.0	1.0	4.1	3.6	1.6	1.7

Source: Cornia *et al.* [1987]
Notes: [a] Preliminary
[b] UN Secretariat forecast

9.3.1. *Rural impoverishment*

Robert Chambers [1983] has argued that due to a number of inter-locking social mechanisms the extent and depth of rural poverty in the Third World has been continuously underperceived and under-estimated. Pushing his argument somewhat further, one may venture the proposition that the degree of (rural) impoverishment has also not been adequately assessed by whatever observers have taken the time and trouble to try and direct their attention to the 'unseen and unknown' people. The Indian sociologist M. N. Srinivas after having spent one year in an Indian village describes in his famous monograph *The Remembered Village* the situation in a few well-chosen words [1976: 257]:

Patience of an almost superhuman character, deep cunning and an ability to mask one's real feelings and intentions, were the only weapons which the desperately poor and exploited villagers had in their struggle against oppressors of all kinds, local landowners, tax collectors and invading armies. If they were unenthusiastic about an innovation which urban officials and local or foreign experts had thought up, it was because the latter were insensitive to the full implications of the innovation at the village level. While the ploughman thought of how well the new blade penetrated the soil, the worms underneath may be pardoned for taking a different view.

An important—although somewhat older—study suggesting stat-istically the existence of a Fourth World in Asian countries is that of Griffin and Khan [1977] who have studied rural poverty and landlessness in seven countries in Asia (Bangladesh, India, Indonesia, Malaysia, Pakistan, Philippines and Sri Lanka). Together these countries account for about 70 per cent of the rural population of all the non-socialist underdeveloped countries. For India separate studies were made of four states, Punjab, Uttar Pradesh, Bihar and Tamil Nadu. The conclusions which, due to the unreliability of data, should be interpreted cautiously, refer roughly to the sixties with a few extensions into the seventies or the fifties. They run as follows:

1. In each country a substantial proportion of the lowest income groups appears to have experienced a decline in its share of real income over time.
2. In almost every case a significant proportion of low-income households experienced an absolute decline in its real income, particularly since the early 1960s.

The second conclusion is based upon three different findings:

(a) Drawing up a poverty line—based on a minimum food intake— Griffin and Khan find in six cases an increase (in one case a modest increase) in the proportion of the population falling below this line, and in two cases a roughly constant proportion.[5]
(b) The average level of real income of the lowest decile or quintile groups (depending on the case concerned) has declined over time.
(c) In most of the cases for which measurements could be obtained real wages of agricultural labourers either remained constant or declined significantly. Only in a few cases was the trend ambiguous (see for these conclusions Griffin *et al.* [1978]).

Taking the study of Griffin and Khan as a point of departure Stewart [1978] has analysed the factors underlying impoverishment, and comes to the conclusion that this is due to the interaction between what she calls the payment system,[6] the capital-intensive nature of technology and rate of demographic growth.

[5] Together there were 10 cases (6 countries + 4 states of India). Poverty lines have been drawn up for only 8 out of these 10 cases.

[6] A payment system is defined by Stewart as a set of rules determining the (primary) distribution of income. These are:

– rules governing how income from work is determined
– rules concerning access to work
– rules governing accumulation of assets.

Lack of access to productive resources (especially land), lack of employment opportunities, the penetration of capitalism (especially in the functioning of the labour market) combined with a high growth of population make large parts of the population very vulnerable. One may object that it is mainly population growth which has to be blamed for that, and not development. More particularly one may argue that precisely a lack of economic development has resulted in the growing imbalance between the expansion of employment and the growth of labour supply. However, such a diagnosis would be short-sighted, as it neglects the crucial factor which Stewart calls the payment system. We will not go into the details of Stewart's analysis here, but it may be sufficient to underline that the penetration of a capitalist payment system greatly increases the vulnerability of the poorer social groups in society, as it destroys the protective social mechanisms ruling under a pre-capitalist payment system.

Historical evidence about the causes of impoverishment in the now industrialized countries (Adelman *et al.* [1978]) supports the thesis that during the period in which traditional social structures providing protection against extreme deprivation have been eroded, and before the state has taken up effectively the responsibility for a minimum of social security, the plight of at least a sizeable group of the poor tends to worsen. The economic history of the presently industrialized countries has been characterized also by substantial periods of impoverishment, before eventually the trickle-down process reached the mass of the poor. Moreover, the balance between population and labour force growth on the one side, and the nature of technology on the other was definitely much more favourable in these countries, as they passed through that specific period in which decumulation of assets made large parts of the population very vulnerable. Amartya Sen [1981] has termed that period PEST (Pure Exchange System Transition).

Recognizing the logic of the argument presented by Stewart we should note the hazardous natuie of the statistical data of Griffin *et al.* to which Stewart refers. Even about the measurement of poverty in India, a land with relatively good statistical data, there has been

---

In any human society these rules are linked together into one system forming a core element in the social order. Stewart then proceeds to distinguish four different prototypes of payment systems: (1) pre-capitalist (pre-industrial) system, (2) pure capitalism, (3) mixed system, (4) socialism.

a prolonged academic debate (see Cutler [1984], Deepak Lal [1984], and most recently J. Bhagwati [1988]) on the question whether or not poverty has been reduced.

This state of affairs is not surprising. Apparently, the picture is a mixed one. Bhagwati, who tends to support the proposition that poverty in India has been reduced due to growth, attaches great value to the anthropological-cum-longitudinal approach. He refers for that to the analysis of Gilbert Étienne [1982] and summarizes as follows (p. 544):

... The results are what we did expect: Growth has indeed pushed several of the poor on in life. Doubtless, some poor have been left behind; others have been impoverished even further. But then, as Arthur Lewis has wisely remarked, it is inherent in the development process that some see the opportunities and seize them, leaving others behind until they wish to and can follow . . .

It is important to note in this context that the phenomenon of impoverishment, as far as it refers to a decline of welfare of people living already below the poverty line, cannot be registered by the widely used poverty indicator of 'proportion of population living below poverty line' (see for a critique of this poverty measure Sen [1981]).

Jan Breman [1985]—on the basis of longitudinal research in South Gujarat—has come to the conclusion that impoverishment—and even pauperization, had occurred among a sizeable group of landless labourers *under conditions of rapid agricultural growth*. His observations are worth taking note of and therefore we will briefly elaborate on them.

In the central and fertile plain of South Gujarat capitalist modernization of farming has proceeded rapidly during the last few decades. It has caused substantial changes in the rural economy, crop diversification, and the widespread application of new seeds, fertilizer and irrigation. However, according to Breman, meanwhile serious impoverishment has occurred among the Halpatis, the caste of landless rural labourers who under the traditional hali-system formed the most important source of labour supply for the landowning castes. They experience a decline in their income due to lack of employment and a low wage rate both resulting from strong competition in the rural labour market caused by the greatly expanded stream of migrants coming from the poverty stricken Eastern parts of the state. Due to population growth and lack of agricultural progress marginal farmers from these drought-prone districts are pressed to migrate in large numbers seasonally or even permanently, to the prosperous central plain, where they outcompete the local landless labourers. An important aspect is the social change in the relation between the Halpatis and their former masters. Under the traditional hali-system the Halpatis—who are of tribal origin—were bound by indebtedness to a farmer, and in exchange for subsistence performed any task given to them in field and household. Breman has extensively studied this system and has concluded that although the system was very exploitative towards the Halpatis, it did provide them a minimum of security (p. 219):

. . . the master-farm servant relationship was also characterized to a significant extent by elements of patronage. The master who was under obligation to guarantee a subsistence livelihood to his farm servant and to protect him against third parties, could conversely claim unconditional loyalty and total submission from his client . . .

With the penetration of the capitalist mode of production the hali-system disintegrates. The relation of mutual dependence starts to erode. As landowners become much more profit-oriented they are keen to economize on labour costs and tend to consider the hali-system, with its implied social obligations, as an economic burden. They prefer to hire migrant workers who can claim only a daily wage. On their part, because of a growing sense of self-respect, the Halpatis want to move around more freely, but they have then to compete on the rural labour market with the incoming migrants. As mechanization of farm operations proceeds rapidly, not enough work is available all through the year for the large labour supply. The legislation of the state government on the minimum daily wage for rural labour is defective and badly implemented. On the basis of a comparison of wage rates paid in 1983, the evolution over time of food prices and the traditional 'entitlements' (under the hali-system) of a farm servant in 1961–62, a decline in the level of consumption of these poor households is apparent. This and many other observations lead Jan Breman to the following conclusion: 'To be sure, the Halpatis have always been poor, but the only term which adequately describes their present retrogression is pauperization'.

One may object that the very competition in the labour market which causes this impoverishment at the same time contributes to opportunities and access to work for the migrants from the backward Eastern districts. Is this not a redistribution of poverty rather than impoverishment per se?

There may be some truth in this, but Jan Breman makes it also clear that the labour regime to which the migrants are subject is extremely exploitative. Both migrants and Halpatis have become part of a workforce in surplus which is now employed according to the logic of capitalist accumulation. Work will be given only to those who can be exploited most profitably.

9.3.2. *Ecological degradation*

Rural impoverishment is severely exacerbated through ecological degradation. This refers particularly to the patterns of land use of poor farmers, and the problems of deforestation. The following long quotation from the Brundtland report describes the dramatic situation prevailing in many parts of the world. (World Commission on Environment and Development [1987: 29–30]).

Within countries, poverty has been exacerbated by the unequal distribution of land and other assets. The rapid rise in population has compromised the ability to raise living standards. These factors, combined with growing demands for the commercial use of good land, often to grow crops for exports, have pushed many subsistence farmers onto poor land and robbed them of any hope of participating in their nations' economic lives. The same forces have meant that traditional shifting cultivators, who once cut forests, grew crops, and then gave the forest time to recover, now have neither land enough nor time to let forests re-establish. So forests are being destroyed, often only to create poor farmland that cannot support those who till it. Extending cultivation onto steep slopes is increasing soil erosion in many hilly sections of both developing and developed nations. In many river valleys, areas chronically liable to floods are now farmed.

These pressures are reflected in the rising incidence of disasters. During the 1970s, six times as many people died from 'natural disaster' each year as in the 1960s, and twice as many suffered from such disasters. Droughts and floods, disasters among whose causes are widespread deforestation and overcultivation, increased most in terms of numbers affected. There were 18.5 million people affected by droughts annually in the 1960s, but 24.4 million in the 1970s; 5.2 million people were victims of floods yearly in the 1960s, compared with 15.4 million in the 1970s. The results are not in for the 1980s, but this disaster-prone decade seems to be carrying forward the trend, with droughts in Africa, India, and the Andean region of Latin America.

Such disasters claim most of their victims among the impoverished in poor nations, where subsistence farmers must make their land more liable to droughts and floods by clearing marginal areas, and where the poor make themselves more vulnerable to all disasters by living on steep slopes and unprotected shores—the only land left for their shanties. Lacking food and foreign exchange reserves, their economically vulnerable governments are ill equipped to cope with such catastrophes.

Again, in what follows, we will restrict ourselves to the Indian subcontinent, leaving aside the ecological degradation under much more *unfavourable* economic conditions, e.g. in tropical Africa. The prolonged drought which during previous years has afflicted India in particular has pointed again to the fragile environmental conditions underlying the whole subcontinent's development. Discussing the causes of the ecological crisis in the Indian subcontinent Rao *et al.* (1988) state (pp. 126–7):

Increasing demographic pressures on limited and non-expanding land resource is often suggested as an important explanation for much of the ecological crisis. There is no doubt that population pressure is one of the factors behind extension of cultivation of marginal lands, encroachments on forest lands, overuse of common lands, etc. But population growth at best offers only a partial explanation of the ecological crisis. The demand for forest products from the high income population has been a major cause for the depletion of area under forests. It must be stressed that if population had grown slowly, per capita income would have grown faster, and the high income-induced demand pressures for forest produce would still have persisted. Therefore, while population pressure is real, there are clearly more fundamental processes at work induced by the patterns of development that accentuated the ecological problem.

A similar assessment is made with respect to the depletion of groundwater resources which is mainly due to over-exploitation by private adopters of new irrigation facilities, and with respect to the steady erosion of land under common ownership due to 'market forces and institutional changes'.

Moreover, Rao *et al.* clearly point out that the poor are bound to suffer most from the scarcity which results from all these types of ecological degradation: deforestation deprives tribals of their most important means of livelihood; the cost of decline in the water table includes the increased time and expense of finding water for washing, drinking and food preparation; and the erosion of common ownership affects the poor who depend upon it for fodder and fuel.

In a case study about the anthropological and sociological dimensions of tribal forestry Schenk-Sandbergen delves more deeply into the consequences of deforestation for the tribal population. (Here we touch on the cultural dimension mentioned in section 9.2.3 above). While the traditional culture of the tribal population in India living in forests attaches high value to the maintenance of the forest through religiously inspired respect and consideration for the life-giving trees, the penetration of commercial interests and gradual intrusion of 'modernization' has forced the tribal population to become the destroyers of their own habitat. What results is the disintegration of their whole socio-economic system:

As a result of deforestation, basic values, attitudes, styles of living and social organizations are changing, resulting in an identity crisis of millions of people (p. 19).

In this context we have also to mention the escape route of urban migration which has been tried by many millions of rural impoverished people. The particular form of environmental decay to which the poor slums in the large Third World cities are subject results on the one hand from the vulnerability of poverty which many rural migrants carry with them almost inseparably when fleeing the countryside, but on the other hand from the incapacity of the urban environment itself to sustain more human lives without serious breakdowns and crisis.

9.3.3. *International dependency*

During recent years the vulnerability of the Third World's children to the international economic environment has been brought emphatically into the open through the study of UNICEF 'Adjustment with a Human Face' (Cornia *et al.* [1987]). In this study inter alia convincing evidence is presented that the severe recession which hit many developing countries in the first half of the eighties has contributed significantly to 'a widespread and sharp reversal in the trend towards the improvement in standards of child health, nutrition and education'. A deterioration in child welfare has occurred in at least 8 countries in Latin America, 16 in sub-Saharan Africa, 3 in North Africa and the Middle East and 4 in South and East Asia.

This is to be attributed to three different sets of factors. First of all, the world recession has hit the countries of the Third World hardest, as their economies—especially those in Africa and Latin

America—are extremely dependent on the growth impulses (or the lack of them) of the industrialized world. The International Monetary Fund's estimates suggest that a 1 per cent change in the real economic growth rate of the latter is associated on the average with about a 3.5 percentage change of the same sign in the growth of export earnings of developing countries (de Larosre [1986]). Secondly, the adjustment programmes which many countries of the Third World implemented were insufficiently growth oriented. While they were mostly effective in improving the current account balance, the growth performance deteriorated and investment levels declined in the majority of the countries. Thirdly, the measures taken to adjust to the recession have led to direct negative effects on the welfare of the poor through indiscriminate cuts in government expenditure, reduction in food subsidies, sharp increases in food prices and regressive fiscal policies. For a penetrating and, in particular, political analysis of the developmental crisis of sub-Saharan Africa we refer to Moyo and Amin.

9.4. Prospects

The grim reality of the Fourth World shows itself in various forms as we have seen in the previous section. In this section we face the question about the future of the Fourth World, or to put it differently: *what can be done about it?*

No easy answer is to be expected. More particularly, the previous sections have shown that what is conventionally considered to be an answer to the problems of the Third World, namely economic development, may lead to a Fourth World. On the other hand negative growth rates clearly exacerbate problems of vulnerability even more, as we have seen in section 9.3.3. Such are the vexing contradictions underlying the Fourth World's vicious circles.

In section 9.4.1 we will say a few words about the relationship between 'growth' and 'the protection of the vulnerable' by comparing the value premises underlying two important reports published in 1987; in section 9.4.2 we will then try to indicate a few policy directions; and finally in section 9.4.3 we will draw attention to the Third System as an ally in solving, and preventing, the problems of the Fourth World.

9.4.1. *Growth and the protection of the vulnerable*

In 1987 two major reports were published which are relevant to the present subject, and from which we have already quoted extensively in the foregoing (World Commission on Environment and Development [1987] and Cornia *et al.* [1987]).

A basic value premise underlying the reports 'Our Common Future' (also called the 'Brundtland report') and 'Adjustment with a Human Face' is apparently similar: protecting the vulnerable. The reports differ in their time-perspective and focus on different threats to the survival of the poor (the one being the vicious circle of environmental degradation and poverty, the other being the pressures for economic adjustment). However, 'sustainable development', which is the core value around which changes in institutions and policies are proposed in 'Our Common Future' apparently has to start with 'Adjustment with a Human Face'. (See 'Our Common Future', p. 43 and 'Adjustment with a Human Face', pp. 131, 132). There is in both reports the explicit notion that poverty—apart from being morally unacceptable and politically disruptive—is economically destructive: it destroys the creative capacities of people and forces them to destroy environment. Underlying this assessment there is thus a similar definition of true human progress, namely the development to the fullest extent possible of human capacities in harmony with the environment. So sustainable development should be viewed as the natural consequence of adjustment with a human face. Both reports complement each other as the short- and long-term perspective of one overall vision of 'alternative development'.

The main point which we would like to stress is the two-fold choice which each of the two reports makes: namely the choice in favour of growth-oriented policies, and the simultaneous change in the nature of the growth towards protection of the vulnerable. Both changes are seen as reinforcing each other.

Are such options based on a satisfactory assessment of the present situation?

From the discussion in the previous sections it has become clear that to change the nature of economic growth in the desired directions is not an easy task given the unevenness of the present growth patterns. That such a task is political, is clear. But what should be stressed also, is the underlying value problem involved. In order to change the nature of growth, growth itself should be viewed from a radically different perspective.

Growth is not an absolute goal. Its value and quality are related to what it socially does to people, no more and no less. There is no inherent value in the expansion of material wealth as such. Such a dethronement of economic growth implies a kind of cultural revolution (see Goulet [1971]) and will not come about easily. Elsewhere an analysis has been given of the current 'development consciousness', as a biased set of values reflecting a Western experience of technologically dominated 'progress' (Terhal [1987: 270–80]). Focusing, in particular, on problems of rural poverty Chambers [1983] has made a case for 'a reversal of professional values' as a necessary condition for effective anti-poverty programmes.

A reversal of values would have to be complemented by radically different techniques for monitoring progress. Unless more adequate ways are found to monitor economic progress by relating it far more closely to what it does to people, now and in the future, economists will continuously have to keep watch against misguiding the politicians. Where material output expands, but at the same time the natural habitat of numerous people is irrevocably damaged, the growth records have to be rejected as indicators of progress. When the lives of whole sections of the population are becoming more precarious, ways have to be found to express that change and to balance it with whatever wealth acquisition other sections may experience. In the multi-dimensional process of change which 'economic development' is, the central questions are how the most vulnerable fare, and what happens to the capacity of the environment to protect human lives.

9.4.2. *Three types of changes*

What is needed is not only economic development, but simultaneously a radical redefinition and redirection of its principal components. That this cannot be brought about immediately is clear enough. We may distinguish three sets of changes depending on the time lag involved: policies which alleviate in the short term the conditions of the Fourth World; policies which restructure economic development in such a way that economic development does not create a Fourth World; and policies which in the long run prevent the conditions leading to the emergence of a Fourth World.

Examples of policies of the first type are given in the report 'Adjustment with A Human Face'. In particular the creation of (temporary) employment for low-income groups through public works, and the improvement of the productivity of small-scale low-income activities through targeted credit schemes, training and technological support can contribute substantially to the social protection of the poor (See F. Stewart, in Cornia *et al.* [1987]). In this context reference may be made to the proposal of Hans Singer [1989] to increase international food aid to sub-Saharan Africa from 4–5 million tons to 11–12 million tons in 1990. This food aid would have to be used to make the structural adjustment support extended by World Bank and IMF more 'growth oriented' and with more of a 'human face'.

A policy of the second type is that advocated by I. Adelman [1979], who argues that, in order to prevent impoverishment concomitant with the productivity increasing innovation of the critical factor of production, the distribution of this factor of production should be made more equal, before the innovation occurs (see section 9.2.1). Here we touch on 'the question of socialism', i.e. the feasibility and appropriateness of a more radical approach to issues of distribution and resource ownership. These issues cannot be avoided. While each country will have to choose its own path, as a rule the adequate protection of the vulnerable without constraints on the acquisitiveness of the strong does not seem to be feasible. Difficult political choices thus have to be made, which need to be supported internationally as well as promoted by indigenous groups belonging to what we will call 'the Third System' (see section 9.4.3).

Policies of the third type are mainly of an institutional and long-term nature. They challenge even more fundamentally the present patterns of economic growth propelled by international capitalism. More particularly, the Brundtland report strongly argues in favour of a global redirection of attention in henceforward giving priority to the needs of the poorest, and protecting the environment for future generations. Such a redirection would reflect the absolute priority to create adequate living conditions in those geographical areas of the world where the overwhelming part of the world's population will live in the near future. This would call for a different type of world order.

More particularly, in the case of international dependency, within the present setting of the international financial and monetary system, developing countries have certain possibilities to choose from for 'adjustment with a human face'. But these options are

very severely constrained by the international system. Cornia *et al.*
[1987] argue '. . . developing countries have no alternative but to
adjust, one way or another . . . .' And the authors then significantly
add:

. . . unfortunately, there is little to compel appropriate changes in international conditions, in spite of the very great human—and economic—
gains that could result.

International adjustment, i.e. a realistic adaptation of the world
economic monetary and financial system to the present day's realities and urgent needs of the majority of the world's population
would be a change of the third type, *preventing* large-scale human
suffering in the future. Therefore the valuable book 'Adjustment
with a Human Face' would have to be complemented by a companion volume of the same title, dealing more fully with this type
of change. The Brundtland report expresses the same concern as
Jan Tinbergen and others [1987] have stressed time and again: the
actions which are most urgently needed in order to avoid massive
human suffering in the future seem to be 'simply beyond the reach
of present decision making structures and institutional arrangements,
both national and international'. Changes in the latter are therefore
imperative.

9.4.3. *The Fourth World and the Third System*

In this context it seems appropriate to consider a broader spectrum
of actors than what is normally under the review of development
economists. In the design of economic policies attention is usually
concentrated exclusively on what Marc Nerfin has called the First
and the Second Systems. With the First System Nerfin means the
state, the public authorities and the Government; with the Second
System, the organized economic agents and the business community.
In symbolic language he speaks about the Prince and the Merchant.
Without denying the overwhelming power invested in the First and
Second Systems Nerfin [1987] points to the growing importance of
a Third System,[7] which is loosely organized, but at the same time
very vital. He defines it as follows (p. 172):

---

[7] The term Third System is not arbitrarily chosen. It evokes—as the term Third
World does—the 'third estate' of the French ancient régime (le Tiers état). Before
the 1789 revolution French society comprised three estates, the nobility, the clergy
and the third estate.

Contrasting with governmental power and economic power—the power of the Prince and the Merchant—there is an immediate and autonomous power, sometimes evident, sometimes latent: people's power. Some people develop an awareness of this, associate and act with others and thus become citizens. Citizens and their associations, when they do not seek either governmental or economic power, constitute the third system. Helping to bring what is latent into the open, the third system is one expression of the autonomous power of the people.

Over the years the International Foundation for Development Alternatives has documented in the IFDA Dossiers the emergence and growth of numerous associations nationally and internationally. Marc Nerfin lists a whole range of examples of 'people's organizations'. People, in the struggle to express their will to improve their lives and that of others, individually or collectively, are motivated in many ways. Apart from the more traditional manifestations like the trade unions, there are, according to Nerfin, only a few deep seated mobilizing themes:

peace, women's liberation, human and people's rights, environment, local self-reliance, alternative life-style and personal transformation and consumers' self defence as well as in some industrialized countries solidarity with the people of the Third World . . . .

In the Third System there is now at least part of a beginning response to the crisis of the Fourth World. In various forms people's associations are taking up the struggle in aid of the vulnerable, in order to try to challenge and change First and Second System choices and activities, to set up autonomous projects for self-defence and survival. As Nerfin notes (p. 182):

The third system does not seek governmental or economic power. On the contrary, its function is to help people to assert their own autonomous power vis-à-vis both Prince and Merchant. It endeavours to listen to those never or rarely heard and at least to offer a tribune to the unheard voices.

People's organizations play a role in advocating changes both in developed and developing countries which would redirect economic policies towards the protection of the vulnerable. While often linked to political parties they remain in essence autonomous. Coalitions with other more or less independent organizations such as university departments, students' organizations, religious organizations and even supra-national organizations such as United Nations' departments, are taking place. Probably neither the Brundtland report nor the report 'Adjustment with a Human Face' would have been written without the continuous influence of Third System activities permeating into the First and Second Systems.

In developing countries the so-called informal sector could be considered as an economic expression of the Third System. Essential is the autonomy which characterizes the Third System: its initiatives are expressions of people's own 'power' and capabilities. The conclusion of Cornia's own contribution [1987] is worth quoting in this context (p. 104):

In conclusion, policy support should unreservedly be extended to those survival strategies emphasizing the growth of employment and productivity of small-scale, informal sector manufacturing; support to communities for self-production and exchange of food, shelter, and community-based services; and increasing communal efforts in basic needs. Because of the comparative efficiency of this group of survival strategies, policy support would be likely to produce better results than where support is exclusively concentrated on the formal sector. . . .

Returning now to the concluding section of the paper of Moyo and Amin we note their arguments in favour of the independent self-reliant organization of the poor outside the control of the state, both in economic and political terms. With respect to the economic component of self-reliance Moyo and Amin point to people's 'survival strategies'. They do not argue, however, in favour of any role of the state in supporting these strategies, as Cornia does. In the field of politics they place emphasis on the emergence of people's autonomous power, as an essential element in solving the crisis of sub-Saharan Africa.

Moyo and Amin's framework of analysis—the national African state as part of imperialist structures—leads their political prescriptions towards what they call 'a national democratic revolution' as a way out. Even while the term 'revolution' may raise expectations beyond what is feasible, the idea of *self-reliance* seems, in the end, to be a perspective for the Fourth World. In a world which is subject to a process of dualistic integration (see Terhal [1987]) dominated and controlled by the First and Second Systems, there is no other alternative.

The analytical and operational implications of the perspective of self-reliance are too broad to deal with here. Certainly they extend beyond the traditional disciplinary boundaries of development economics.

We have no arms to cause pressure, the only thing we have is the right to cry for our dignity and the need to live in our land.

Thus, the quotation with which we started this paper, summarizes its content and message.

References

Adelman, I, and C.T. Morris, [1978], 'Growth and impoverishment in the middle of the nineteenth century', *World Development*, vol. 6, no. 3.

Adelman, I, [1979], *Redistribution before growth: a strategy for developing countries* (Leyden University Press).

Bhagwati, J.N. [1988], 'Poverty and public policy', *World Development*, vol. 16, no. 5, May 1988.

Breman, J. [1985], *Of peasants, migrants and paupers, Rural labour circulation and capitalist production in West India* (Delhi: Oxford University Press).

Chambers, R. [1983], *Rural development. Putting the last first* (London: Longman).

Cornia, G.A., R. Jolly and F. Stewart (eds.) [1987], *Adjustment with a human face*, vol. I. Protecting the vulnerable and promoting growth, (Oxford: Clarendon Press).

Cutler, P. [1984], 'The measurement of poverty: a review of attempts to quantify the poor, with special reference to India', *World Development*, vol. 12, nos. 11/12.

Étienne, G. [1982], *India's changing rural scene, 1963– 1979* (Delhi: Oxford University Press).

Goulet, D. [1971], *The cruel choice* (New York: Atheneum).

Griffin, K. [1969], *Underdevelopment in Spanish America. An interpretation* (George Allen and Unwin Ltd).

Griffin, K. and A.Z. Khan (coord.) [1977], *Poverty and landlessness in rural Asia* (Geneva: International Labour Office).

Griffin, K., and A.Z. Khan [1978], 'Poverty in the Third World: ugly facts and fancy models', *World Development*, vol. 6, no. 3.

Hirschman, A. [1981], 'The rise and decline of development economics', in: A. O. Hirschman, *Essays in trespassing: economics to politics and beyond* (Cambridge University Press).

Kuznets, S. [1973], 'Modern economic growth: findings and reflections', in S. Kuznets, *Population, capital and growth* (New York: Norton and Co.).

Lal, D. [1984], 'Trends in real wages in rural India 1880–1980' Discussion paper, report no DRD103, Development Research Department, World Bank.

Larosre, J. de [1986], Address before the Economic and Social Council of the United Nations, Washington DC, IMF.

Nerfin, M. [1987], 'Neither Prince nor Merchant: Citizen—An introduction to the Third System', *Development Dialogue* (1).

Myrdal, G. [1957], *Economic theory and underdeveloped regions* (London).

Rao, C. H., Susanta K. Ray and K. Subbarao [1988], *Unstable agriculture and droughts: Implications for policy* (New Delhi: Vikas Publishing House).

Schenk-Sandbergen, L., 'People, trees and forest in India. Anthropological and sociological dimensions', Annex 2, in: Report of the Mission of the Government of the Netherlands on the identification of the scope for forestry development cooperation in India.

Sen, A. [1981], *Poverty and famines. An essay on entitlement and deprivation* (Oxford: Clarendon Press).

Singer, H. [1989], 'Food aid and structural adjustment in Sub-Saharan Africa', paper presented to the EADI-workshop on The performance and economic impact of food aid, Oslo, 19–21 February, 1989.

Srinivas, M. N. [1976], *The Remembered Village*, (Delhi: Oxford University Press).

Stewart, F. [1978], 'Inequality, technology and payment systems', *World Development*, vol. 6, no. 3, March 1978.

Terhal, P. [1987], *World inequality and evolutionary convergence*, (Delft: Eburon).

Tinbergen, J. and D. Fischer [1987], *Warfare and Welfare: Integrating Security Policy into Socio-economic Policy* (Brighton).

World Commission on Environment and Development [1987], *Our Common Future* (Oxford University Press).

Index